I looked down on my mother as she lay in a coma on her deathbed. I gently lifted my hand to her forehead and felt her taut and cool skin. I stroked her hair like she might have stroked mine while I slept as an infant. I heard the wissssh, whoosh *of her ventilator and smelled the distinctive antiseptic scent of her hospital room. Then I held her limp hand and said, "Hi Mom, it's me, Teresita. I'm home!" I began talking to her as if she were perfectly well and understood everything I was saying.*

I summoned all my courage and apologized for the past. "I'm sorry that I ran away. Please forgive me. I forgive you . . . I'm sorry that we never bonded with each other, and I'm sorry I never bonded with my son. . . . I had an abortion, Mom. . . .

"The apple doesn't fall very far from the tree, does it? But it's never too late. You know, without that bond Mom—the special grace instilled in us mothers by God—there wouldn't be any continuation of the human race.

"It seems unnatural that the child should re-establish the bond with the mother, but that's what you and I need to do. We need to make peace with each other. We need to love one another. So as your daughter who really loves you, I'd like to restore the bond that we should have had all along.

I held her hand in both of mine and said, "I love you, Mom. Life is full of second chances. We can make up for our bad choices by making good ones. Let's make up for our estrangement by bonding NOW."

As I said this, she squeezed my hands. She had heard me, and she was responding to my love . . . at last. We were no longer estranged. I felt great relief . . . and then my tears began to flow.

Library of Congress Control Number: 2001126174

ISBN: 0-9647988-3-2

Published by:
THE MISSIONARY IMAGE OF OUR LADY OF GUADALUPE, INC.
144 Sheldon Road
St. Albans, Vermont 05478
Phone: 1.802.524.5350
www.ourladyofguadalupe.org

The song "Old Cape Cod." Copyright © 1956 by George Pincus and Songs Music Corp. Used with permission.

The song "What a Wonderful World." Copyright © 1967 by Range Road Music Inc., Quartet Music Inc. and Abilene Music Inc. Used with permission.

The song "Sunrise, Sunset." Copyright © 1964 by Sunbeam Music Inc. Used with permission.

Printed in the United States of America.
"God Bless America"

Teresita's Choices

A Testimony of Life, Healing, and Hope

By Dan Lynch

THE FAMILY RESOURCES CENTER
Family Resources Center
415 NE Monroe,
Peoria, IL 61603 (309) 839-2287

Can a mother forget her baby,
be without tenderness for the child of her womb?
Even if she forgets,
I will never forget you.

Isaiah 49:15

Their wealth remains in their families,
their heritage with their descendants;
through God's covenant with them their family endures,
their posterity, for their sake.

The Book of Sirach 44:11-12

Foreword

There can be no family without life, and there can be no life without the family.

When the family, which Pope John Paul II has called "the sanctuary of life," is weak and unstable, life itself is threatened and often destroyed. On the other hand, when the dignity of life is rediscovered, that discovery can provide the basis for rebuilding the family. That is what this book teaches us.

The family is the basic social unit, and it begins with the bond that is established between a mother and her child. Abortion breaks that bond, and its effects ripple out in harmful waves from the mother into her relationships, and indeed, into society as a whole. The good news is that there is hope that the mother who has had an abortion can find healing and peace. The bond with her aborted child can be reestablished through faith, hope and love.

Teresita's Choices, a drama with many surprising twists, illustrates this truth with riveting clarity. In this book, many of the abortion issues that are currently debated are given a name and a face. They are explored in the context of people on their own unique, personal journeys. While feminists claim that a key aspect of feminism is to "listen to the voices of women," ironically, those who support abortion fail to listen to the voices of those women who testify to the pain and devastation it brings. Teresita is one of those voices.

Teresita, in the course of her dramatic journey, also becomes a pro-life activist. The suffering she endures in her witness for life is a fitting tribute to countless unsung heroes throughout our country. I have been greatly enriched by knowing many of them. They deserve the gratitude and esteem of us all.

Reading this book provides numerous stepping-stones to prayer, and I invite you to read it in that way. Pray for the conversion of the hearts of those who support abortion. Pray for the many young men and women who feel they have no choice but to have their child aborted. Pray for those seeking forgiveness and healing from the wounds of abortion. Pray for abortion survivors, and for people whose families lack the love and communication that should be there. Pray for pro-life activists.

Above all, pray to Our Lady of Guadalupe whose motherly presence pervades this book, and indeed, the whole pro-life movement itself. She is the Protectress of the Unborn, and as her image brought an end to human sacrifice several centuries ago, so shall it do again in our times.

Fr. Frank Pavone
National Director, Priests for Life
January 22, 2001

Preface

This book is an expanded and revised version of a journal that I wrote at my lawyer's insistence. He wanted it for legal support in a case he was handling for me. After reading it, my lawyer said, "Teresita, this story is too amazing to be heard by only twelve jurors. Everyone should hear this!"

I hope that you agree with my lawyer's assessment of the book. I am allowing my story to be published now so that other women might be inspired *to make the right choices.* And that the men in their lives will support them in those choices.

No other book will tell you the whole truth about the consequences of the choices for premarital sex and abortion! It's as simple as that.

I want to thank Dan Lynch for his rewriting and editorial assistance in making my journal "come alive." Without his help, it would be gathering dust on my bookshelf. He polished up my rough draft, gave it a body and soul, and got it published. Dan said, "This is a story that has to be told. No one could make up a story like this. This truth is stranger than fiction. It's also timely for the Hispanic culture since it's an epic that covers five generations with the rejection and reestablishment of their traditions. You're a survivor Teresita! I hope that I can portray your mind and heart and do justice to the incredible and compelling experiences in the twists and turns of your life." I think he did.

This is my personal testimony. It is the story of my life, my choices and their consequences. I rejected my Hispanic values to become "my own person" and to make my own choices. I was hurt badly and it took me a long time to heal. I had the help of a good friend who was always there for me. Her belief in me helped me to believe in myself and that, with God's help, I would be healed! And I was. I forgave all those who had hurt me, and I accepted full responsibility for all of my bad choices and their consequences.

Maybe I can be a friend for you. I'm not looking for sympathy, I'm looking to help. If the sharing of my story makes a difference in just one person's life, it'll all have been worthwhile. In this testimony, I honestly confront the consequences of my choices, detail my healing process, and demonstrate how it is possible to live on in hope.

We are not just victims of our past, our parents, and our environment. We all are accountable for our free will choices, actions and their consequences. We have to take personal responsibility for them. Choices have consequences. Perhaps by reading about the consequences of my choices, others will be able to make wiser ones.

Please join me on the journey and choices of my life from growing up on Cape Cod, to running away as a teenager to Miami and on from there as a changed wife and mother to a new life in Vermont. Join me as we travel the path of heritage, culture, family, and faith.

Teresita Gonzalez
Burlington, Vermont

Feast of Our Lady of Guadalupe
December 12, 2000

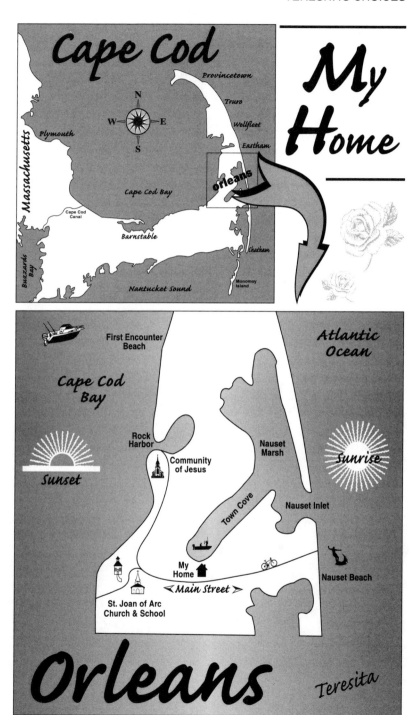

One

Raaah, erraaaaaaaaah! The raucous and healthy cry of a newborn baby broke the expectant silence of the farmhouse bedroom. With joyful relief, the young mother laid back on the birthing bed. Her rugged husband smiled down on her and their new child with pride and tenderness. I quickly dried the little one off and asked, "What have we got here?"

"A girl!" the father yelled tearfully. I suctioned the baby's mouth and gently placed her near her mother's exposed breast. Her father cut the umbilical cord while caressing the baby's head. He was an experienced Vermont farmer who had helped birth many calves. Now he had assisted in delivering his own child. The mother gently guided the baby's searching mouth to her nipple and stared deeply into her eyes. Instant love!

It was early in the morning one day in August 2000, and I was a midwife performing my first delivery. While performing my professional duties, I couldn't help but notice the warm and wondrous intimacy that radiated from the little family as they celebrated this new life in the safety and comfort of their own home.

Soon feeling like a bit of an intruder, I limped off toward the bathroom to wash up. As I bent over the sink and looked into the mirror, I saw a young-looking, 32-year-old woman. I looked tired from the long night birth vigil. My shoulder-length black hair, a bit disheveled, framed the cocoa brown face and bright blue eyes of a fourth generation Latina.

Reflected in the background of the mirror I could still see the young mother nursing her newborn. I always marveled at the sight of a nursing mother and child as they locked eyes with each other. I was reminded of the fact that humans were the only species in the animal kingdom that were designed so that mother and child could gaze at each other during the intimate act of nursing. I envied the bond being established between this mother and daughter—one which I had never known.

I took a deep breath, and I collected myself. Despite a tinge of regret because my own mother had never established such a bond with me, a soft smile formed on my lips. I was genuinely happy for this mother and child. But as the warm tap water rushed over my hands, I experienced the flash of a recurring memory—a silent scream that rose like mist from my earliest awareness. . . .

I am floating freely under water . . . like an underwater ballerina or a weightless astronaut. I bounce off the trampoline-like walls that closely surround me, somersaulting effortlessly. Then I rest and feel happy. But I sense another presence, someone very close.

Is someone else with me? It's dark . . . I can't see. I have this strong feeling that I'm not alone. But I'm not frightened. It seems that I have a companion—a friend nearby. I feel peace.

Suddenly, it seems like my water sanctuary is invaded. I sense aggression. I feel a cold fear. I get agitated. It seems as if something is searching for me. The water gets rough. I am in a vortex of chaos. My body is agitated like a washcloth in a washing machine on spin cycle. Instinctively, I try to swim away. But I can't.

I feel an incredible torrent of fluid rushing around me. It feels like I'm white-water rafting out of control. I'm terrified. I don't know what's happening to me.

I want to communicate my terror, but I can't. I scream but it's a silent scream—nobody can hear me. I am completely helpless. I can't help myself, and I can't help my friend. The sense of my friend's presence diminishes. Then there is only emptiness, a void. But it's quiet again. I feel sad that I was unable to help. I try to get to safety but my left leg is wrapped around my neck and I feel a newly experienced sensation—excruciating pain!

I still felt some pain in my left hip as I stood before that Vermont farmer's mirror years later. And I could still feel that emotional terror and the excruciating pain of my earliest memory that became a recurring nightmare for me. The cause of it remained unknown to me until I was 16 years old. It was then that my mother solved the mystery, but discovering the truth at last was both a relief and a painful shock.

I stared at myself in that mirror for what seemed like an eternity, facing my reflection with trepidation but also with courage. I resolved to head home to my own family, get some sleep, and finally finish writing the story of this memory. I had been at it on and off for over 12 years. Painful as it was, I felt morally obligated to provide hope for others. If even one person could learn from my choices and their consequences, I reasoned, the effort would be well worth it.

I left the smiling couple with their firstborn child and drove to my home in Burlington, Vermont. My husband, Miguel, and my two children, Lupe (pronounced Loo-pay) and Mickey happily greeted me. We lived in a large old farmhouse which we made into separate quarters for ourselves, my mother-in-law, and my retired father. We were one big and happy family now — but it wasn't always that way. Miguel watched the children while I took a nap. An hour later, I got up, refreshed, and sat right down at my computer, determined to finish my story.

On the advice of a lawyer who was representing me in a medical malpractice case, I began the process of putting my memories on paper in January of 1988. I was then 20 years old and living in Miami, Florida. He told me to write the whole story down, detailing my pain and suffering, so that I'd be prepared to answer the defense lawyers' questions in the pretrial depositions. I told him that I wasn't much of a writer, but I was willing to try in the hope that it would help our case and just maybe prevent someone else from going through the suffering that I had. Getting started was always difficult for me, and once I did start, I found it hard to keep at it for very long.

Then in the summer of 2000, something happened to move me to action. It was the national *Encuentro*—Meeting 2000. These Catholic meetings had always been exclusively for Latinos. But the Church decided to use the Latino leadership to open the *Encuentro* in 2000 to all races for the first time.

In his *Encuentro* homily, Boston's Cardinal Law confessed the errors of Church members in failing to recognize the equality of all men and women before God. The theme of the meeting was "The Many Faces in God's House," and in a beautiful tapestry of brown, white, black, red and yellow faces, the diverse children of God came together to tell their stories. I decided that it was now or never for me to show my face in God's House. At last, I was finally able to say, "This is *my* story."

Two

"*T*eresita, Teresita Lowell, *Ven acá!*—Come out here!"

On a late Saturday morning in the summer of 1981, I groggily dragged myself from my bed and made my way downstairs. At 13 years of age, I would have preferred to sleep in longer, but my grandmother was excitedly calling me. I obediently responded and found her on the front porch of our family home at 92 Main Street, Orleans on Cape Cod, Massachusetts.

Grandma said, "You should get up in the morning, Teresita. You sleep too late and you miss life. Look at the show that you're missing!" She pointed to the packed carloads of families going to the ocean at Nauset Beach and exclaimed, "Look at the *turistas*—tourists! They bring everything but the kitchen sink to the beach! Umbrellas, chairs, coolers, surf boards, fishing rods, radios, life jackets, floats . . . everything!"

"They want to have some family fun, Grandma."

"Then they should travel light and enjoy one another. They don't need all that junk!"

"Right, Grandma."

"They're off to the *Atlantic* Ocean. But did I ever tell you how I traveled to the *Pacific* Ocean? Since I'm only with you for a couple weeks every summer, I can't remember what I've told you and what I haven't."

"No, I don't think I've heard that story." My interest perked up. "I thought that you were *born* in L.A. Let me get some breakfast and then you can tell me."

"Wait a minute, not so fast, Teresita. I wasn't born in L.A. I was born in Mexico! Don't you know anything about your heritage? Didn't your mother tell you anything?"

"Honest, I thought that you were born in L.A."

"Teresita, I'm part Tarahumara Indian." Grandma paused. She must have noticed the look of surprised interest on my face. "They're the indigenous people of Chihuahua, Mexico," she continued. "In Tarahumara, the word *chihuahua* means 'place of the workshop.' That was the place where my father and mother lived and worked, a place that was built on silver mines by the sweat of our ancestors. Now it's known only for its miniature dogs!"

"Oh yeah, I've seen those dogs. Don't they have a high-pitched bark?"

"Forget the dogs. My mother, your great-grandma, was a poor *comadrona*—a midwife. She helped to support our family with her income from midwifery and the sale of her *sarapes*—shawls in the plaza. They were beautiful, roughly woven, natural-colored *sarapes*. And my father was a tenant farmer in the almost barren fields. My parents and I, along with my five brothers and sisters, lived in a three-room shanty. There were no jobs and no future in Chihuahua for a young girl like me."

"Hold it, Grandma. I have to get some breakfast. This sounds like it's going to take a while. I'll be right back."

"Well, don't eat any donuts! You should lose some weight, you know. You eat too much junk food and not enough healthy stuff."

I left her on the porch in her rocking chair watching the parade of tourists traveling to the beach. She was my mother's mother. Grandma was short and squat with jet-black hair and eyes. Her almost black face was wrinkled and creased with some deep crevices along her high cheekbones. Her hands were rough and gnarled from all her work as a maid and cook. She walked with a cane that also served as a prod when I didn't move fast enough. And Grandma was always throwing some Spanish phrase at me in the hopes that I'd learn the language. I loved and admired my grandma very much. She was kind, but she was also very wise. She didn't have a formal education, but she was self-educated and had an impressive knowledge of history. But until this day, I never really knew that much about her or her life.

After eating my breakfast in the kitchen, I came back out to hear Grandma's story. I brought a cup of hot tea for her and a glass of lemonade for myself. Unlike my mom, Grandma was very talkative. I knew her story wouldn't be brief. So, I sat on the rail of our front porch and faced her as she rocked back and forth in the rocking chair. A prevailing west wind blew across the porch to cool us from the late morning sun. And a slight smile formed on her face as Grandma began her tale.

"I was only an 18-year-old *señorita* in 1938 when I began my walk from Chihuahua to El Paso, Texas. It was almost 300 miles. After that, I ended up traveling on to L.A. I left with nothing but my meager savings and my mama's *bendición*."

"What's that, Grandma? You know I don't understand Spanish, so why do you keep talking in Spanish when you can speak good English?"

"Because maybe if I say these things often enough, you'll learn some Spanish."

"Wishful thinking, Grandma."

"It's a sin that your family doesn't speak Spanish. A *bendición*, Teresita, is a blessing. My mother blessed me and prayed over me. She said, 'May *La Virgen de Guadalupe* watch over and protect you and your children and theirs—to the fourth generation!'"

"*La*-what?"

"Don't tell me you don't know anything about *La Virgen!* She's the Virgin Mary, the mother of Jesus, who appeared from heaven in Mexico to an Indian named Juan Diego in 1531. Shame on your mother for not telling you such things! You need to learn your heritage and the history of your people, Teresita!"

"That's why I'm here with you, Grandma. I could be at the beach, you know."

"All right, then, listen and learn. I walked off from my home in search of *El Gran Sueño Americano*—'The Great American Dream'—money and security with liberty and justice for all! I thought to myself, *La Tierra Prometida eres tú*—'You are the Promised Land!' The road to the north burrowed straight through the center of Mexico. There were only small villages along the way, and the distances between them were long. I walked through the blistering hot desert by day. I prayed for safety from snakes and from the *bandidos* who roamed the desert at night. My mother had warned me about the *bandidos* who enjoyed raping pretty young girls. She said, 'First and foremost, my daughter, guard and protect your virginity.' That's good advise for you too. Remember that for yourself, Teresita.

"Don't forget, I was once a pretty young girl like you—you with your twinkling blue eyes. Your father is right when he says that they're as blue as the sky on the Fourth of July! And from whom did you get your blue eyes, Teresita? From your *gringo* father, of course! And why do we call whites *gringos?* Because when the American soldiers camped outside Mexico City during their siege in the Mexican-American War, they sang the song "Green

Grow the Lilacs, All Covered With Dew" around their campfires at night. The Mexicans thought that they sang 'gringo' instead of 'green grow.' And so the Americans became *gringos*.

"Our eyes are the windows of our souls," she rambled on. "And when I look into your *gringo* eyes I see *aguante*—Hispanic determination and endurance. Hold onto it, Teresita. Someday you'll be old and round like me. Enjoy your youth while you can, but always be on guard and protect your virginity. Remember that! With *aguante!*"

"Okay, Grandma. Weren't you going to tell me about your walk?"

"Well, anyway, my days of walking were long, and I yearned for the coming of night with its beautiful sunsets and cool evenings for roadside rest and sleep."

"You must've been very brave, Grandma. I don't know if I could do something like that."

"Well, I made a *promesa.*"

"A what?"

"I promised *La Virgen* that if she protected me and guided me safely to El Paso, I would name my first daughter María in honor of her, *La Virgen María*. I walked on in faith. *La Virgen* watched over me in answer to my mother's prayer in her *bendición*. So that's how your mother got her name. When she was born, I fulfilled my promise and named her María."

"I never knew that. Mom never told me. That's a neat story, Grandma."

"It gets better," she continued. "Almost three long weeks after I began my pilgrimage, I approached the city of Ciudad Juarez on the U.S. border with my blistered feet. This city was originally named *Nuestra Señora de Guadalupe del Paso del Norte* in honor of Our Lady of Guadalupe. It was built around a mission church dedicated to her. Remember, Teresita, it's pronounced *gwa-da-loo-pay.* It's part of your heritage."

"What's 'Guadalupe' mean?"

"In Aztec it means, 'she who crushes the stone serpent.' Our Lady of Guadalupe turned our Aztec ancestors away from the stone serpent they worshiped with human sacrifice and brought them to the knowledge of the one true God. Remember that, too, Teresita."

"Human sacrifice?!" I gasped and scrunched up my nose in disgust.

"Yes, the Aztecs sacrificed almost 10 million people over a period of 200 years to their stone idols until Our Lady stopped it in 1531."

"How could they do such evil?"

"How can Americans have killed more than 10 million in only *seven* years by abortion? When people don't follow God's ways, they're capable of doing great evil very easily. Think about it.

"Anyway, as I approached Ciudad Juarez, I saw The Good Neighbor Bridge which spans the Rio Grande River, the natural border between Mexico and Texas. It connects Ciudad Juarez to El Paso, Texas. But there was no welcome sign out for me, Teresita, from the 'Good Neighbor.' I was a 'wetback,' an undocumented, illegal alien. No, I was not welcomed into the United States. You know, later, I read that they wrote on the Statue of Liberty, 'Give me your tired, your poor, your huddled masses yearning to breathe free . . . ' But they didn't mean *all* of the 'tired' and 'poor.' They didn't mean 'wetbacks.' You had to have legal documents and come by boat through New York harbor," she added bitterly.

"Our kind were called 'wetbacks' because our backs got wet crossing the Rio Grande River at night. The U.S. Border Patrol was waiting for a *tonk* like me."

"Tonk?" I interrupted.

"Yes, it's the sound that a flashlight makes when a Border Patrol agent hits a 'wetback' over the head—*tonk!* "

"They really hit them over the head?! They should have called that bridge the 'Good Neighbor *Fence.*' "

"What do you mean?" Grandma looked perplexed.

"You know, Robert Frost's poem, 'Good fences make good neighbors.'"

"Yes, that's exactly what it was, 'The Good Neighbor *Fence.*' " She scooted down in her rocking chair and wrapped her arms around her drawn-up legs. "I crouched down like this in the bushes on the Mexican side of the river and waited for it to get dark. The Border Patrol waited on the American side with their flashlights. For a dime, a boatman ferried me by rowboat across the river. I was now an official 'wetback.' I scurried up the slippery riverbank, evaded the Border Patrol and made it to my *tío* and *tía's*—uncle and aunt's—tin shanty in the *Segundo Barrio.*"

I sat in quiet awe listening to this story of a brave young woman making her epic journey. "Then what?" I asked.

Grandma was quiet and stared at the wall with squinting eyes and pursed lips as she kept rocking in her chair. "You know, it was cruel for me to have to sneak like that into the U.S. After all, Texas and most of the American Southwest were originally part of Mexico. It was all taken by the United States after we lost the Mexican War in 1848. Even your own President Grant, who was one of its veterans, said it was an unjust war."

"But," I burst in, "we learned in history that it was part of our Manifest Destiny to have this land. It was America's destiny to rule from sea to shining sea. We even sing about it in 'America the Beautiful': 'Crown thy good with brotherhood from sea to shining sea.'"

"Brotherhood!" she replied with a look of disgust on her face. "That's a lie."

"Well, Grandma, I guess this is the part of the story that we didn't hear in school."

"It sure is. I was just reading Grant's *Memoirs* last night, trying to figure out how we lost half of our country. It's up on my bed stand. Please go and get it, and I'll read you what he said."

Dutifully, I went up to her bedroom, retrieved her book and brought it out to her on the porch. She turned to a bookmarked page and began to read:

I regard the war as one of the most unjust ever waged by a stronger against a weaker nation. It was an instance of a republic following the bad example of European monarchies, in not considering justice in their desire to acquire additional territory.

"I'll bet you didn't learn *that* in history! But there you have it from one of your own presidents—an unjust war for more land. Sounds just like Hitler's Lebensraum—more territory for a stronger nation. What's the difference?" she said shrugging, opening her palms and lifting her outstretched arms.

"You know what my *tío* told me? He said that the members of his family were *Tejanos*—Mexican Texans who had lived in Texas for many generations. 'We never crossed the border, the border crossed us!' he would argue. 'Texas used to be a part of Mexico. When we lost Texas, the Mexican border moved to the south, but my family never moved!'"

Grandma unfolded her arms and legs and continued with a smug smile. "The Rio Grande was like my Red Sea. As the ancient Jews were the first 'wetbacks' who crossed the Red Sea in their Exodus to seek freedom and their dream of a Promised Land, so I crossed the Rio Grande. The Jews were 'illegal' and undocumented aliens in a foreign land, and so was I. And I wasn't ashamed.

"Soon, I got enough money by waitressing in a cafe to buy a bus ticket to Los Angeles. I was welcomed there in the *barrio* in East Los Angeles by another *tío* and *tía*. Their attitude was, *Mi casa es tu casa*—'my house is your house.' So I ended my pilgrimage safe and sound. *Gracias a Dios por mi familia!*—'Thank God for my family!' Don't ever forget to thank God for your family, Teresita."

As if on cue, the intimacy and peace of this shared moment was shattered by my mother's ear-piercing shriek: "Teresita, get in here and help me with lunch!"

"Excuse me, Grandma. I think Mom wants me."

The disapproval showed on Grandma's face. "Okay, we can continue the story later." She shook her head, casting a concerned look in the direction of the kitchen and shuffled toward her bedroom to wait for lunch.

THWAT! My mother slapped my face without warning as I walked up to her.

"You knew that I was in the kitchen making lunch by myself. You waste your time out there talking to Grandma when you should be in here helping me. Now get started and make a salad."

"Okay," I said sullenly.

In bewilderment, I scratched the bottom of my right earlobe with my thumb and forefinger. I was suddenly reminded of scratching behind my ear as a little girl when I would pick at the scabs that had formed there—scabs from wounds my mother inflicted upon me whenever she angrily pulled on my earlobe and dragged me to wherever she wanted me to go. Sometimes I felt like she would pull my ear right off my head. I thought that I must've been a pretty bad girl to deserve such scabs. But now I knew that I hadn't done *anything* to deserve such physical abuse.

For some reason I didn't know, my mother had these "spells" when she'd fly off the handle, yelling, screaming, and slapping me. I felt like I always walked on eggshells around her because I never knew how she would react. I could never figure out when the next slap was coming. When it did, I just accepted it in sullen silence. I survived, but my bitterness against my mother just grew.

That night I needed to get out of the house. So I went with Julie Snow, my only real friend, to watch the Orleans Cardinals play baseball under the lights at Eldredge Park. The teams in the Cape Cod Summer League were composed of college kids who were Major League hopefuls. But Julie and I didn't go to watch the game. We went to watch the cute guys. When we got there, we bought hot dogs and sodas and sat as close to the dugout as we could. By the time the umpire yelled, "Play ball," I had forgotten all about my mother and that afternoon's "spell." I had other things on my mind.

Three

The next morning, as Grandma once again watched the parade of tourists from our front porch, she continued her story. She told me that she had lived in L.A. with her uncle Joaquin who worked in West Los Angeles. He was a groundskeeper who kept white men's lawns and shrubs pretty. They anglicized his name, and he simply became known as "Joe." Grandma worked as a maid, nanny, and cook. Every day she crossed the bridge to Los Angeles to work while the white men's wives played golf and bridge.

"Later, I married your grandfather at the outbreak of World War II. He was a Mexican-American named Ed Lopez. We rented a little bungalow and planted a vegetable garden behind it. He enlisted in the Marines, leaving me alone to give birth to our first son in 1943. Then I started working out of our home, cooking for the neighbors."

"How did you do that?" I asked.

"You just put your charcoal grill on the ground, outside the bungalow, and start cooking. Pick up the wet corn tortilla dough, plop it on the grille, pat it out like a pancake, carefully curl up the edges with your fingertips, and when it bubbles, add the filling of the customer's choice and sell it hot off the grill. Soon I had a little restaurant going, serving tables outside the bungalow. My menu expanded to include tacos, enchiladas, tamales, and burritos.

"When Grandpa Lopez came home from the war, he got a job for good wages at a foundry. Los Angeles was booming. My home businesses picked up, and life got better for us. I even had time to learn English and to read up on Mexican-American history." She paused thoughtfully.

"Spend time at the library, Teresita. It's America's free higher education. Especially read literature and history—it'll help you understand human nature. I taught myself English. And I would've liked to go to real school, to college maybe. But my family came first: *Mi familia!* My family meant everything!" Grandma said with conviction. "The meals, the dinner and bedtime prayers, the work, the celebration . . . the love—that's family.

"That's how your mother grew up in the fifties. But the money . . . there was better money after World War II. Even the Hispanics dreamed the American dream. Your grandpa and I bought a home. It wasn't much, and it was small, but it was better than the bungalow we'd been living in . . . and it was ours, Teresita. Soon we filled it with three more sons. In 1946 I had my first daughter, your mother. I named her 'Maria' as I had promised Our Lady, like I already told you. When your mother grew up, she studied hard, and her teachers said she should try for a scholarship so she could go to college. She won a scholarship and was the first in our family to go to a college! We were so proud of her—even though she could hardly speak Spanish!"

"Why couldn't she?" I asked.

"For the same reason you don't speak Spanish. Too much English, always English. Spanish just slowly disappeared. Grandpa spoke Spanish but only broken English. I taught myself English and your mother spoke English, but only broken Spanish, I'm sorry to say—just the opposite of her father. In high school your mother didn't even study Spanish. She took French! And now you don't even understand simple Spanish!" Grandma sighed and with a frown said, "So now I have to explain everything to you myself."

"I'm sorry, Grandma."

"Well, never mind, Teresita. But try to remember your roots. Now I'm going in for a cup of tea. *Adiós!* " She stood up straight and tall, chin up, and I saw a grin break over her weathered face.

"What's that mean, Grandma?" I asked with a smile.

With feigned exasperation, she threw her hands up in the air and went back into the house. After she left, I sat there and thought, *Wow, what a woman! Not even a high school education, and she knows so much! Mom never told me anything about Grandma's journey or my heritage. I wonder if she's ashamed of it . . . now that she's so Americanized.*

Four

O h, my God!" My mother let the phone slip down the side of her face, and I could clearly see a tear squeeze out of her left eye and run down her cheek. It was a breathtakingly beautiful autumn day, and I had just walked in the door from school. Immediately I knew something was wrong. My mother never cried. So I stood very still until she composed herself. "Teresita . . . oh . . . Grandma . . . she's dead. Grandma's dead."

A gasp escaped from my open mouth, and I remember feeling as if I were in shock, anaesthetized—like a deer caught in the headlights of an oncoming car. "No! . . . how? . . . why now? . . . it's not fair!"

"She had a stroke. Don't ask too many questions . . . I don't have any answers."

I felt like someone had kicked me in the stomach, and I ran to the bathroom in tears and vomited. The only one who really cared for me was dead. I was only 13. I didn't realize then what a loss it would mean for me and how much I could have used her wisdom and advice in the future.

We went to L.A. for the funeral. It was my first airplane ride and my first and last trip to see my mother's family. The funeral reception was held at Grandma's home. Relatives came from all parts of L.A. The young family members lined up by age to endure the kisses from our aunts and the rough handshakes from the work-hardened hands of our uncles. I felt conspicuously awkward and embarrassed because I had never met any of them before.

In contrast to my discomfort, the house was filled with laughter, singing, dancing, and storytelling, which got wilder the more that the wine flowed. I didn't feel at all like I was at a funeral reception. It was more like a birthday party. Grandpa told of Grandma's epic pilgrimage from Mexico to Los Angeles, while the uncles told of their macho feats as young men. Meanwhile, the aunts were busy preparing and serving the food.

Later in the evening when it got dark, Grandpa told the young children a ghost story called *La Llorona*—"The Crier." Out of curiosity I followed my grandpa and cousins into a darkened bedroom for the telling of the tale. He began in a slow and scary voice: "*La Llorona* was a widowed mother, and she was supposed to take care of her children. But she just wanted to have fun and go out and dance with men. She didn't want to stay home and take care of her children. So one day she killed all three of them! Soon after that, her neighbors heard cries coming from her bungalow at night. One night there were no cries so they went to investigate. They found her lying dead on her bed next to a bottle of pills with a note: 'I killed my children, and now I've killed myself because I'm so sorry and lonely.'

"Then her ghost haunted that bungalow, and you could hear her cries at night, *Mis hijos, mis hijos!*—'My children, my children!' Nobody ever bought that bungalow because it was haunted and even today at the lot where the bungalow once stood you can still hear *La Llorona* crying at night, *Mis hijos, mis hijos!*"

There was utter silence, and then Grandpa turned on the lights, hugged all of the frightened children in his big arms and said, "Our family is not like *La Llorona* because we love all of our children and all of you! So don't be frightened. Just remember the moral—'Love the children!'"

Then he led us back to join the rest of the family. It didn't seem to be a very appropriate story for a funeral reception or for children, but it kept them occupied and gave the adults a break from their running around inside the house. The celebration continued, and instead of mourning Grandma's death that evening, the family seemed to be rejoicing in it.

There weren't many family celebrations like that for me on Cape Cod. I had no aunts or uncles there. My mother's relatives all lived in California. Like my father, I was an only child. Grandma was the only relative that ever visited us. So I never heard any more family tales or ghost stories. No more lessons on my heritage or maxims of adult wisdom. Instead, my father and mother spent most of their time working and socializing. There wasn't much time or interest in family communication. We just sat around and watched television in lonely, isolating silence.

Five

I don't have the time or the inclination to sit down and be interrogated," my mom said with obvious irritation.

"It's not an interrogation, Mom. Couldn't we try to make it a *conversation?*" I asked.

"Not with that pad of paper and your pen in your hand, Teresita." She pointed at the school notebook that lay innocently in my lap.

It was near Thanksgiving, shortly after my grandmother's funeral. And after seeing all the relatives in L.A., I wanted to learn more about my family. My English teacher assigned an essay on "My Mother's Life" which was due after the school break. I was actually thankful for this homework because it gave me an excuse to actually "talk" to my mother.

At first, she was very resistant. I followed her around the house for days and pestered her to give me at least a short interview. But she was always too busy and impatient. Finally, after supper one night I literally begged her to help me with my assignment, appealing to her from an academic standpoint. Eventually I convinced her that it was a non-threatening "interview" and not an intimidating "interrogation." With obvious reluctance, she gave in and sat down—surprisingly in "Grandma's" rocking chair. With paper and pen in hand, I sat directly across from her, as I used to with Grandma, and started the interview. It was a little rigid and formal at first, but it was the best conversation that we ever had. I learned things about her and her family that I had never known before.

My mother began by nervously tapping her fingers on the arm of the rocking chair. She crossed and re-crossed her legs. With downcast eyes and an anxious voice, she finally said, "I don't know where to begin."

"Just start with your happy memories," I suggested.

She haltingly began, punctuating her sentences with long pauses. "Uh . . . my happy memories are of my family. They all begin with my family. You know all about the family roots from Grandma, but maybe I can tell you about some things that bring back happy memories from my girlhood . . . those traditions are all gone now, though." Her eyes seem to moisten with regret.

"For example, take December, which should be meaningful to you because it's the month of your birthday. The first tradition in December was always the Feast of Our Lady of Guadalupe. This is on your birthday, December 12. I can still hear Grandma saying, 'Remember it's pronounced *gwa-da-loo-pay*—it's part of your heritage!' The whole family would go to a special Mass to honor Our Lady as our patroness and protectress. You've heard from Grandma how she and her mother always prayed to her for protection and how she always came through for them. We called her *La Morenita*—'The Little Brown Girl' because she appeared in Mexico as a *mestiza*—someone who is both Spanish and Indian. She came to bring reconciliation between the Spanish Conquistadors and the conquered Indians. *La Morenita* did this by forming *La Raza*—the Mexican people from their intermarriages. Well, anyway, we'd all go to this special Mass on December 12th to thank her.

"We were poor, but we spared no cost for *La Virgen*. The Church altar was filled with beautiful, fresh, fragrant, roses. That was because when *La Virgen* appeared in Mexico City on December 12, 1531 to the Indian Juan Diego, she gave him fresh roses."

"Where'd she get them in the middle of the winter?" I asked.

"They suddenly and miraculously bloomed right in front of his eyes. She gave them to him as a sign for the Bishop so that he would believe and honor her request for a church to be built on that spot. Juan carried the roses to the Bishop in his *tilma*—a poncho-like cloak. He dropped them at the Bishop's feet and as the roses fell, *La Virgen's* image miraculously appeared on Juan's *tilma*. The Bishop believed Our Lady's request and built the church that she requested. That's why we believed that we too were helping to honor her request to 'build a church' by going to church ourselves on her Feast Day."

"How come *we* don't do that?" I interrupted. "We could do it for my birthday! Please, Mom! I'd really like—"

My mother put her hand up as a sign that I should be silent. "Teresita, don't be so impulsive. You get yourself so worked-up. If you're going to act that way every time I tell you something, I'm going to stop right now."

I felt embarrassed because I had allowed myself to get caught up in my mother's story. I got too close to her. And she criticized me, as she had so many times. It always felt like rejection and it was painful. "All right, all right, Mom. I won't say anything."

My mother waited for at least a minute before she began again. The interruption had changed the tone of our conversation and the silence was very uncomfortable, like an unspoken punishment which she wanted to make sure that I knew I deserved. She seemed as if she were considering whether or not she wanted to continue. When she felt that she was in control of the situation again, she slowly and purposefully continued.

"We don't celebrate the Feast of Our Lady of Guadalupe any more, Teresita. Times have changed, and traditions disappear. So let's just acknowledge that and move on." I shook my head in reluctant agreement, with my eyes fixed on my paper as I didn't want her to sense my disappointment.

"So anyway, *mariachis* with guitars and trumpets would lead a great procession to the rose-covered altar with the priest and the altar boys who carried a large image of *La Virgen*. She looked so beautiful with her hands folded in prayer, her head lowered in humility wearing a mantle covered with stars and surrounded by the rays of the sun.

"All of the Hispanic families would be there dressed up in their Sunday best. We'd sing songs in honor of *La Virgen* and make *promesas* just like your grandma's *promesa* to name me 'Maria' if she made her pilgrimage safely to El Paso."

"And she did! That's a great story. How come you never told me about Grandma's *promesa*, Mom?"

"I don't know. Maybe I thought it was an old wives' tale. Or maybe I thought it was too "cute." Either way, I guess it embarrassed me every time my mother talked about it."

"How come?"

"Anyway," she went on, ignoring my question, "after Mass people would give testimonies of how *La Virgen* had helped them during the past year—how they stopped drinking, or became faithful to their wives, got jobs, had healthy babies, or received healings."

My mother shifted in her chair and looked up at the ceiling, obviously avoiding my disappointed and questioning eyes. "It was all so long ago. It seems like another lifetime when I was another person. But I can remember . . . how it felt to be Hispanic."

"How did it feel, Mom?"

"That you were loved . . . by *La Virgen* and Jesus and other Hispanics. There were so many others, like one big family. You could feel the warmth.

"I'm sorry I didn't tell you about these traditions before," she winced. "It was like I started a whole new life when I married your father. I left L.A. behind, came to the Cape, and transformed myself into an Anglo. I didn't want anybody to know . . . that I was Hispanic. So I kept my origins and traditions under wraps. Pretty awful, huh?"

"No, I can understand it. There aren't many Hispanics here on the Cape, and we didn't have any relatives to celebrate those traditions with. I don't think you're terrible, Mom. Tell me some more."

"Our next December tradition," she continued as the memories flowed, "would be celebrated the week before Christmas, *Las Posadas*—'The Lodgings.' My friends and I would get together and imitate Mary and Joseph who looked for lodging on the first Christmas. We would put on costumes and go from house to house like you used to on Halloween. Only we didn't say, 'Trick or treat.' We'd ask the people if they had lodging for us. Someone from within would shout, 'No! There's no room in the inn.' But then they'd invite us in to eat *pan dulce*—sweet rolls—and to drink Mexican hot chocolate. It was all so exciting. It also helped to remind us that Jesus came through Mary as a poor and humble baby. And that we should welcome everyone, especially babies. . . . " Her voice trailed off, she winced and rapidly started up again.

"It all climaxed at midnight on Christmas Eve with *El Abrazo de Navidad*—'The Christmas Hug.' We gave each other Christmas hugs because Jesus was born at midnight, and we were happy about his birth that brought peace to the earth. For us, Christmas was about being together as family and showing respect and love to God and each other. It was a very emotional event, Teresita. We never believed in Santa Claus, and we gave more hugs, food, and drink than gifts. Grandma used to say, 'Sharing ourselves is more important than giving expensive presents.'"

My mother seemed to be seeing her memories. Her eyes were focused on something I couldn't see. "We decorated the house with *faroles*—tissue-paper lanterns—and the tree with popcorn strings and colorful *Ojos de Dios*—'The Eyes of God.' These were homemade triangular decorations that looked like God's eyes watching over us when they were placed on the tree. Then on Christmas morning, we'd open our simple gifts. We were poor, but Mama and Papa always made sure that we had a good Christmas. Then we'd go to the poinsettia-filled church for Mass and celebrate the birth of Baby Jesus.

"Since Grandma's funeral, I've been thinking about the old days and the traditions . . . and my family back in L.A. So much has changed. We don't even go to Mass any more, Teresita."

She was silent and thoughtful for a moment, and then she seemed to snap out of it, continuing, "When I was about your age, my parents were very strict with me. They weren't permissive like we've been with you. It was very different then. My parents still lived the old-fashioned Mexican values. I couldn't smoke, drink, or even date until I was 18. When they did let me out, I had to be home early. So I ended up rebelling. Papa tried to keep such a tight reign on me! But he had his hands full. I lied about where I was going and sneaked out of the house to meet guys. I just wanted to be like the other girls. The times were changing in the sixties, and I guess the movements for sexual freedom and social justice had a great influence on me. The changes were everywhere around you in the music, the movies, the books and the television. It was a different time. You can't possibly know what it was like unless you lived through it . . . as a young person. It was powerful, really powerful."

I was a bit shocked with her revelations since she'd never opened up like this with me before.

"The idealism of my youth," she mused, "was all stirred by President Kennedy's inaugural challenge in 1960: 'Ask not what your country can do for you, ask what you can do for your country.' I thought to myself, 'What could *I* do?' But I didn't do anything, not until I got into college later. It takes a while for idealism to crystallize into action."

"Well, what happened to crystallize your idealism?" I asked, as I shook out my cramped hand from all the writing.

"George Wallace, the Governor of Alabama! I'll never forget his speech, 'Segregation now, segregation tomorrow, and segregation forever.' And this led to Dr. Martin Luther King, Jr.'s marches against discrimination and for the right to vote. The blacks marched for the right to be treated as human beings equal in dignity to the rest of society. My mind was filled with the television images of them marching in the South. They marched, and the cops mowed them down with high-pressure water from firehoses and attacks by German Shepherd police dogs." My mother's voice seemed to get higher pitched, her eyes glassed over, and her speech was rapid, as her emotional momentum built up.

"It reached its high point with Dr. King's stirring 'I Have a Dream' speech in the front of the Lincoln Memorial In Washington, D.C., in the summer of 1963. I read that speech over and over and almost memorized it. He gave us an image of his American Dream of racial harmony and freedom where a person would not be judged by the color of his skin but by the content of his character, where little black boys and girls would be able to join hands with little white boys and girls and walk together as sisters and brothers. I can still hear him chanting . . . It reminds me of the Pilgrim heritage here on the Cape . . .

Land of the Pilgrim's pride, from every mountainside, let freedom ring . . . and speed up that day when all of God's children will be able to join hands and sing in the words of the old Negro spiritual, "Free at last! Free at last! Thank God Almighty, we are free at last!"

"That's pretty heavy stuff, Mom. But what did *you* do?"

"I'm getting to that." She began to rock faster and faster in the chair. "Before I could do anything, my ideals began to dissolve. When I was a senior in high school, we were discussing the Civil Rights Movement in my history class when the principal abruptly walked in. She whispered into Sister Joan's ear. Then a tear dropped from Sister Joan's eye as she announced in anguish, 'President Kennedy has just been shot in Dallas, Texas.' It was November 22, 1963 . . . *eighteen* years ago this very month," she said, closing her eyes and placing her hand to her lowered forehead, shaking her head in disbelief, "the beginning of my disillusionment."

There was a long silence and then my mother opened her eyes, looked down at her watch, abruptly got up from the rocker, and said, "Well, Teresita, I gotta' run. I'm going to be late for a house showing. I'll tell you the rest some other time."

I gathered some more bits and pieces of the story over the next few days from short conversations I had with my mother while we prepared dinner or did the dishes. I wondered why she was so mean to me when she seemed to have had such a normal and happy childhood herself. As it turned out, she went through high school, got a scholarship, and proudly entered U.C.L.A. in 1964. She said that her professors challenged her to forget the Great American Dream. But she didn't explain what this meant until her schedule slowed down at Thanksgiving.

Six

*T*hanksgiving on Cape Cod was a big celebration because the Pilgrims came there in 1620. They had the first Thanksgiving meal at Plymouth, just up the coast from my hometown of Orleans. Orleans was known as the Second Pilgrim Colony because many of them settled there after Plymouth got too crowded. The Pilgrims were convinced that there was a divine purpose for their settlement in the new world. It was like a new Eden for them. So they gave thanks to God at the First Thanksgiving for their safe arrival, their homes and their food.

My family never prayed, so I assumed my parents had forgotten how to give thanks. And my mother wasn't much of a cook. So we always went out to a restaurant for our Thanksgiving turkey dinner. We were conspicuously one of the few families there. Most people, after all, had dinner at home with their family. I remember feeling like a jerk eating alone in silence with my parents on Thanksgiving Day.

When we got home, Dad turned on the football games and I managed to corner my reluctant mother in the kitchen, asking her to explain what her professors meant about forgetting the Great American Dream. She poured some tea for us and began.

"My professors told us that the Great American Dream was really a nightmare, Teresita. A nightmare of war, discrimination, and injustice. They challenged us to get involved in protests against the unjust war in Vietnam and in social activism for the oppressed. In their liberal vision of social justice, they believed in the unlimited potential of all people. Since I wanted justice for the Hispanic migrant workers, this philosophy gave me hope. I fed my hope by voraciously reading books about peaceful civil disobedience for non-violent social change. Books by St. Francis of Assisi, Thoreau, Gandhi, Martin Luther King, Jr., and Cesar Chavez.

"But some of the activists weren't patient or peaceful. In August 1965, the blacks in the Watts section of Los Angeles exploded in rioting, looting, and arson. It lasted six days! People were killed, hundreds wounded, and millions of dollars worth of property was destroyed. It took thousands of National Guardsmen to quiet things down.

"The politicians demanded that the blacks have patience and respect. That reminded me of how my mother said she learned from her mother the character traits of *aguante* and *respeto*. *Aguante* is to have determination and to endure suffering. *Respeto* is to respect your parents, teachers, and employers. But, like the blacks, my mother said that there was too much *aguante* and *respeto* and not enough justice, especially for the migrant farm workers. They had endured suffering for too long, and there was no reason to respect the unjust farm owners. So I took up my cause for justice in defense of the migrant farm workers."

Mom obviously wasn't finished with this statement; she was just picking up steam.

"The migrant farm workers moved from farm to farm and picked certain crops as they ripened at different times of the year. My inspiration for their cause was Cesar Chavez. He was a union organizer and a former migrant worker himself. I even took notes of his speeches and kept them. I reread some of them last night."

"You did? Cool. But why was he so important to you?" I asked.

"Well, he was a man after my own heart. He said, 'The love for justice that is in us is not only the best part of our being but it is also the most true to our nature.'"

"I agree with *that!* "

Mom smiled proudly at me and continued, "The migrant workers were Mexican-Americans who lived in tin shanties or their cars and trucks. They ate whatever they could get their hands on and worked in the scorching sun for hours on end picking unsafe pesticide-laden fruits and vegetables in the San Joaquin Valley for low, piecework wages. They had no medical insurance, no workers' compensation, and no benefits. They called it, *en el labor.*"

Without a word, she raced out of the room and came back carrying a scrapbook that I didn't even know existed. She looked into it with nostalgia and said, "Chavez appealed for justice for them. Listen to what he said." Then she read from a news clipping.

Today, thousands of migrant farm workers live under savage conditions—beneath trees and amid garbage and human excrement—near fields that use the most modern farm technology and pesticides—all unsafe and unhealthy working conditions. Vicious rats gnaw on them as they sleep. They walk miles to buy food at inflated prices. And they carry in water from irrigation pumps. Almost 800,000 of their under-aged children work across America. Migrant workers are not agricultural implements. They are not beasts of burden to be used up and thrown away. They are human beings with inherent dignity as children of God and have natural rights to good living and working conditions and fair pay!

"Now that was enough to get my blood boiling and get me going to help them get those 'good living and working conditions and fair pay.'"

"So did you finally do something? What did you *do?*"

"Chavez used the great Indian leader Gandhi's methods of peaceful marches and boycotts to raise public awareness of the workers' plight, all in the hopes of gaining better conditions for them. He gave the Hispanic people a sense of *coraje*—righteous anger—and urged them to unite in a union. This resulted in the formation of the United Farm Workers.

"I joined *La Causa* Pilgrimage in March 1966. I marched 300 miles from Delano to the state capitol of Sacramento. I did it in memory of my mother's 300 mile walk from Mexico to El Paso. Cesar Chavez and a five-foot banner of *La Virgen de Guadalupe* led the Pilgrimage. Hey, I've got a newspaper article about it in my scrapbook.

"Look, look!" she said in restrained frenzy, pointing to a news photo in her scrapbook, "here's Cesar standing on the capitol steps with the banner of Our Lady of Guadalupe and our supporters. By then our ranks had swollen to 10,000. It was Easter Sunday, 1966, and a great day for all Hispanics and all seekers of justice. My idealism and social activism came to a head. I never reached that high again . . . never," she said somewhat regretfully.

"Why not?" I asked.

There was a long, uncomfortable pause. My mother cleared her throat, seeming to collect her thoughts and weigh her words.

"Because, Teresita, things changed in my life. In the middle of the Pilgrimage, I met your father. He was a Berkley student from Boston. We started a relationship . . . "

She hesitated and then stopped in mid-sentence. But the suspense was unbearable. Finally, I broke the silence. "And . . . "

" . . . and a year later I discovered that I was pregnant."

I heard my mother's words, and yet they didn't seem to register. Immediately I started to calculate dates in my head. When the math didn't add up, my jaw dropped open and my breathing became fast and difficult.

"Pregnant? With me!? You told me I was born prematurely!"

But instead of responding with maternal compassion, she became instantly defensive. "Yes, Teresita, pregnant with you! You *were* born prematurely but you were also conceived before our marriage."

It didn't take me long to realize that there would be no apologies or explanations given. In fact, my mother responded with her characteristic irritability and impatience, as if shifting some unspoken blame right back to me. When she finally realized I was left speechless by her revelation, she hurried through an explanation so that we could close the conversation.

"Actually, I probably should have told you before this. You're a big girl now. You would have found out someday anyway. It's better that you know, Teresita."

But I didn't feel like a "big girl" at that moment. I felt like crying, but there were no comforting arms to run into if I let the tears begin to flow. I would have preferred never knowing that I was conceived out of wedlock and that my mother was having sex with my father before they were married.

Though I was already obviously shaken by her comments, she was determined to get the burden off her chest. At this point, I regretted having asked her for her life's story. I really didn't want to hear this part. I felt like running out of the room, and finding some hidden place to hide for a while. But I could tell there was no escape.

"Maybe it's more information than I need, Mom."

She looked me straight in the eye and said in a low monotone voice, "In June of 1967 I got pregnant. I dropped out of college to go to work. Your father and I got married in August and you were born with your handicap on December 12th. Dad finished his last year at Berkeley and graduated in June of 1968. Right after that, we moved to the Cape. That's the story, Teresita! I hope you get a good grade on your essay. I should go watch the game with your father."

With that, she left the kitchen to join my dad in front of the television. Once again, she had rapidly finished her story as if she wanted to skip over a big part of it, get to the end and get it over with. But there still seemed to be something missing from Mom's story—a big gap. I didn't move or breathe or think for a while. I was paralyzed. She almost seemed angry with me, or at the very least, she somehow made me feel I was to blame. Like usual, it was my fault. Everything was my fault. Being born was my fault.

I tried to rationalize with myself, but my emotions were too strong. I thought, *Why should she be angry with me? Why should she blame me for her own choice to have premarital sex? Oh, I get it. I probably ruined her college career. I had made her social activism impossible. Maybe that's why she hates me . . . maybe that's why she still blames me whenever she's unhappy. . . .*

Seven

*T*eresita, come out and see my new toy!" It was a late spring evening in 1982, and I was 14 years old. I obediently walked out to the driveway, and there stood my dad in boat mocs, white duck pants, and a blue blazer all crowned by a white hat with gold cords around its brim and the word "Captain" written in blue lettering across the front. It all went well with his sky-blue eyes, close-cropped blonde hair and perennial preppy look. I was so taken by surprise at his get-up, that it took me a few moments to notice the brand new boat sitting on a trailer next to him.

"This is my Dream Machine," he proudly announced, "the BMW of the boat world. It's a 22-foot Grady White walk-around cabin with twin 150 horsepower Evinrude outboard motors, and it can do 45 miles per hour. I've named it *On Business.* That way, if anyone calls my office when I'm fishing, my secretary can truthfully say, 'He's out *on business.'* Get it? Can't let people know that I'm playing. Image is everything, Teresita. Well, what do you think?"

"Pretty nice," I answered. But I felt like saying, *You look like a nerd, and you and your dumb-named boat don't impress me at all.* Dad thought he was funny and clever. I thought he was corny and that he shouldn't tell lies. *What's wrong with moderate leisure and recreation?* I thought. *Are you embarrassed by it? Why are you so concerned about appearances? Why do you always act like you're busy?*

Of course, he was always too busy for me, too. I got the same excuse his clients did. I took piano lessons, and I loved to play. It was soothing and peaceful. I enjoyed being creative, composing my own songs from poems that I had written. But Dad never had the time to come to my piano recitals. He'd always promise to, but never did because, as he always said, "Something came up at the office." The only time that he spent with me was doing things that *he* liked to do—like Bluefishing on his boat.

I'll never forget our first trip out. The boat was berthed at Rock Harbor on Cape Cod Bay. We left the dock and cruised north toward Provincetown for about an hour. Dad was an amateur historian and perhaps the only thing that I inherited from him was my love of history. When we got to Provincetown, Dad pointed out the harbor and said, "This is where the Pilgrims signed the first governmental compact in America aboard their ship the Mayflower. That's why they called it the *Mayflower* Compact."

"Duh," I replied.

"Hey, it's important history, and I thought you liked history. This was the first document of self-government in this country. They agreed to work together and pass laws for the common good of all in their colony. You should know things like this."

"I *do* know things like this, Dad. I go to school, and I take State and Local History."

"Okay, let's go down toward home past First Encounter Beach. I'll show you something that I bet you *don't* know."

The history lessons continued as we approached the beach. "Here is where the Pilgrims had their 'first encounter' with the Indians. They left Provincetown and were looking for a place to settle. A party landed on this beach and was met by an Indian scouting party. It was their 'first encounter' with the natives."

"And that's why they named it 'First Encounter Beach,'" I interrupted sarcastically.

"Right. Then the Pilgrims fired their guns and drove the natives off."

"Oh," I interrupted again, "was this the beginning of racism in America?"

"What do you mean?"

"Whites meet reds and shoot."

"Hmm, I never thought of it that way," he shrugged.

I felt like saying, *Why don't you think of real people and tell me some of your own history, something real, something about you instead of some abstract history?* But that wouldn't have been safe for Dad.

This much I did know. His name was James Lowell, and he was born in Boston where he attended private schools, eventually going on to college at Berkley in California—much to the dismay of his parents. His father was a wealthy third generation lawyer in an established downtown law firm. He wanted my dad, his only child, to follow in his footsteps and attend Harvard Law School. Dad could've done it, but he opted for a radical break from his family's tradition to choose his own path. As he often said, "I followed Horace Greeley's nineteenth century advice, 'Go West young man!'"

So he went to Berkeley, met my mother on the Great Pilgrimage where they shared their ideals, got married, and then came back East in what was a radical break from my mother's family tradition. But it was also the *end* of Dad's family tradition. His parents disowned him after he married my mom who, they told him, "was a colored Catholic girl, far beneath your station, and an embarrassment to the Lowell family." Mom and Dad moved from California to Orleans, on Cape Cod, Massachusetts in the summer of 1968.

As Dad and I cruised along in his new boat, I asked him why they moved to the Cape. He said, "I spent my childhood summer vacations here, and I wanted to return to the land of the Pilgrims away from L.A. and crowded cities, away from California's dull weather, and back to the four seasons. Back to our country's roots in small town life. Back to the happy memories of my childhood. That was my idealistic hope anyway."

"Well, what was the problem with L.A.? Mom said you were into the migrant farm workers' cause."

"Yeah, I was. But ideals change, Teresita. Especially as you get older."

"Did anything happen out there to change them?"

I could tell he didn't want to handle that one, so he became evasive and suddenly and excitedly pointed farther out on the bay and said, "Look at the flock of gulls feeding over the Blues breaking water. Let's go get 'em!"

With that, he gunned the boat and sped out to a school of feeding Bluefish. They are rapacious predator fish that can weigh up to 20 pounds. They are built streamlined for speed to catch schools of baitfish. They travel in schools themselves and herd and corral the schools of menhaden and sand eel bait fish which they attack and slash with their sharp teeth. They could easily bite off a child's thumb. That's why they call them "Choppers." Their attacks on the baitfish schools drive them to the surface. This attracts flocks of seagulls to feed on the baitfish. So flocks of seagulls are a dead giveaway for the presence of Bluefish.

Dad ran his boat to the gulls. They were hovering over the churning water where the Bluefish slashed at baitfish from below while the gulls attacked them from above. The helpless baitfish were left floating in pieces, swirling in pools of blood on the water's surface. We cast floating lures into the churning water and reeled them back as fast as we could. The lures splashed and looked like baitfish trying to escape. This attracted the killing instincts of the Bluefish that slashed at the lures and hooked themselves. Dad yelled at me, "Tip up, tight line, and take your time! That's 'The Three T' tips for landing Blues!"

They fought real hard, jumping and running. It took me a while to bring them to the boat where Dad hooked them with a gaff—a sharpened six-inch hook on a four-foot stick. Then he lifted them into the boat leaving a trail of bright red blood on his clean white boat. But the whole scene was too gross for me. I didn't do much Bluefishing with Dad after that. The one activity that he allowed me to participate in was too bloody and violent for me to want to do with any regularity. After that, my Bluefishing days were over—and so was my "quality time" with my dad . . . with one exception.

Eight

O n the Fourth of July weekend, we took a family vacation to get away from the summer madness on Cape Cod. My parents wanted to escape from the Cape's thousands of tourists, overcrowded beaches, traffic jams, and long shopping lines and try the simplicity and quiet of Lake Champlain in Vermont. They rented a small cottage on the western shore of Isle La Motte, the northernmost island of Lake Champlain. It was as close to the northern boundary of the United States as Orleans was to its eastern boundary—ten miles.

On the long ride up, Dad gave me another history lesson. He told me that Samuel de Champlain discovered Isle La Motte, and the lake was named after him. Lake Champlain is the American *outlet* to the Atlantic Ocean by way of the St. Lawrence River. Ironically, Champlain also discovered Nauset Inlet in our hometown of Orleans almost 400 miles to the south where the Atlantic Ocean has its first American *inlet*.

On Isle La Motte we were disconnected from the rest of the country. We had no telephone or television. It felt really different especially since we spent most of our time at home in Orleans watching television. We stayed in a nice rustic log cabin that had warm knotty pine floors and paneling and a huge fieldstone fireplace. It was located on a bluff overlooking the lake and was surrounded by tall evergreen trees. On our second night, Mom went for a ride in the car to watch the sunset on the lake. While I read, Dad had a few Scotches and then abruptly said, "Hey, Teresita, let's play a game of Scrabble."

This was totally out of character for Dad since we never played board games or had much conversation or anything. So I acted like a good sport and agreed to play with him. He set up the board and we picked pieces to see who would go first. As he laboriously tried to show that he was enjoying the game, I tried to ease the tension with conversation.

"Dad, if the Cape is such a hassle in the summer, why did you and Mom move there?"

"Well," he said, "two months of hassle isn't too much to pay for ten months of a beautiful temperate climate. Besides, we knew that I could make a good living in real estate on the Cape, unlike this island where the economy is limited to the summer tourist trade."

"So you went for the climate and the economy? Didn't you have that in California?" I kept probing for the real reason my parents left L.A.

"Actually, it was more than just that. My parents always took me on family vacations for two weeks every summer on the Outer Cape. Those vacations gave me some of the happiest memories of my life. We'd do things together there like swim, hike, bike, fish, and clam. We'd finish the day by watching the sunset on the bay from First Encounter Beach. By the way, did you know that beach was named after the 'first encounter' between the native Nauset Indians and the Pilgrims?"

"Yes, Dad, I know. You showed it to me when we went Bluefishing, remember?"

"Oh, yeah." He coughed nervously. "Anyway, after the sunset we'd go back to the cottage and play board games like we're doing now. You know, I'm kind of sorry that we haven't done more things together. I guess I've been too busy with my work. They say if you don't control your work, it'll control you."

We continued playing amidst a smattering of conversation until I spelled out my game-winning word and triumphantly said, "No more pieces, I win!"

Dad groaned, saying, "Nice move." He clinked the ice cubes against the sides of his glass and took another sip of his Scotch. He leaned back and looked up at the ceiling. I could tell the alcohol was loosening him up, and I felt a little apprehensive. I wanted to know the real reason my parents left L.A., but I couldn't forget my last reaction to a parental revelation.

Somehow, I always sensed that something was off kilter in my family. Maybe the lack of communication made me feel that there was something my parents were trying to hide. And I was determined to find out, not so much out of curiosity, but out of a genuine concern. On the surface, we seemed like the perfect American family. But I knew the truth. We were three lonely people.

Dad started to open up. "Now that we're talking about it, our move to the Cape wasn't just for the climate or to relive boyhood memories. Your mother and I needed stability. We were out in California in the sixties into all kinds of idealistic causes to make the world a better place to live in.

"Your mother told me that she told you that she got pregnant with you in L.A.—and we weren't married. Honestly, Teresita, I got scared. I hate to

29

admit it, but fear drove me back East. Not just fear of offending my parents or of taking responsibility for you, but fear of getting swallowed up in permissiveness where anything goes and there are no rules. Fear of using up my energy in one cause after another. Fear of being cast adrift on the waters of life without an anchor. So Cape Cod was a move I made to find an anchor in life, someplace where there would be social stability and security."

I was amazed that Dad was talking openly like this. He'd never really spoken about himself to me before. The pace of his talking quickened. "But family values were sacrificed for the work ethic and I made a lot of money but lost a relationship with you. And I'm truly sorry about that. I don't know why I'm saying all of this except that I feel that I should be honest with you."

He began to slur his words ever so slightly. "I think that I've always been emotionally handicapped—not in touch with my feelings. I've operated from my head and not from my heart. That may be good for business, but it's bad for personal relationships. I just hope that it's not too late for us, Teresita."

I didn't quite know how to respond to this. I wanted to cry; I wanted to hug him; I wanted to believe that things would change. But I knew they wouldn't.

"Better late than never," I answered rather glibly. "I'd like to get to know you better, too, Dad."

I had trouble opening up to him. I felt so vulnerable and afraid to trust him. But despite his attempt at emotional intimacy, I still felt like he was holding something back from me. I wanted to ask him for the whole story and get to know him and maybe even ask him about boys and his advice on how to handle their sexual advances. I wanted to be prepared, but my stomach was queasy and I didn't have the guts to ask him.

Suddenly, the door opened. "You guys missed a beautiful sunset!"

And I missed my opportunity with my dad. Mom came in and interrupted the only real conversation I ever had with him. When we got back home to the Cape, the television went back on, and Dad didn't open up to me like that again. I learned to accept my parents' explanations about why they had moved to Cape Cod. But I still wasn't satisfied.

Nine

*If you're fond of sand dunes and salty air, quaint little villages here
and there, you're sure to fall in love with Old Cape Cod. . . .*

*P*atty Page's song rang out from the dusty jukebox later in the
summer of 1982 at the "Hole in One Diner." I was working there
as a waitress.

When I first saw the diner's sign, I thought it was meant to attract the
many Cape golfers. But I soon found out that it stood for the hole in the
middle of a donut, and that's what we sold to the local carpenters and
fishermen—early morning fresh donuts and good strong coffee. These were
real homemade donuts and real homemade men, unlike the mass-produced
donuts eaten by seemingly mass-produced men at the fast food chains.

Patty Page's song was from the fifties, but it was still played on the
Cape's remaining jukeboxes. The song evoked familiar images of the
Cape with its winding roads, skies of blue, moonlight over the bay, and
"church bells chiming on a Sunday morn that remind you of the town
where you were born."

As the words of the song drifted through my head, I filled sugar jars and
reflected on the town where I was born—Orleans, right in the center of Cape
Cod. I was thinking about the sand dunes.

"Hey, instead of just listenin' to songs about san' dunes, ya wanna' see
some *real* san' dunes?" One of my cute customers snapped me out of my
daydream and waved me over to his table.

"Can I help you?"

"Yeah, you can come with me and see some real san' dunes."

I thought that he was trying to make a move on me, so I said, "No
thanks, I see 'em all the time when I go to Nauset Beach."

"Yeah, but I bet you've never seen the whole ten miles of 'em."

"No, just near the swimming beach. But I'm really not interested, thank you."

31

"Come on, I won't hurt ya'. I drive a dune taxi—'Doug's Dune Drives.'
I'm Doug, and I'll give you a ride that you'll nevah forget . . . for free!"

I felt a little safer, but I couldn't figure out why he made the offer. So I
said, "Well . . . maybe if I can take my friend Julie with me."

"Sure , take anybody ya' want . . . plen'y 'a room."

"Why free?"

"Well, if you'd mention my business to *your* customers, maybe they'll
become *my* customers."

"I get it. I think I could help you there —"

"Fine, I'll pick you and your friend up at 9 a.m. on your day off."

"That'll be Thursday."

"See ya' then." He put his money on the table and left with a smile.

On Thursday morning, my best friend Julie Snow and I stood outside
the diner. We had been friends since grammar school and did everything
together. Promptly at nine, a bright yellow Suburban four-wheel drive taxi
drove up and suddenly stopped. Doug jumped out of the driver's side with a
big smile on his tanned face. He walked around the front of the car, pointed
at the painted sign on the front passenger's door and said, "Welcome to
Doug's Dune Drives, Driver Doug at your service." Then he opened the rear
door and held it for us. We climbed into the back seat, and he got into the
front. He put his right arm on the back of the seat and started our drive
towards Nauset Beach.

He started right in on his spiel. "Well folks, here we are on Main Street
in the Town of Orleans, Massachusetts. Some of the Pilgrims settled here in
1644. They moved here from their original settlement at Plymouth
Plantation because of their small land grants. Orleans became known as the
Second Pilgrim Colony. The name goes back to Orleans, France where St.
Joan of Arc ended an English siege in the thirteenth century. Today her
statue stands overlooking this here town from the front of the Catholic
Church named after her —"

"We know. Julie and I went to grammar school there. Now we're going
to Nauset High."

"Nice church, huh?"

"Yeah, that's where we were baptized and received our First
Communion. Don't see much of it anymore. But . . . I always admired Joan
of Arc. I thought she was a great feminist."

"A *feminist?* How's that?"

"She tried to follow God and not her culture. She even wore men's
clothing and led them into combat! She was also a virgin—the Maid of
Orleans. She believed that the French would beat the English invaders only

through purity. So, she banished prostitutes from her camp and made her soldiers go to Confession before they went into battle."

"Whoa! . . . you sure know your history."

"Yeah, thanks to my grandmother . . . and the French drove the English out of France."

"Well I'm gonna' drive *you* down to the beach. But first, I gotta' stop here at the parking lot to let some air outta' my tires."

"Why?" asked Julie. "Won't your tires get flat, and we'll get stuck in the sand?"

I thought, *Julie, maybe you should let some of the air out of your head, so you don't get stuck in your ignorance.* But I didn't say anything. She wasn't the brightest girl in my class, but she was kind to me and not prejudiced against my race like some of the other kids. I enjoyed her company.

Doug explained the air situation to her. "When I let some air out, we'll have *more* traction over the sand, not less. Now that we're stopped, I want you to look around. Orleans is only 5 miles wide from the ocean to the bay. These sand dunes hold back the ocean. The strong winds carve them up, and their shapes are always changing.

"Look north over there towards Nauset Inlet," he continued. "That's where the ocean comes through to form Nauset Marsh. Check out the glowing chartreuse colors of the marsh grass. The light here's very unique. The sun reflects off the sea and gives brilliance to the light. Colors look more brilliant. It's like the sunlight passes through a magnifying glass. It also makes the cranberry bogs fiery red and the blueberry and goldenrod fields brilliant. The Cape landscape is a kaleidoscope of colors. The sun rises here from the ocean and sets over there on the bay. Ya know, it's one of the few places on the east coast where the sun sets over the water."

"Cool."

"Okay, now Ill let the air out of my tires and we'll drive south down to the next inlet—that's Chatham Inlet where the ocean flows into Pleasant Bay. We'll see the dunes, Pleasant Bay and its islands on the right and the ocean on our left as we drive along the beach."

As he started off along the beach, we bounced along the ruts formed by other cars. Doug was quiet for a change. He just let the wind blow his long blond hair, and he sucked up the salt air. It gave Julie and me a chance to talk.

"Speaking of St. Joan of Arc, I don't see you there anymore, Terry." She had anglicized my name.

"Nope, I stopped when I graduated. My parents don't go, so why should I? My mom said it was my choice . . . I couldn't believe it . . . my first real choice. She let me make it."

"What about Confirmation? Are you going to go to the classes on Monday nights?"

"Hadn't thought about that. But . . . no, I don't think so. Why should I, if I don't even go to church? It won't do anything for me. I've got better things to do with my time —"

"My mom said that you need the graces of Confirmation to stand against teenage temptations for booze, drugs and sex," Julie said softly, testing for my reaction.

"That won't be a problem for me. I'm strong. My grandma said I have *aguante*—endurance. I'll be fine without —"

"Look, Terry . . . there's some Nauset kids having a beach party—volleyball, surfing and piling up the driftwood for a bonfire tonight."

"Oh, I can't wait, Julie! I hope that I hurry up and meet a guy with wheels. I'm tired of riding my bike to the beach, looking like a nerdy grade school kid."

"Me too! It won't be long before we're driven to our own beach parties."

"Hope so."

"Now look out to the ocean," Doug chimed in again. "There are a lot of shallow sandbars out there. Many sailing ships were wrecked on 'em. They called it the 'Graveyard of the Atlantic.' Even the Mayflower almost wrecked on 'em, and it had to sail back with the Pilgrims to Provincetown. Sometimes shipwrecks lead to safe harbors."

"That's something to think about," I said.

"Yeah, but not all of 'em made it to a safe harbor. The survivors of the shipwrecks who made it to this here shore were called 'washashores.'"

"What's that mean?" asked Julie.

"They called 'em 'washashores' because they were washed ashore, and then they decided to settle down here."

I thought about that for the rest of the ride as Doug droned on with his tourist talk. I stopped listening to him and listened to the roaring sound of the surf. I could smell the salty air. I saw the now deserted beach as we went further south. It was 100 yards wide from the surfline to the dunes. Beyond them you could see the islands of Pleasant Bay set like green emeralds in a sea of cobalt blue. On the way back to the parking lot I could feel the wind in my face with its occasional stings of blown sand. I felt much more alive than when I rode my bike to the beach. Finally, he dropped us off at the diner.

"How'd I do?" he asked.

"Fine," I said. "But it's more for a tourist than a townie like me. How long have you been doing this?"

"It's *supposed* to be for tourists. Remember? That's why I took you, so that you could get me some tourist business. And guess what? You're my first trip. I just bought the Suburban."

"Well, it was a good first trip . . . the tourists will love it. Have a great season."

Julie and I went in to the "Hole in One," sat down and ordered some cokes. I said, "When Doug called those shipwreck survivors 'washashores,' I thought of my parents right away."

"Why?"

"Well, it seems like they got shipwrecked out in California in the sixties, survived and washed ashore here in Orleans. That's what they told me and that's what I've been thinking about all the way back here in the car."

"What shipwreck, Terry?"

"It's like they were on this ship of ideals that wrecked and they survived it and came here like washashores. My mom said that they had great idealism in the sixties that vanished when they realized that they couldn't eliminate poverty, discrimination, and injustice. When the sixties ended with the assassinations of Martin Luther King, Jr. and Bobby Kennedy, they were completely disillusioned. After that, they put all their frustrated energies into their careers.

"That's why they're preoccupied with work, social life, and me—in that order. Their ideals gave way to reality. Don't you see? There were no more causes. They just wanted the good life."

"And that's why your dad is rich?"

"Yeah, if you can't make justice, you might as well make money."

"Is that what the sixties did to them?"

"Yeah, but the seventies weren't much better. Remember when we learned that the seventies began with the National Guard killings of the student protesters at Kent State University? It all went downhill from there, and then it ended with the Iranian hostage crisis and the failed attempt to rescue them. It was a decade of disasters—of oil embargoes, the Watergate scandal, the toppling of Nixon's presidency, and our defeat in Vietnam. Put that all together and you've got a real crisis of the spirit."

"Crisis of the spirit?" asked Julie.

"Yeah, that's what President Jimmy Carter called it. He complained on national television about a crisis of the spirit that had led Americans to forsake God and family for the worship of self-indulgence and consumption. . . . He was talking about my parents.

"So my dad's a rich real estate broker . . . always working . . . I never see him. He's always showing some property for sale or socializing to get people to list their properties with him.

"And my mom's cut off her Hispanic roots and Americanized herself . . . climbing into the upper middle class with my dad. She helps him part-time in his work and full-time in his socializing, mostly at cocktail parties and dinners.

"She never allows herself to get close to me, emotionally or physically. You don't know how many times I've wanted to hug her or kiss her, and all I get is her cheek turned toward me or her shoulders hanging limply while I do all the 'hugging.' I really want to be held by her, but she always keeps her distance. The only time she gets close to me is when she gets into one of her weird 'spells.'

"For no reason at all, she'll fly into a rage, yelling and slapping me for no reason. Then it's like she gets all sorry, and breaks down, and for a minute, she'll let me see that she doesn't hate me . . . but even that doesn't last, and it's almost worse, 'cause when she does let her guard down for one minute, the next minute she's twice as bad, as if she's trying to prove to me that I did something wrong. I just want to feel her love, to feel her arms around me, and to hear a gentle, tender voice. I act tough, as if I don't need these things . . . but really . . . I do."

"Geez, Terry, I had no idea. I get along fine with my parents. No problems."

"You're lucky, I wish I had it like you. Only a few more years and I'll be in college and out of the house. Can't wait! I just hope that the eighties will be better for us than the sixties and seventies were for our parents."

"So do I. Let's hope that the messes are all behind us. We've got a lot of fun to look forward to, but right now I have to get home for lunch. Come on . . . let's go."

We left the diner, got on our bikes and rode home.

Ten

My teen life in the early eighties focused on studying, surfing, and skiing. Fortunately, my limp handicap didn't stop me from participating in these sports. I just had a difficult time running, so I didn't play basketball or soccer. But I could stand on my surfboard and skis. Julie and I would surf in the summer sun and ski in the winter snow. We also canoed the marshes where we picked mussels from the mud banks and dug for soft-shelled clams on the mud flats. Then we'd steam them in a little broth of garlic, butter, and wine for a delicious dinner. When the shells opened, they were ready, and we'd dump them into a large bowl, fork out the meat, dip it in the broth and eat them with some crusty garlic bread.

Like Julie, the other kids at Nauset High soon started to call me "Terry," despite my objections. It seemed like what I had left of my Hispanic heritage was being taken away from me. Because of this, I tried to hold on to my heritage even harder by studying Spanish. I also followed my grandmother's suggestion and used the public library to study the history and sociology of my cultural roots, which I was honestly confused about. So, one day after school during my freshman year, I asked my mother about it.

"What am I, Mom?"

"What do you mean, 'what am I?'"

"I mean, what race am I? What is my nationality? You can't go anywhere if you don't know where you came from. You can't be anybody if you don't know who you are."

"You're an American. Why do you ask?"

"Then what are you?"

"I'm a Mexican-American."

"Why?"

"Because my mother was Mexican and my father Mexican-American."

"What was Grandma?"

"She was a Mexican-Indian because she was born in Mexico with Indian blood."

"Then why aren't I a Mexican-American since I was born in America with Mexican blood."

"Because all of that blood got mixed into plain American. Your father is American and so are you."

"Well, I don't think I am," I replied adamantly. "I feel like the Afro-Americans must've felt when they went through their identity crisis. First they were Negroes, then they were blacks and now they're Afro-Americans. I think that my race is Mexican-American because I've studied this and my blood is *mestizo*—mixed blood—Mexican and American."

"Believe me, Teresita, you don't want to be a Mexican-American. It's too hard. That's what I am and I know. The Mexicans don't accept you, and the Americans don't want you. You're in a racial twilight zone of half-breed brown-colored people. You don't fit in the light of the whites or the dark of the blacks. So you face discrimination unless you can be more Mexican than the Mexicans and more American than the Americans. So that's what I did. I became more American than the Americans, and I don't face any discrimination. With my coloring, I simply pass as someone of Italian descent. And that's all right with me."

"Well, it's not all right with me! And how can someone like you, with your dark black eyes and hair and chocolate-colored skin, pass for an Italian?"

"It all depends on how you present yourself, Teresita."

"Well, I don't think that you should be ashamed of your roots or your color or who you are."

"Look, Teresita, didn't you learn in school that America is a 'melting pot'? That means that all of the nationalities blend into one, and you simply become an American."

"Yes, but you don't have to believe that. It's not really true. It's just a myth."

"No, it isn't. Your grandma was a Mexican-Indian, I'm a Mexican-American and you're simply an American. So you have the transition from the country of origin, to a hyphenated American to a full American. And that's what you are, and you should be proud of it."

"Well I'm not. I'm proud to be a *Mexican*-American, just like you should be. But I'm still a little confused about my culture. I thought that I was Hispanic . . . but the word is too macho."

"Macho?" Mom asked.

"Yeah, it goes against my feminist leanings. It's not inclusive. If I'm *His*panic, I can't be *Her*spanic," I joked.

"That's a good one."

"So then I read that the name Latino covers everyone of Spanish and Native American Indian or black descent from Mexico, Central America, South America, and the Caribbean. That's about as inclusive as you can get, and the best part is that a female Latino is a Latina. So that's what I am, a Mexican-American Latina, and I'm proud of it! I'm a Latina who is racially mestizo, culturally Latino and patriotically American."

"Okay, Miss Latina," Mom sighed, "but I think that you'd be better off being just a plain old American."

How prophetic were her words.

Eleven

*T*his is the shape of Cape Cod," Mr. Flint, my freshman geography teacher, said as he made a fist and a muscle. He held out his left arm. He looked like a guy in an ad for bodybuilding. I'd had a crush on him since school started. He was so kind to me and so handsome that my eyes bulged out of my head from gawking. On this particular day, he was wearing a short-sleeved white shirt and his bicep was stretching his shirtsleeve out to its limit.

He pointed with his right hand. "Here's the end of the Cape at Provincetown where my fist is. Chatham's at my elbow. My bicep is Barnstable, and my shoulder is the Massachusetts mainland." Then he pointed to the inside of his elbow and said, "And right here is our own town of Orleans."

I didn't hear anything else that he said. Hot flashes shot through my body. I didn't understand what was happening to me. I just stared at handsome Mr. Flint and his muscle and felt hot all over.

When I got home that afternoon, I ran up to my room, changed into my jeans, flopped down on my bed and stared at the ceiling thinking about Mr. Flint and how he made me feel.

He always smiles at me and pats me on my back to encourage me. He pays more attention to me than my own father. Maybe he feels the same way about me as I feel about him. I can see him holding me and saying, "It's okay, Terry, I'll take care of you, and everything will be all right." And my body got hotter as I imagined his caring words.

That's ridiculous, I continued to think, *he's in his thirties and I'm only 14! Even though he's single, I don't stand a chance. I'm probably just a kid to him. But I'd show him otherwise if he gave me a chance. I'd love him forever. . . . Teresita, you've gotta' stop thinking like this! I know . . . I'll think about my hometown and what he taught us today. That should distract me from these crazy thoughts.* Then I started to reflect on how much I loved my hometown.

I lived where Mr. Flint showed us, right in the crook of his elbow on Main Street. It had brick-lined sidewalks that led to the white-steepled Congregational Church in the center of town. Surrounding the church were quaint little shops with their flower boxes full of bright red geraniums and white and blue petunias.

My family lived in a white clapboard two-story colonial house with a wrap-around front porch. Behind it was Town Cove's shoreline. Town Cove was at the inland end of the waterway that led from the ocean at Nauset Inlet—Mr. Flint's forearm. Samuel de Champlain discovered it in 1605. The tidal water comes from the Atlantic Ocean through Nauset Inlet, which is a cut through Nauset Beach. The water then flows through Nauset Marsh and continues like a river until it ends in Town Cove. And that was my backyard.

From my house I could row out into Town Cove or ride my bike along Main Street east to the ocean at Nauset Beach or west to the bay at Rock Harbor. Either way it was only a short ride of two and a half miles because we lived right in the center of town. I loved to ride my bike. The pace was slower than riding in a car, and I could appreciate the scenery more as I rode along. I loved the sense of freedom, the feel of the sun on my head, the wind in my face, and the smell of the flowers and the salty air. Sometimes in morning fogs you could even taste the salt in the air.

The ocean and the bay had different moods that were affected by the variables of nature—temperature, barometric pressure, tide, wind force, and the amount of sunshine. The ocean greets the new day with magnificent sunrises and shouts at you with the roar of its crashing waves. The gentle bay whispers to you at the close of day with its awesome sunsets and stillness.

Their moods were like the changes in people who have their ups and downs like the tides, who are buffeted by the shifting winds of life, frozen by deep cold and warmed by sweet sunshine. I learned that if you're sensitive to the variables of nature, you're sensitive to the variables in yourself and other people, and you can better understand yourself and others.

I'd ride my bike to the ocean or to the bay and allow myself to become sensitive to the variables of nature. There were no better places to feel on the inside what you see on the outside. When the sun reflected off the water, I saw it as a symbol of all the happiness that radiated outward from my joyful spirit. When the clouds cast long shadows, I saw it as a symbol of my own darkness.

I'd ride to Nauset Beach on the ocean where the snack bar was famous for its hot dogs, fries, and malts. I'd meet my friends and we'd spend many a summer weekend enjoying eating, swimming, surfing, and volleyball until almost sunset. From Nauset you looked to the endless horizon towards Spain, the land of my ancestors. The sun rose over the ocean for a new beginning every day. It was open and free, and you felt total liberation just being there.

Then we'd ride our bikes over the twisting road to Rock Harbor to watch the beautiful sunsets. We'd pass the sandy lanes that branched off the main road with their cute names like "Captain Doane Way" and "Penny Lane." We'd pass the gray-shingled cottages and white clapboard homes with their split rail fences and climbing rosebushes with vibrant red, pink, and yellow roses. Then we'd arrive at the Harbor parking lot.

Rock Harbor was named after a ten by ten-foot rock that marked the harbor's entrance to the bay. The Community of Jesus was situated on its left to the south. They were an ecumenical Christian community of Brothers, Sisters, and families. Here they prayed and tended their beautiful lawns and gardens. They had a sandstone monastery that matched the color of the harbor's beach sand. The sounds of their Gregorian Chant Evening Prayer floated from the monastery over the peaceful stillness of summer evenings.

Here the sunset beckoned onlookers to reflect. Every day before dusk, tourists came on pilgrimage, packing the parking lot with their cars, so they could experience this unique sunset. They actually applauded when the sun's farewell ended. Once I overheard a lady say, "How can you watch this and not believe that God's behind it all?"

Despite my reflection on my hometown, thoughts about Mr. Flint kept breaking through. Every time this would happen, I would feel flush and warm, my breathing would get heavier, and my heart would start beating faster. I could feel it thumping. Both my mind and my body were running wild, and I thought I was losing control of my senses.

What I wouldn't give to feel that muscle! But I can't think like this! I've gotta' stuff these thoughts and get out of here.

So I ran downstairs, got on my bike, and went for a ride to Rock Harbor. When I got there, the tide was coming in. The water level rises and falls every six hours because of the gravitational pull of the moon and the sun. At Rock Harbor it rises and falls ten feet. When it falls, it leaves behind all that is dead—rotting seaweed and decomposing shellfish—and as a result, it smells terrible. When the water rises, it covers all the dead sea life and drowns out the smell. Everything looks and smells fresh again. And as I sat down with my back to the large rock and watched the tide come in, my thoughts rose with it. I too felt fresh again.

I'm not going to think about Mr. Flint. I'll wait for Mr. Right. But I hope that he'll be someone just like Mr. Flint. I'm going to always remember what Grandma said, "Guard and protect your virginity." And I'm not going to drink or take any drugs. I'm going to keep my body pure! I want to be clean and pure like St. Joan of Arc. She wasn't a wimp. She was a virgin and *a feminist. And if she can be both, so can I! I won't care what my friends say, and I won't follow them if they do it. Grandma and St. Joan will help me. I'll wait and Mr. Right will come. He'll hold me and take care of me. My parents give me every material thing, but they really give me nothing because they don't give me themselves. He'll give me himself. I'll be his virgin queen. We'll have a lot of kids. . . . I'll never get an abortion . . . I love kids! This is my* promesa *just like Grandma made. Our Lady of Guadalupe, watch over me!*

My husband won't care that I'm a brown girl in a sea of white ones. My color won't matter. He won't lust after my body either. He'll love me for myself, for my character, and for my heart. We'll raise our family in a little gray-shingled Cape cottage. He'll probably be somebody like a maverick lawyer who won't care about money but who will fight for right, for truth and justice, for the underdog—just like Mom and Dad used to before they went mainstream. I'll wait for Mr. Right, I promise!

Twelve

*H*ere's another one," said Julie as she lifted a flounder into my wooden rowboat.

"Now this is what I call fishing," I said as I pulled out the hook and threw the fish into my cooler. Flounder are flat fish that lie quietly in the mud on the bottom of calm waters, protected from the wind. It was May of 1983, and we were both 15 years old.

From the shore behind my house, I rowed Julie out 100 yards to the middle of Town Cove. We were in my 14-foot rowboat. I loved to row. It was very soothing and rhythmical to dip the oars just below the water's surface and pull them through the water as the boat moved slowly forward and the water rippled away from it, leaving a gentle wake. When we got to the middle of the cove, we set the anchor, baited our hooks with sandworms, and dropped our lines over the side to the bottom. This was Julie's first fishing trip, so I explained things for her.

"This is called 'stillfishing,' unlike Bluefishing, which is all action. You patiently wait to feel a telltale nibble and then reel in a one or two pound 'flattie' without any bloodshed. It's calm, peaceful, nonviolent, and bloodless. Sometimes I'll catch fifty and sometimes only five. When it's slow fishing, there's time to sit and think. You can breathe in the fresh salt air and breathe out all your problems."

Many of my early teen troubles were resolved during my flounder fishing expeditions. This particular day was a slow fish day, so Julie and I had some time to talk. We talked about my earliest memory that had been a recurring nightmare for me since I was a little girl. I couldn't figure it out.

"Julie," I said, "I have these dreams . . . I keep seeing these images of me swimming and doing gymnastics underwater. I'm aware of the presence of a friend, and then I sense intrusion and aggression. The water gets agitated and swirls powerfully around me like a whirlpool. The image ends with my leg wrapped around my neck and I feel excruciating pain in my left hip. I want to scream but it's a helpless silent scream because I'm under water. It all seems so real and I always wake up in a cold sweat. Maybe it has something to do with my limp handicap. What do you make of it, Julie?"

She just sat there, looking at me with her head set back, her eyes squinted and her nose scrunched up—as if to say with her face that I was some kind of a weirdo. So I prompted her, "Hey, what do you think? I don't have a clue."

"Sounds pretty weird to me. You know, dreams don't have to make sense. Most of the time they're just bizarre images and scenes."

"But sometimes, don't they try to tell us something . . . or can't they be a suppressed memory?"

"Yeah, but it would take a psychiatrist to figure it out . . . it just isn't worth it."

"Maybe you're right, but I still think this dream means something. It's too real."

"Don't worry about it." She seemed bored with the subject of my dream and more bored because we weren't catching any fish.

She stared at her line and said, "Where are all the fish?"

I said, "Often, when it's slow like this, I'll call them."

"Call them?" she asked, giving me an incredulous look.

"Yeah, like this." And I stood up in the boat and yelled out over the water, "Flouuuuuuuunder! Here, flounder, here, flounder! Come on flounderrrrrr!" And then I sat down.

Julie said, "I didn't know that flounder could hear!"

I was surprised at her air-headedness, but I decided to play on it. "Not only can they hear," I said, "but if they're around, they'll obey and come. You know, like when you call your dog. Sometimes I can call them right off the bottom, and they'll come right up to the top, and I'll just scoop them into the boat with the net. That's when it's easy. Today there aren't many around. So we'll have to work at it with these slimy worms."

"Yuck! . . . You know Terry, you seem to know a lot about practical things like fishing, but not a lot about guys."

"What do you mean?"

"Well, you know, like, you're still a virgin. Right?"

I could see where this was going. She was going to play "one-upmanship" with me and shift into her favorite topic of sex.

"Guess what?" she said, as she cocked her head to the right and raised her eyebrows. "Bob and I . . . finally . . . well, we finally did it! She brushed her long brunette hair back behind her head and waited for my reaction.

"Really?" I said, as if I were interested.

"Yup. I was wondering when he would make his move. I waited and I was ready. You know, he wasn't the first and he sure won't be the last either. When are you going to get with it and do it, Terry?"

Many of the girls in my class were already sexually active. I was still a virgin—one of the holdouts. But Julie was putting increasing pressure on me to join "The Club." I resisted because I remembered my heroine, the feminist virgin St. Joan of Arc, and my grandmother's advice to protect and guard my virginity. Also my Catholic education, which I hadn't completely forgotten, taught me that sex was something reserved for a marriage that was open to accepting children. Any other sex was just two people using one another for their own satisfaction.

"You know what I think," Julie said as she reeled in one of our few flounders, "*Carpe diem*—seize the day! Get it now or waste the best part of your life waiting for the right guy. I'm serious! Why wait, Terry?"

"You know me, Julie. I'm Miss Romantic. I don't want to be used goods. I'll wait for the right guy who will come at the right time, and we'll do the right thing and wait. I think that God made sex for bonding and babies. And there's no bonding except in marriage, so I'll wait." I winced as I recalled my parents' revelations of their failure to wait.

"Sure!" she said sarcastically, "dream on . . ."

"It's no dream for me Julie. It's reality. My parents had sex before they got married, and I was born four months later. I don't feel too good about that. And I don't want my child to feel like I do."

Julie sat in the back seat of the rowboat thinking. She held her rod in her right hand. put her left hand up to her hatless head to protect her eyes from the sun, and squinted at me. "I think sex is okay before marriage if you really love the guy. You try on a pair of shoes before you buy them, don't you!?"

"Yes," I quickly countered, "but you'll never know if they fit until you tie the knot and walk in them. Anyway, who wants to buy used shoes? I'll stay a virgin."

"You're out of it, Terry. You don't know what you and Brian are missing."

She was referring to my boyfriend, Brian Boyce. But despite all my good, noble, and romantic intentions, Brian and I would eventually find out what we had been missing.

Thirteen

The next year on Memorial Day, when we were both 16, Julie and I watched the parade come down Main Street. The Community of Jesus' "Spirit of America Band" led the parade and played "Stars and Stripes Forever." One of the floats had a large sign that read, *Join Us and Walk in the Footsteps of Thoreau.* We took a flier and read that they were leading a hike the next week out on Nauset Beach, following Henry David Thoreau's famous nineteenth century walk to Provincetown. Julie and I decided to join them. We had a great Memorial Day but, like my childhood, it ended too soon at dusk with fireworks over Rock Harbor.

I spent the next day researching Thoreau's Walk at Nauset Library, and then I went surfing at Nauset Beach. The name "Nauset" honored the original settlers, the Nauset Indians. Julie and I planned to hike along with the Thoreau reenactors from Nauset Inlet to Truro—a distance of about 20 miles. I had read about Thoreau's famous hike in his book, *Cape Cod,* and was anxious to follow his example. He described the ocean as "naked nature, inhumanely sincere, wasting no thought on man, nibbling at the cliffy shore, where gulls reel amid the spray."

We started off on our hike in great spirits and began walking north on the golden sand alongside the dunes that hold back the Atlantic Ocean from Cape Cod. A lonely cargo ship slid along the cobalt blue edge of the ocean's horizon. Seagulls hovered and screeched overhead, and Bluefish churned the water chasing baitfish.

We fell behind the group and walked at the water's edge where the sand was cooler and harder and the walking was easier. The white foamy wash of the water licked our bare feet as we walked past Coast Guard Beach, Nauset Light Beach, and Marconi Beach. Here Guglielmo Marconi sent the first wireless message across the Atlantic Ocean to England in 1903. We walked past the remnants of his transmission towers and continued on past small brown-flecked sandpipers that fed on tiny morsels at the edge of the foamy wash. We picked seashells and listened to the roar of the surf—and we talked.

We talked about our families, our girlfriends, our next year at school, and the clothes that we'd buy. Then we talked about the girls who were having sex and that led to the subject of abortion.

Julie led into it and said, "My older sister had one when she was only 15 over in Hyannis. My mother took her. My sister said it was a piece of cake, Terry—nothing to it. It was too early in her pregnancy for it to be a baby—it was just 'products of conception,' they told her. She said it was over in a jiffy, and it only hurt a little bit."

"Well . . . I think it was her choice, right?" I said, while kicking the water's edge. "I don't think we should have sex until we're married and ready for children. But if you do it before marriage and you get pregnant then it should be your choice. After all, it's your body, so it should be your choice. I mean *I* wouldn't do it because it's against the Catholic Church. But I don't have a right to tell somebody else that *they* can't, especially if they're not Catholic. I can't impose my values on someone else. So I guess I'm personally opposed to abortion, but I think each woman should be able to make her own choice. That's the feminist way."

"Well, blow me away. I thought you'd freak out over abortion the way you do about premarital sex. I thought you were gonna' say something like, 'What about the *baby's* choice? Nobody asks the *baby* if it wants to live or die—that's not choice . . . ' But you didn't say that. You've got the right idea, Terry, at least on abortion. I think women have a right to choose, too—about sex *and* abortion."

We walked on and got as far as the Wellfleet Town beaches—about 10 miles—when our conversation, my hip, and our spirits gave out. I had bitten off more than I could chew. I thought that I could make it to Truro, but my limp got worse and my hip hurt so we called it quits and let the reenactors finish the hike. We crossed over the dunes to the highway and hitchhiked back home.

As I fell asleep that night, bone-tired from our walk, I wondered, *Will I really wait for Mr. Right? Will I ever have sex before marriage? My parents did, and they ended up getting married. And they must be happy—they're still together. Will Brian be the one? He keeps pressuring me. I like making out with him because he makes me feel loved. But he's never satisfied. It's hard to stop him when we're parked alone on the back roads. Our relationship started innocently enough with bowling and going to the movies with friends. But now that he has a car, we spend more time alone, and I don't know where this is leading. If I do have sex with him and I get pregnant, would I ever consider the possibility of an abortion? . . . No way!*

A couple of days later, I was surfing some high waves at Nauset Beach. I leaned too far forward on my board and too far ahead on the wave, and I lost my balance. I pitch-poled forward and wiped out. I can still feel myself somersaulting under the waves as they crushed me to the bottom, ground me in the sand, and threw me up into a white water maelstrom that left me high, dry, and helpless on the beach. A lifeguard had to rescue me.

I only realized in retrospect that this foreshadowed what was about to happen in my life. I got too far ahead on my wave, lost my balance, and wiped out. My future would be just as tumultuous as my near drowning experience. Little did I know then that I would end up being as beaten and bruised as a "washashore," barely making it to shore, and waiting helplessly for a "lifeguard" to come and rescue me.

Fourteen

Y ou're still up?" my mother asked with disapproval on her face.

It was a late Friday night in late June of 1984. I lay awake reading an article in a teen magazine, "Sex by Seventeen." I was only 16. My parents had been out all evening at a cocktail party promoting Cape Cod tourism. I heard them return home about 11:30 p.m. and come up the stairs. My light must have shown through the bottom crack of my closed door because my mother abruptly opened it. I reacted by quickly turning the magazine upside down on my bedspread.

"I was just reading an article about some cool fashions," I said with mock calmness.

She came in and sat on the edge of my bed. It was unusual for her to get so close to me, unless she was going to let loose and wallop me. As she leaned over, I could smell the wine on her breath. She slurred out, "Let's see what's cool in fashions." And before I could stop her, she picked up my magazine—right to the article I had been reading.

"This is what's cool and in fashion? Sex by seventeen?! Look dear," she stammered, "I uh . . . I've been meaning to talk to you about this. I guess I shouldn't have put our little talk off for so long. But now's as good a time as any. When I was your age, it was the beginning of the Sexual Revolution. 'If it feels good, do it. Make love not war.' That's what we said. So we did . . . your Dad and I. We made love. It was one more establishment barrier that we broke down.

"Grandma always told me, 'Stay a virgin; guard and protect your virginity; no sex before marriage.' But we did our own thing. So now it's your turn. *You* have to decide. It's your own choice, but make sure that if you choose sex, Teresita, that it's safe sex—safe for your body and safe against pregnancy. Make sure that he wears a condom and that you take the pill. Ask me if you need some. Okay? Promise? I don't want you to get hurt. I want my girl to be safe. No diseases and no pregnancies! Understand?"

I just stared at her and slowly shook my head up and down in silence.

"You know," she hesitated, "I wanted to talk to you about something else before this. But I . . . uh . . . never got the chance. It's kind of a follow up to your assignment on 'My Mother's Life.' I think that I should tell you now."

I didn't think I would like what she was going to tell me now any better than I liked what she had to say the last time she opened up to me. But there was no stopping her, especially when she was this close to me.

"Remember I told you I was pregnant with you before I got married? And that your father and I were both still in college? Well, here's the part that you don't know." She stopped for a moment, closed her eyes, and breathed in deeply. When she let out her breath, it was slow and measured. "Your dad really pressured me, Teresita. And I was so scared. I wanted to finish college. I didn't want to lose your father. Everything was crazy. I didn't know what to do. And I couldn't ask Grandma."

"What are you saying, Mom?"

Her voice became panicked and shrill. "Try to understand, Teresita. Your father said, 'I've got to finish college. I can't shame my parents. I can't take on this responsibility. I can't afford to support a child. And you can't take care of a baby on your own. I'll pay for everything.'"

I could feel my eyes open as wide as possible. I couldn't blink. I couldn't talk. But I clearly remember my thoughts at that precise moment. I will never forget them: *What's my mother saying? Nooooo! What am I hearing? I'm not hearing what I'm hearing. Stop it, Mom. Why are you telling me this? Why do you hurt me? Why have you always hurt me? Why do you hate me? Why don't you love me? Why? Why?*

"Really, Teresita, he really pushed me into the abortion. Believe me, I didn't want to do it. It was against my family's moral values and religious beliefs. It was against our traditions. But I felt like he held a gun to my head and said, 'I have an offer that you can't refuse.' So I didn't refuse. I had no other choice! Did you hear me? I didn't have a choice!" A tear squeezed out of her left eye as she choked, "I need to tell you the truth about your damaged hip. It wasn't just a birth defect like I told you."

My heart started beating faster as it began to dawn on me . . . *Is this the part of her story that she hurriedly skipped over in the interview for my essay? She tried to abort me and I was hurt by the abortion! Oh, my God! My God! Stop, please stop! I don't want to know this! I don't want to know!*

Mom struggled on, certainly more for her benefit than for mine. "Of course, abortion was illegal in 1967, but you could always find an illegal abortionist. I found one . . . and I had an abortion. My doctor falsified the report and wrote, 'D&C consequent to miscarriage.' A month later, I was lying on my couch reading. I laid down my book on my stomach and it jumped! I was shocked. I actually felt a baby kicking! It was you, Teresita!" And for a brief moment, her face, twisted in pain, gave way to a sad smile.

"I called the doctor and he said, 'You must've had twins and we only got one of them. You better get in here right away, or it'll be too late to finish the abortion. This other one can't survive. If it does, it'll be permanently deformed or brain damaged.'

"For some reason, I hesitated. I told him I'd call him back. Then I called your father and told him. Teresita, I never expected him to say it, but he did. He said, 'Maybe . . . maybe we should re-think this. Let's see what's in there.' So I went to the doctor, and he examined me and found you! He heard your heart beating!

"It was a miracle that you survived the abortion. So, your dad and I thought maybe you were our miracle, and God was giving us another chance to make a choice for life—to make up for our choice for the abortion. Maybe this was a sign of His love and not His condemnation. So we decided against the abortion, and I carried you until your birth.

"But, Teresita, you had been hurt during the abortion. The agitation caused by the vacuum tube severely dislocated your left hip and you were born prematurely with your handicap. They placed you in an incubator, operated on your hip, and the rest was up to you. You fought for your life. The nurses could see your determination to live. We visited you, cheered you on, and you survived. That's the real story, Teresita. It's the whole uncensored story with nothing left out. I'm sorry . . . I'm so sorry."

With that, she got up, patted me on the head, and said, "Good night. Sleep well." Then she left the room and closed the door behind her without waiting for any response or reply from me. I felt cheated.

Sleep well? I thought. My heart was crushed inside my chest, and I was trembling uncontrollably. I couldn't process, couldn't understand, couldn't accept or even believe what my mother had just said. I lay awake the whole night thinking of my nightmare, my dream memory. Now it all made sense.

My mother tried to abort me. But she was pregnant with twins and didn't realize it. That's why I sensed a companion in my dream! The abortionist killed my twin and hurt me. My limp . . . it's because of a botched abortion!

The water that I was swimming in was amniotic fluid. I was bouncing off the uterine wall. The abortionist's vacuum tube was probing for me and then the fluid began churning. I couldn't scream because of the fluid. I ended up with my left leg wrapped around my neck and my left hip severely dislocated. Now I understand why Mom and Dad didn't come clean with me about their radical move to the Cape. Mom told me I was premature and had a birth defect. All these years I've struggled and suffered with this limp. She could have apologized, but instead, she lied to me!

She tried to kill me. She killed my twin. No wonder she always acts like she doesn't like me. No wonder she never wants to hug me or show me her true feelings. She never wanted me. She's never loved me. I was a mistake, and she made me know and feel it even before I was born! No wonder I always take the blame around here, I'm always at fault. No one loves me because they want to, I'm just something Mom puts up with because she feels guilty for her premarital sex, guilty for killing my twin, guilty for trying to kill me. How can she love me if she tried to get rid of me?

I lay there in a flurry of emotions. I was angry, hurt, and shocked. I felt utterly rejected and abandoned—so unloved. *Do I even love myself?* I thought. *If I did, this sure changes things . . . why should I love myself if my whole reason for being here is some freakish accident . . . and every time I limp a step, I remind her of it. . . .*

I wanted to hate her and run to her at the same time. I wanted her to still be there, crying and holding me, begging me for my forgiveness and just telling me she loved me. And I wanted her to know I did love her anyway, and that I would forgive her . . . but she hadn't asked for forgiveness, hadn't even hinted that she knew I had been badly hurt. Just a look of love, a few words of love, would have been balm on my soul, healing ointment on my heart. But instead, she just walked away and left me there, bleeding, with a mortal, spiritual wound.

Something inside of me felt very different, very confused. My strength, my resolve, and my purpose felt all screwed up, out of whack. The path was no longer as straight or as meaningful . . . or as important. Mom had dropped another bombshell on me without warning . . . just like she used to hit me—without warning. And now I knew why.

Fifteen

I lived in a stupor for days after Mom's new revelation. On the third day, I got up early before Mom and Dad and was greeted by a foggy Sunday over Orleans. I rode my bike to Nauset Beach and walked barefoot over the cool, moist sand to the water's edge. Visibility on the Atlantic Ocean was only about 50 yards. Dense fogs were a frequent occurrence here when the warm moist air evaporated over the cooler ocean water.

I carefully scooped out a hole in the sand to sit in. I didn't need all the beach chairs and equipment that caused Grandma to make fun of the tourists. They lugged their chairs to the beach with their coolers, umbrellas, and other unnecessary cargo. But I traveled light. I sat down in my natural seat in the sand, and looked into the foggy mist over the ocean. The damp, salty fog settled over my body. And my mind wandered. . . .

How can Mom think that sex is just another choice? She's so different from her own mother. Grandma told us both to guard our virginity. But if sex is really just another choice like Mom said, then why don't I choose it? Sex is the deepest expression of love. I need to feel loved. I need to know that I'm loved. I wonder if Mom really loves me. How could she if she tried to abort me? My left hip—every time it hurts, every time I limp, it will remind me that my own mother tried to kill me!

Brian really wants to have sex with me. He wants to love me—all the way. He keeps saying, "If you really love me, you should prove it and go all the way with me." I need to be loved; I want to be loved; I deserve to be loved. Mom had sex before she was married, why shouldn't I? I'm almost seventeen. Maybe I will. Why shouldn't I? Mom said, "It's your own choice." Maybe I will. . . . Maybe I will. . . .

And then my thoughts drifted off with the fog and an image of Brian came to mind. I daydreamed that he was walking toward me at Nauset Beach dressed in his black tight nylon bathing suit. He was carrying his surfboard beneath his right arm and waving to me with his left to come and join him.

He had bright blue eyes, sun-bleached blonde hair and suntanned dark skin. He had the trim, lithe body of a surfer. And that's what he was—a beach boy. And I was his girl.

Brian and I had spent time together during the previous winter going bowling and to the movies. We rode bikes or our parents drove us. But after he got a car for his birthday in March, we began riding in the car, and our entertainment became parking on lonely dark roads. The Cape is full of rutted sand roads that pass through forests of scrub pine and past secret ponds unknown to most everyone except high school kids. Brian and I started by making out, and soon it became heavier and more frequent. By late spring, I was beginning to enjoy it and look forward to it. The pressure was always there. So many other girls had already done it—gone all the way. And my mother didn't seem to care. She said it was my choice.

I didn't really notice that our relationship had become more physical and less communicative. We also started drinking beer and smoking pot together. Brian kept the pressure on, telling me how much he loved me. And he insisted that if I really loved him, I'd let him love me completely. "Then," he said, "we would belong to each other." His persistent persuasion began to wear on me. I didn't want to lose him.

One night in early July, a week after my mother's little talk on sex, Brian and I were at a beach party at Nauset Beach. There were no stars out and the full moon rose in splendor over the Atlantic Ocean. It looked like an orange paper pumpkin pasted on black construction paper, the kind you see hanging on kindergarten bulletin boards during Halloween.

We had a driftwood fire going near the water's edge. It was all very romantic as I sat next to Brian and our friends in a circle around the fire. We sang along with the rock songs on the radio, drank beer, and smoked pot. We passed the joints around the circle and took long drags that we held in as long as possible before exhaling. I got pretty high. The light given off by the fire flickered across Brian's dark and handsome face. He seemed to glow in the dark. I felt mellow and very warm and loving.

Brian gently took my hand and said, "Let's go for a walk." Everything seemed to move in hazy slow motion for me. I let him pull me up and lead me back into the darkened dunes away from everyone else. He laid me down in the sand and said, "I love you, Terry, and it's time for you to show your love for me."

Before I knew what was happening, it was over. All I remembered was Brian saying his line and me feeling the pain of him inside of me. He abruptly pulled me up and said, "We better get back to the fire or they'll start talking about us." So ended my virginity. I had experienced sex—but not love.

As I lay in bed later that night I thought, *I feel dirty. Something's gone, gone forever. It wasn't like "Sex by Seventeen" pictured it at all. What happened to your great resolutions, Teresita, to wait for Mr. Right? Why didn't I follow Grandma's advice to guard and protect my virginity? Why did Mom make it sound like sex before marriage was all right? She made it seem like it really didn't matter, like it was no big deal—"It's your own choice," she said. Some choice! I just let it happen. I let my guard down.*

Where were you when I needed you, Grandma and St. Joan of Arc? I feel so empty. My romantic dream to remain a virgin was just a disappointing and unrealistic illusion. I thought that I could. But now my only real gift to my husband is gone forever. I guess I just didn't have the determination Grandma saw in me. I'm weak; I'm damaged goods now. So much for my great ideals when they were actually tested.

Soon I started getting sick in the mornings. I felt nauseous and vomited almost on schedule every morning. The smell of Julie's cigarette smoke began to make me sick to my stomach. I began missing my periods—one month, two months, three months. Finally, I couldn't deny it any longer!

One morning in early October, I started the day out as usual. I got up, vomited, showered, dressed, made my bed, grabbed a quick muffin and coffee for breakfast, and caught the bus to school. But after school, I went over to the Hyannis Family Planning Clinic and had a pregnancy test. At first, I didn't want to believe it, but then I realized I had no choice. I was pregnant. That was the end of normal days for me.

The next day I rode my bike down to Nauset Beach. A typical Nor'easter was blowing onshore in full force. The surf was at least 15-feet high and the breakers pounded the beach in a confusion of crashing booms. These storms came in the fall from the northeast. They collapsed the foundations of the great sand cliffs of the outer Cape causing them to erode. The currents washed the eroded sand down the Cape to Nauset Beach.

I felt like that Nor'easter had come personally for me and was symbolically showing me that my sex with Brian was a brief storm that collapsed the sandy foundation of my virginity and eroded my life into sandy pieces washed by the current to where . . . I didn't know. I sat on the beach, absorbing the full brunt of the storm, and began to think. . . .

My whole world has collapsed! How could this have happened? How can I be pregnant? I only had sex once! I thought that you had to have a lot of sex before you got pregnant. I just want to be myself again. I just want everything to be the way it was before.

Pregnant! I can't talk to Mom. I wish we were close. I wish that she could hug me tight and tell me everything would be all right. I'd feel safe and loved, and I'd tell her everything—my guilt, my regret, my pain, and my fears. But there's no chance of that. I'm feeling self-pity, frustration and isolation.

Dad would kill me if he knew! It would be such an embarrassment to him and hurt his business reputation. This just happens in the movies . . . to bad people. How can it be happening to me? Why did Grandma have to die? I need her advice. She'd know what to do. I need SOMEBODY. I'm all alone on this one. I am so alone. Isn't there someone who can tell me what I should do, where I can go for help?

God won't help me. How can He forgive me after I promised to be a virgin like St. Joan of Arc? Choices have consequences. And I've got to pay the price. But I'm so scared. My classmates have done the same thing I did. But they're laughing and having a good time. They don't have to pay the price. And they certainly don't care about me. What will happen to me? I've gotta' finish school.

I feel like this storm. My mind is swirling and my head is killing me. It's more painful than the time I took the radiator cap off Brian's car when it overheated after he warned me not to touch it. I thought I could handle that, too. But the hot water exploded out of the radiator and burned my hand. My insides feel like that boiling water. I'm ready to explode. The pain from that burn was on the outside but this pain is on the inside. I've burned my soul! Maybe I should tell someone. Julie? Brian? Maybe Brian will marry me.

But I'm only 16 years old. Do I even want to get married? I can't take care of a baby. This thing growing inside me it's just a fetus now. It's not a "real" baby. It's just a blob that won't be a baby until later. . . . That's what Julie said about her sister's pregnancy. So I better do something now. Before it's too late. What will I do? God, what will I do?

That's the question that I asked myself all the way home. Of course, I never admitted that I carried a real baby, and I never thought of having the baby and letting someone else adopt it. Nobody ever told me about that option. Nobody mentioned that there were places that girls like me could go and be protected during their pregnancy, until their babies were born. That there were people—kind people, selfless people, genuine people—who wanted to help take care of them and their babies. Nobody even told me that it was a baby.

Sixteen

The next day after school, Brian and I went out for a ride in his car. We rode all the way to the end of the Cape at Provincetown and parked at McMillan's Wharf. We sat and watched the whale-watching boats that brought the tourists back into the harbor from the open sea. I broke the tense silence between us and told him the news.

"Brian, I'm pregnant." I waited for a reaction, but there was none.

"What should we . . . uh . . . *do,* Brian?"

What I can only describe as anger and irritation appeared on his previously blank face. "What do you mean *we?*"

"Well, you're the *father!*"

"How do you know that *I'm* the father?"

"BRIAN!" I screamed in a hysterical voice, "I haven't made love with anyone else but *you.*"

"Yeah, but how do I know that? You could just be trying to trap me."

"I don't believe what I'm hearing. . . . You *know* me!"

"Believe it, Terry. I *thought* I knew you!"

I tried to calm myself before the conversation got worse. "Brian," I took a deep breath, "we've got to talk this out rationally."

"I've got nothing to talk about," he said with glassed-over eyes. He was looking right through me. I was invisible to him and so was *our* problem. I wasn't getting through to him. He was in complete denial.

"Look, Brian . . . I'm your girlfriend. I'm *pregnant,* and *you've* got to help me decide what to do. Maybe . . . maybe we should get married?"

"Are you *crazy?!* We're only 16!! What do you think, I should quit school, get a minimum wage job and give up everything to support you and a baby? No way!"

"Well, if you're old enough to be the father, you're old enough to take some responsibility."

"Okay," he said in a calculated and measured tone, "I'll pay for an abortion."

"But, Brian—"

"Look, I have to go to college. I can't deal with this. My parents would kill me if they found out. There's no way you can have this baby, Terry. Find out where you can get an abortion, and I'll pay for it."

"I can't have an abortion! I made a *promesa!*"

"A what?"

"A special promise . . . to Our Lady . . . of Guadalupe," I mumbled.

"Whatever. I'm not changing my mind, Terry. It's a done deal. I'll scrape together the money for the abortion—that's *my* promise." It was the only time I heard any sincerity in his voice that day.

"I thought you loved me . . . If I had known, I never would have let you . . ." He looked down in what I thought could have been shame. I felt abandoned. I knew our exchange was over, so I said, "Julie will help me. You only care about yourself. I'm outta' here. Have a nice ride home and have a nice life."

With that, I jumped out of his car, slammed the door shut in his face, and caught a ride home with one of the departing whale-watchers. I felt so *used*. Brian, who had been so kind and gentle, now became someone I didn't know—or even worse, someone whom I had never really known and who apparently didn't want to know me. Now he had shown his true colors.

The next day after school, Julie and I went window-shopping and stopped at an ice cream shop for malted milks. As we drank them, I slowly told her the whole depressing story. She replied by saying, "Look, Terry, Brian's totally irresponsible, but he's right, you know. You don't have any other choice. You have to have an abortion to take care of this problem. Get it over with and move on with your life. Just like my sister. She had one and she's doing fine."

"How? Where? I don't know anything about abortions."

"You can get a quick abortion up in Vermont. It's your body, and it's your choice, Terry. I read in the papers that in Vermont, you don't need your parent's consent, and they don't even need to be notified! Nobody will ever know. It's too early in your pregnancy for whatever's in there to be anything. It's not even a baby yet. But you've got to do something quick before you're too far along. We can go up on Columbus Day weekend. My dad will let me take my car. We'll say we're going hiking to check out the fall foliage. We can even stay with my aunt in Burlington. She's cool."

In a panic, I told myself, *Brian won't marry me. I can't tell my parents. It's all for the best. I don't have time to think, just act. Be strong, Teresita, and just do it!* So I took Julie's advice and said, "Okay, then, that's my choice. We'll do it." This was the second time I had made a choice to do something that I had promised not to do. So much for my promises.

I went into the phone booth, called the Burlington clinic for an appointment and found out the fee. Then I called Brian for the money he promised. Ironically, he kept *his* promise, but I had broken *mine*—my *promesa*.

He gave me the money after school the next day and said coolly, "I don't think we should see each other anymore."

"Oh, screw you, Brian!" I clenched my teeth and glared at him as I stuffed my rage and hurt.

I went straight home to my room and fell onto my bed in tears. And that's what I did every day after school until Julie and I went to Burlington. I didn't want to see anyone or go anywhere or do anything. I just wanted to be alone. I was sick and tired and cried all the time. Mom and Dad never even noticed.

Seventeen

*J*ulie and I left Orleans on Columbus Day weekend and began our journey to Burlington, Vermont. We crossed the Sagamore Bridge over the Cape Cod Canal and left the Cape behind. We went up Route 3 to Boston and took Interstates 93 and 89 through the White Mountains in New Hampshire and the Green Mountains in Vermont.

It was the height of the fall foliage season and carloads of tourists were traveling for "leaf peeping." As we drove along, the scenery took my mind off the reason for the trip. I saw the riotous blood red of the sugar maple leaves and the flaming orange of the oaks. I remember the stark contrast of the bright yellow of the birches with the deep green of the pines. The spectacularly painted countryside was dotted with quaint little villages hidden away in the hollows along the way. Each village seemed dominated by the high pointed steeple of a white clapboard church. And each church seemed to be nestled amid a cluster of tidy homes and well-kept stores.

On the outskirts of the villages were green meadows kept neatly manicured by the black and white Holstein cows that grazed there. Small farms with their red barns, tall navy blue silos, and white houses could be seen off in the distance.

As I watched this breathtaking scenery, I thought back to the last time I came by this way on our family vacation to Isle La Motte. *Those were the times that my life was as idyllic as these little villages. Now I just can't wait to pass them by, get to Burlington, and get this over with. I wish I were on my way home instead of on my way there! I just want to hurry and get this over with so everything can be all right again.*

"How far is it anyway?" I asked Julie. She began to calculate the distance in her head: "Well, it's about 300 miles from Orleans to Burlington."

That struck me in the heart! *That's the same distance that my grandmother walked alone from Mexico to Texas. It was the same distance that my mother walked to Sacramento with Cesar Chavez. They walked for freedom and justice, and here I am covering the same distance, in a car, on a pilgrimage for what? For myself! To get rid of a problem as quickly as possible and to forget it! Their pilgrimages were about hope and building up. Mine's about despair and destruction. Maybe this isn't the right choice. Don't think about it, Teresita! Just do it!*

We drove directly to the Feminine Health Clinic in Burlington. I'll never forget how its dark brown, dead-blood color contrasted with its Victorian round tower entranceway with its black steeple-like roof. It reminded me more of a witch's hat than a medical facility.

Julie and I courageously walked in. The receptionist handed me an information sheet and a small paper cup. Without looking up from her book she said simply, "Fill this out and fill this up with a urine sample." So I filled out the sheet, went into the bathroom, came out and gave her the sheet and the sample.

"Sit down and wait," she said flatly. I did. She came back a few minutes later and announced, "You're pregnant. The procedure will cost $250 in cash. You can come in tomorrow at nine. We'll have you in and out of here in less than an hour."

I got no counseling, no parental consent forms, and no information—I gave no informed consent. I was only 16 years old! I got nothing except some painkillers that I vomited on my way to the clinic the next morning.

When we got there, I was nervous, scared, and numb. And that's how the other girls looked to me. They held their heads down. I handed the cash to the receptionist. She slowly counted it out. I told her that I had vomited the painkillers, but she said that I'd have to go ahead without any because there was no time for a new dose to take effect. I told her that I was only 16 years old. But she said that my parents didn't need to know and that I didn't need their consent—everything would remain confidential. She told me to sit down and wait.

Deep down inside, I didn't really want the abortion. I was hoping that someone would help me and stop me. I was grasping at excuses to avoid it. I wanted Mr. Right, or Julie or even my grandmother's soul to come and rescue me. But the receptionist had fielded all of the excuses that I threw at her with her complete confidence and reassurance that I was doing the right thing.

After waiting for what seemed like hours, I started to nervously flip through some old teen magazines that lay scattered on a beat-up coffee table. Ironically, I opened to "Sex by Seventeen," the same article I had been reading the night my mother came into my room and turned my whole world upside down. I read through it this time with bitterness, and with a new wisdom. I could see through its lies—how beautiful and "right" it made everything sound!

Sex by seventeen. . . . I thought to myself. *And that's why I'm sitting here right now. The article never mentioned that sex would hurt, that doing it one time could get you pregnant, that it would make your boyfriend wind up leaving you, that—*

"Ms. Lowell?"

Just then, the receptionist called my name. Julie gave me a hug and said, "Don't worry. Everything will be just fine."

In a monotone, almost foreboding voice, a nurse repeated my name. I got up on shaky legs and mindlessly followed her. She led me to a room that was completely bare except for a cold metal table covered with white paper. She said, "Strip, put on this gown, sit on the table, and the P.A. will be right in."

I obediently followed her instructions, trembling as I wrapped the thin cotton gown around my body. Just then, a woman dressed in white entered. Without any introduction she said, "Lay down, spread your legs, and put them up in the stirrups." As I lay down, I noticed a picture of a Teddy Bear smiling at me from the ceiling, probably hung there as a distraction. *How inappropriate,* I thought. Ever since, I cringe whenever I see a Teddy Bear.

Then she gave me a shot in the cervix to numb me. I cried. She shoved a tissue paper at me to cover my tears and said, without looking at me, "I'm going to cover up this clear vacuum tube because some people aren't comfortable seeing the contents. Ready? Here we go!"

And with that, she rammed the tube up my vagina—such pain! I heard this horribly loud and menacing vacuum sound that sounded like the engine on a jet plane—*Whoosh!* She vacuumed my womb, pulling and pushing the tube back and forth. I heard the "plops" going into the vacuum jar. I could feel her scraping inside me. It hurt so much. But it ended as quickly as it began. The abortion was quicker than the sex with Brian, but it hurt a lot longer. I felt broken and empty inside.

Just as it was beginning to register with me that it was over, I felt a warm wetness dripping down my legs. I looked up at the P.A. with concern, and she nonchalantly told me that I might have some vaginal bleeding. After handing me a pad to absorb the blood and a couple of painkillers to ease my pain, she told me to get up and get dressed. When I sat up, I immediately crumpled backwards like a wet rag. I saw my blood all over the table, and I felt woozy. I saw spots before my eyes, and my hearing went out. I had to lie there a long time before I could get up.

No one helped me up or even helped to dress me. No one comforted me or told me I was going to be all right. The P.A. eventually popped back in and handed me some juice. I got up, changed my drenched pad, and dressed very slowly, one piece at a time, trying to put myself back together again.

The nurse eventually led my trembling body to a recovery room where some women were vomiting and others looked like white statues. I started bawling. She handed me a tissue box and another pain capsule and said, "Wait here until you feel better; then you can go home."

I waited, but I never did feel better. I just wanted to get out of there as fast as I had previously wanted to get in. We had to keep stopping all the way home so I could change my pads. I bled heavily and long. I cried and cried.

Julie asked me why I was crying. I said, "It wasn't a piece of cake like you said it was for your sister. My body hurts and my heart hurts even more. I don't want to talk about it."

I wanted my mother so much. I thought, *If only she, or Grandma, or Brian, or even Dad, someone . . . anyone was there for me, this never would have happened. My best friend, Julie, didn't do me a favor; she just made the way out too easy for me.*

Little did I know that what was supposed to be "a piece of cake" would wind up being so hard on me for the rest of my life. The sight, sounds and smell of the clinic were permanently engraved on my mind and heart. Fall foliage scenes and even that Teddy Bear would forever remind me that I had miserably broken my *promesa*.

Eighteen

What's a P.A.? I wondered on the way home. I didn't feel any relief at all, and I was in total denial that I had just killed a real live baby—my baby! This time, I didn't notice any pretty scenery. My eyes were closed most of the way. I could only see the dead-blood colored Feminine Health Clinic with its witch's hat which contrasted with the clean, white-dressed P.A.

After I got home, I slept a lot for the first week. It took a month for my vaginal bleeding to stop, but nothing stopped the bleeding of my heart. Things started bothering me that never did before. My food stuck in my throat and I couldn't eat. Sleep wouldn't come until I had cried for hours and exhausted myself from grief. I was in an anguish that I didn't understand. I couldn't talk to anyone about the abortion except Julie, and all she had to say was that I had done the right thing. But it sure didn't feel like the right thing.

Brian never called me again, and he avoided me like the plague. I couldn't believe that he could be so callous. When we looked at each other, it was almost as if we both felt the realization of our own potential for evil. We never said it, never even talked about the abortion, but there was this unspoken disgust over what had happened. It was like we wished we had never met.

I felt like Brian had his fun and dumped me. I felt like he was actually angry with me that I had gotten pregnant. I began to feel unattractive. I began to hate myself. I felt rejected, abandoned, and lonely. And most of all, I needed my mom's love more than ever. But as usual, it wasn't anywhere to be found.

Soon I started to lose interest in school and became oversensitive and paranoid about how the other kids treated me. I also started to notice what I thought was subtle discrimination. Like people didn't come right out and call me a *Spic,* but I no longer got invited to parties and the cliquish sports girls snubbed me. Then one afternoon it all came to a head in the school hallway. As I walked by two cheerleaders, I heard one whisper to the other, "She's just a black slut!"

After that, I felt like I was walking around wearing a day-glow scarlet letter "A" as a badge of infamy. But unlike Hester Prynne's letter, mine didn't stand for "Adulteress," it stood for "Abortion."

Nathaniel Hawthorne's novel, *The Scarlet Letter,* had been required reading in my English class. It was set in 17th century Puritan Massachusetts. I remembered the heroine, Hester Prynne. Her sin of adultery in the woods was publicly revealed in the town square. According to the town's punishment, she had to wear a scarlet letter "A" on her bosom, which stood for "Adulteress."

Like Hester, I felt that everyone was talking and giggling and pointing behind my back—talking about what happened to me in the dunes and the abortion clinic.

What did I do to deserve this? I thought. *Did Brian tell? I can't forgive Brian for using me up and throwing me away. I gave him myself, and first it cost me an abortion and now my reputation. But I'm stronger than them. Who cares what they say about me? Who needs them? Who needs anybody? Screw 'em!*

Then that night I laid in my bed curled in a fetal position and the tears flowed. I was only 16 years old, but I felt that I had already lived a lifetime. For many nights after I would lay awake at night thinking of the abortion. . . .

I was desperate. I was driven by fear and panic. I didn't know what I was doing. It wasn't as if I really had a choice. Julie said that it would be quick and painless, that it would be over in a jiffy—in and out, no problems, instant and easy solution, no consequences. Bull! My body hurts, my mind hurts, my heart hurts, and my choices have consequences—but I've gotta' stuff it. I can't handle this. Don't think about it, Teresita!

Nineteen

"W̶ait a month and it'll come," the P.A. replied. It was November, a month after my abortion and four months after sex with Brian, and my period still hadn't come. I had called the Feminine Health Clinic from a pay phone, and the P.A. reassured me that this wasn't unusual. But when my period still didn't come in early December, the fifth month, I called her again.

"Maybe there are still some baby parts in there. You better get to the hospital, you might need a saline procedure," she said.

"Some *BABY* parts?" I screamed into the phone. "You never said anything about a *baby!* And what's a saline procedure?" My wall of total denial was tumbling down around me.

"Listen," the P.A. said, as if talking down her nose to me, "just call the Green Mountain Hospital in Burlington and get right in there for an exam." I called them and set up the appointment for Saturday, December 11. My mind churned with all kinds of thoughts. . . . *Is this what it was like for Mom? Is life repeating itself? Was I pregnant with twins? Do I still have a baby inside me?*

Once again, Julie got her aunt to cooperate, and we told our parents that we were going to stay with her in Burlington and ski at Stowe for the weekend. Again, we drove the 300 miles north. The pretty foliage was all gone. We passed by a dead landscape blanketed in white snow. We drove straight to the hospital.

Just as before at the Feminine Health Clinic, I was ushered into another bare room with a cold metal table and a sink. The doctor examined me, shook his head and said, "You're too far along for a D&C, so you'll have to stay overnight for a saline injection procedure."

"What's that?" I asked.

"I'll inject some saline into the amniotic sac, and then we'll get everything out."

"Oh," I said, as if I understood. The thought of "some baby parts" haunted me. But I was too paralyzed with horror to ask if by "everything" he meant "baby parts."

Then I lay down on the table. The doctor came and stood over me with the biggest needle and syringe that I'd ever seen. I was very frightened. He didn't say a word. He just shoved it into my abdomen. A wave of nausea came over me and I squeezed that table so hard that it left marks on my hands. He told me to go to my room, drink plenty of water, walk a lot, then lie down and wait.

After I lay down, I could feel something thrashing around inside of me. The next morning I went into labor. I pushed naturally. I could feel something warm and wet and fleshy come out between my legs. I rang for the nurse and waited, but no one came. I didn't know what was happening to my body, so I reached down between my legs to find out what was coming out of me. I felt something like a wet tennis ball. I grabbed it and held it up.

Aaaaaaah!!! I screamed and screamed and screamed. What I saw was the burned and bloody head of my baby boy. My heart beat like a drum in my ears. He was dead. Horror of horrors. I looked at his tiny feet and hands. I yearned to just put him back inside my womb but it was too late. Finally, the nurse came in, picked him up, and without any respect or feeling, dumped him into what looked like a big pickle jar. Then she left me alone with my thoughts. Later I learned that my baby boy had been burned to death by a potent salt poison in what they euphemistically refer to as a "saline procedure."

I kept wringing my hands and gently rocking from side to side on the bed. I felt like I was going into shock, or breaking down, or just going crazy. I didn't even know who I was, or if I wanted to be alive. My mind was numb and at the same time crowded with thoughts. . . . *What's happened? What have I done? Either the P.A. missed my baby or he was a twin abortion survivor just like me. He survived the P.A.'s vacuum. But unlike my mother, I didn't give him a second chance. I killed him the second time around. Two choices, all mine, and neither one was good! Both have killed parts of me, just like they killed my baby or babies.*

Something else is dead beside my baby. My body hurts. But something inside of me, not connected to my body, hurts even worse. Something is dead inside of me. I feel empty with an emptiness that I can't understand. It can't be suctioned out, I can't get rid of it. Something seems frozen inside me like an iceberg—I'm becoming as cold as my mother.

This is a living hell. No, this is just plain hell. I'm dead inside. There is nobody I can tell. How do you explain the burning to death of your own son?

When someone dies, like Grandma, people get together to grieve, and they stick together, help one another and healing comes. But there's absolutely no one for me to tell and healing will probably never come.

I stand alone—and I feel trapped, betrayed and frightened. I want to tell Julie about my guilt, anger and self-pity but there is no way that I can speak out such horror. I hate Brian! He got me in this mess and abandoned me. I feel ripped, wounded and bleeding on the inside and the outside. My baby's been taken out of me, but it feels like my legs have been taken off. I'm slowly bleeding to death. No doctor can help me. They've already butchered me up.

I see an image of shattered glass. That's how I feel—like fragile shattered glass. It reminds me of the time I was driving with Brian and a rock flew out of a dump truck that we were following and smashed his windshield. The glass shattered but it didn't fly into the car, it stayed on the windshield. Brian explained that the glass was safety glass and when it shattered, it held in place. I just hope that I can hold myself together like that shattered safety glass. I'll look the same to everyone on the outside, but on the inside, I'm a shattered mess.

Waves of pain and nausea swept over me as bits of thoughts continued to run through my mind. How I hoped that everything was really fine, like I was planning to tell Julie.

When I left the hospital with Julie, I just told her that everything went fine. I vowed never to tell *anyone* what really happened. I felt that I had left a part of me behind. Something that I could never get back. I felt a surge of love and sorrow for the child I had just left there, a child I wanted to hold and bond with, but instead, one whom I had destroyed. It was as if all the good inside of me had been sucked out and nothing remained except a shell of what used to be me. I felt incredibly lonely and empty inside. I held my stomach and felt the emptiness. It was like there was a gaping hole inside, one which longed to be filled with the baby I had callously left behind.

That night I returned home in total shock. I even forgot that it was my seventeenth birthday.

Twenty

*M*y *milk's coming in!* It was two days later. I was alone in my bedroom and I felt milk come into my breasts. Food was coming in for a baby that I had killed and denied even existed! I sat on the edge of my bed, feeling nauseous and dizzy. I went into the bathroom, vomited, and then went back to my bed and passed out. All this without either one of my parents suspecting that anything other than a simple stomach virus was affecting me.

The next evening, shaky but a bit improved, I rode my bike to Rock Harbor to watch the sunset. It was winter and all the boats had been hauled out of the water. I sat beside the rock that marked the Harbor's entrance to Cape Cod Bay. It sat there like a sentinel. Skim ice had formed around it. This one lonely rock was a ten-foot by five-foot boulder after which the Harbor was named. Geologists call this kind of boulder "erratics." They're oddball rocks left behind by the melting retreat of prehistoric glaciers.

I felt that life had left me behind, just like the rock was left behind. And I felt like the rock looked—abandoned and alone, frozen in at Orleans, Massachusetts.

The Harbor was only a small pond. Ironically, its shape reminded me of a uterus, and it had a small river leading out from it past the rock to the bay. The ebb tide was taking the water out of the pond, and it flowed down the river past the rock as the sun was setting on the bay. I sat down and turned west to take in the show.

The sun gently set on the bay like a giant fireball, double its original size, and reflected on the water like an awesome nuclear explosion. Then the sun set over the horizon, and its tip hung there like a glowing ship of orange-yellow fire. It almost refused to set. When it finally did, there was an encore of a fire-like sky of red, orange, yellow, and violet. I couldn't help opening my eyes and mouth in wonder. I remembered that Mary Higgins Clark, the mystery writer, once wrote, "Seeing the sunset on Cape Cod Bay is like falling into the arms of God." And I thought . . .

God, whoever You are and wherever You may be, please help me. I feel so empty inside. I'm numb, nauseous and I feel like it'll never go away. How did I get into this mess? Where were You when I needed You? Will my pain ever end. . . . ?

God, please just let me die. I have nothing to live for. Why did this happen to me? Was it my mom's fault? Brian's? Mine? Was it worth bringing me into this world? What kind of a god are You? You're supposed to take care of girls like me! Why are You punishing me?

Do You hear my cry, or do my words just flow out like this tide into a great bay of emptiness? I don't think You're listening to me at all. I don't even think I believe in You. Look, there's only me here! I'm sitting alone just like this rock. You're not going to help me. My parents don't care; my schoolmates are freezing me out. Brian has dumped me. I have no one . . . no one! The first chance I get, I'm outta' here, and I'm never going to think about that abortion again!

As I left the Harbor on my bike, it was getting dark. The only lights came from the life-sized Nativity scene on the lawn of the Community of Jesus and the lighted candles in the windows of their monastery from which the sounds of their chanted Evening Song filled the cold night air. Baby Jesus lay safe and protected in His manger by the Virgin Mary, His mother.

I arrived home, went to my room, and made my plan. I decided to quit school, leave Orleans, and make my own way. But where would I go? Once again, my friend Julie had an idea. She said, "My family is flying down to Miami Beach during Christmas Break. You can come as our guest. When we get there, you can scout it out and then leave us a runaway note and stay in Miami."

"Sounds like a plan," I said. "Maybe I can get in touch with my Hispanic roots down there. Yeah, and I could start all over. I'm going to do it!" It seemed like a good plan, but it was really just another bad choice with bitter consequences, some of which I was finally able, with God's help, to turn into blessings.

My parents approved the trip, gave me $500 in spending money, and told me to consider it my Christmas present. Little did they know that I would be using the cash to start a new life.

Twenty-one

*F*ast fruit's healthier than fast burgers," a lady vendor yelled in a singsong voice. Julie and I were checking out Miami's Hispanic section and had stopped at a cart where a lady prepared fresh fruit. She peeled and diced fresh watermelon and strawberries, cantaloupe, pineapple, honeydew melon, and blueberries. She placed them in a plastic bag, added salt and a dash of cayenne pepper, shook them up, and poured them into clear plastic cups in which she placed a toothpick. We each bought one.

The cups were a medley of red and creamy orange, yellow, lime-green and blue—a rainbow of colors. As I ate the beautiful multicolored fruit, I thought, *This is what being Latino means to me—mixed blood with many varieties and colors forming a beautiful rainbow race and culture. I feel that I belong here in Miami. I feel at home.*

Spontaneously, I broke into song, singing the parts I could remember from "What a Wonderful World":

The colors of the rainbow, so pretty in the sky!
Are also on the faces of people goin' by!
I see friends shakin' hands, sayin', "How do you do!"
They're really sayin', "I love you!"

It was the first time in months I felt even a little optimistic.

I had flown down to Miami Beach with the Snow family the week after Christmas. After we checked into our hotel, Julie and I said we were going window-shopping. But we were really going to check out the Miami scene. After catching a cab, we headed downtown and found the Hispanic section known as Little Havana. It was a 30-block strip in the center of Miami that was home to exiles and refugees from Cuba.

Little Havana was also known as *Calle Ocho*—8th Street—in honor of the broad thoroughfare that ran west of downtown Miami. It was a sensual

Latino kaleidoscope. As we strolled the streets eating our fruit medley, the sounds of salsa music and spoken Spanish reverberated through the air from open-windowed apartments and bars. The smells of garlic-laden steak, grilled pork strips, and picante sauce wafted from sidewalk stalls and carts with candy-striped colored umbrellas.

We walked into the middle of a multicolored crowd past open-air markets that served sugarcane stalks and coconut milk fresh from the shell. Churches, theaters, shops, and stalls lined the sidewalks. There were plenty of cafes and restaurants where I hoped to get a job.

So, the night before we were supposed to fly home, I left my runaway note explaining that I was on my own. Julie was to show the note to both her parents and mine. As expected, my parents didn't come running after me, nor did they contact the authorities. Out of curiosity, and maybe a little hope, I called Julie later to find out if my parents were concerned when she told them.

Julie said, "Your mom seemed a little agitated but said, 'If that's her choice, then we respect it.' Your dad just silently nodded his head in agreement."

For Mom it was just another choice. She was such a liberal—at least she wanted people to think she was.

On the surface, all seemed well and good for me. After all, moving to Miami was what I wanted—or so I thought. As I struggled with these thoughts—my "choice" to move to Miami and my mother's reaction—I couldn't help but remember how much easier it was *before* my mom had the talk about sex with me. Then, at least, all these "choices" were taboo, and life was easy. There was a right and a wrong. Grandma had made that clear. The choices just confused me.

That was how I left home in early January of 1985, three weeks past my seventeenth birthday. I started both a new year and a new life. Life on my own. I found a room in an inexpensive hotel and got a job as a waitress at a Cuban restaurant in the *Calle Ocho*. The restaurant served good, simple meals with great *café cubano*.

The restaurant was named "Gloria's Café and Restaurant Cubano" after Gloria Gonzalez, the widowed owner. Her son Miguel managed it, but there was no question who the real boss was. Gloria came in almost every day to check up on him. She'd sit at a table, drink coffee, and smoke cigarettes. From her perch she'd scan the restaurant with an eagle eye to see that everything met her approval. She'd wave me over to join her during my breaks or for lunch. On that, I *didn't* have a choice.

I always felt embarrassed sitting with her. She wore flashy dresses and too much makeup—dark penciled eyebrows and bright rouge and lipstick. She wore gold earrings and bracelets. You could smell her perfume two tables away. And she smoked too much.

Through the smoky haze, I learned from Gloria that Miami was almost half Hispanic, 60% of whom were Cuban. More than a half million Cubans fled Castro's regime in the sixties and another 125,000 in the eighties. Many of them settled in the *Calle Ocho*. There was a Square dedicated to the Cuban 2506th Brigade that invaded Cuba to liberate it from Castro's Communism. They fought at the Bay of Pigs and lost because of a lack of promised American support. Gloria told me that a flame now burned atop a ten-foot column as a memorial to them.

I walked past that flame every morning on my way to work—down SW 8th Street and over the brick-lined sidewalks that reminded me of Main Street in my hometown of Orleans. There were large stars embedded in the sidewalks with the names of famous Latino entertainers in the middle of them. This was to give some recognition to the Latino stars whom Hollywood ignored.

I walked past the many one-story shops, all of which had old-fashioned awnings over their storefronts to protect them from the sun. There were all kinds of businesses—beauty shops, religious goods shops, dress shops and the Tower movie theater. Then I arrived at work and got ready to serve our famous homemade, foot-long, crispy, grilled, Cuban club sandwiches. They consisted of layered ham, sliced pork, Swiss cheese, and pickles, with mustard on one side only. The restaurant had a diner-like counter with stools, and tables for four with simple upholstered steel chairs.

The customers seemed to like my smiling service. I worked hard at it, as I quickly learned it helped to increase my tips. I even managed to pick up some Spanish which helped me communicate. All the while I thought about Grandma and how right she was in advising me to learn Spanish. How I wished my mother hadn't abandoned her heritage!

I was glad that no one could see the sadness that I couldn't seem to shake. The tips got better and better, the days flew by, and I made enough money to rent my own efficiency apartment in a duplex bungalow around the corner on SW 7th Street. It was small, clean, and simple. I imagined that it might have looked like my grandmother's first bungalow—a stucco house painted pastel pink with a red, clay tiled roof. There was a small front lawn with a 3-step stoop leading to the entrance. On the right side of the stoop stood a statue of Our Lady of Charity, Patroness of Cuba.

I furnished my apartment with Salvation Army freebies. I lived in the apartment on the right-hand side, and my landlady lived on the left. I got my meals at the restaurant, and my drinks at the bars where I started to hang out at night more and more frequently.

I drank and danced to forget my memories of the abortion. But I was constantly confronted with it. Every time I saw a baby, I got upset. Not a day went by that I didn't think of my aborted, dead baby. I tried not to, and did what I had to do to get through the day. Though the days ended with sleep, even then, there was no escape.

I had recurrent nightmares of crying babies. One night I woke up in a cold sweat with the piercing sound of a baby's cry still echoing in my ears. The dream was so real that I got up out of my bed and looked around the room for a baby. I tried to stifle those dreams and cries that haunted me. So I danced my cares away—the mambo, the samba, the meringue.

Twenty-two

I'm living out Miami vice, I said to myself one day, *and I don't like it!*

There was a television show in the eighties called *Miami Vice*. During the whole year of 1985, I was like a glossy image from the show—an easy woman strolling the streets and bar-hopping at night against a background of neon lights and the downtown skyline. In the discos, I'd dance to the loud pulsating music in front of the strobe lights to attract men on the prowl.

I let myself get picked up by guys—single guys, married guys, young guys, old guys, black guys, white guys, and brown guys. It made no difference to me. I didn't discriminate. Sex was a payoff for me. In exchange for my favors, I heard some kind words and I was held. When I was with these guys, I felt less alone, less dead. I also think that I subconsciously wanted to get pregnant to "make up" for my abortion.

It looked like a glittering life on the outside, but it was very dark on the inside. I thought of suicide often. One day I almost cut my wrists in my bathroom sink, but the phone rang and interrupted me. I really wasn't aware that I needed help or why. I didn't even know how to ask for help, so I just kept trying to cover everything up.

Things got progressively worse. I had opened up a need in my life for sexual intimacy. I found myself going from man to man. But I didn't have the maturity to establish a relationship first before I had sex. There was no communication, no sharing, and no commitment. I didn't care about anything, not about myself and not about anybody else.

The drinks and one-night stands made me feel loved temporarily, and kept me from thinking about my nightmares and the abortion. I had stuffed that memory so far down inside of me that it was like I couldn't face what I had done. Yet, I lived in devastating inner conflict by trying to ignore it. My conscience was dulled. I just drank, smoked pot, and had sex just to avoid thinking.

But when I woke up I had to deal with reality. There was no covering it up in the morning. I could run all night, but I couldn't hide by day. I woke up not only with the physical pain of a hangover, but in deep emotional pain as well. I felt like an electric eggbeater was grinding away inside me.

When I looked into the mirror, I no longer saw what my dad had seen—"eyes as blue as the sky on the Fourth of July." I saw what looked more like the American flag on the Fourth of July with my blood-shot eyes—red, white and blue. I looked so phony smiling with my lips, while my puffy and bloodshot eyes had dark circles beneath them on my gaunt face.

I knew every morning that my life was all wrong. I couldn't deny it. When I saw pro-life people praying at abortion clinics on the morning news, I shuddered and shut off the TV. When I ran the vacuum or the garbage disposal, I cringed, as the awful noise reminded me of the abortion vacuum. I felt like I should be the one to be vacuumed up or disposed of. I was dirt and garbage!

Maybe, I thought, *if I stopped all this drinking and smoking and indiscriminate sex . . . maybe if I settled in with just one guy, things might be different.*

So I started to pay more attention to Miguel Gonzalez, the young manager of the restaurant where I worked. He was a good prospect and a hard worker. We were both Latinos. Gloria, his widowed mother, told me in one of our "talks" how lucky Miguel was to live in America with her and to be able to take over her restaurant business. Like my grandmother, Miguel's parents came here as immigrants.

One day in January of 1986 Gloria told me the whole story. As usual, she came into the restaurant around noon to check everything out. As usual, she made her grand entry like a Queen, overdressed and wearing too much makeup and perfume. She regally marched to her throne-chair from which she could oversee her restaurant and tell her son how to run it.

"Life was good for us in Cuba. We were on top until Fidel Castro and his Revolution came into power in the early sixties. Then everything changed, and we were with the first to join *El Exilio* and go into exile. Castro conquered Batista's corrupt right-wing dictatorship with the promise of democratic reform. But Castro was a closet *comunista,* and there was no room left in Cuba for restaurant-owner capitalists like us."

"So you came here?" I interrupted.

"Yes, we left everything to come here. We lost our home, our restaurant, our extended family, and our country. We came here and worked hard, saved hard, and got enough capital together to buy our first restaurant. Later, I sold it for this one after my husband died. We were proud Cuban whites who loved this *Calle Ocho* section and the transplanted Cuban culture."

"What do you mean by 'Cuban whites?'" I asked.

"We weren't like the niggers."

I was surprised by her racist remark, but I didn't say anything. Not then.

"Oh, well, what about America?" I asked. "Are you thankful for America?"

"America let Devil Fidel get away with murder. They never helped us. We had to take care of ourselves. They promised our men air cover when we invaded the Bay of Pigs, but the airplanes never came and they left our men to be hunted down by Castro like dogs."

"I didn't know that," I said. "I learned in school that we always tried to help other countries, especially against the Communists."

"Not when *we* needed it," she replied. "The help came later when we *didn't* need it. In 1980 a second wave of Cuban refugees came—the *Marielitos*. This was Castro's revenge on America for the Bay of Pigs invasion and the long economic boycott of his island. The Marielitos were black criminals and lunatics! Castro emptied his jails and insane asylums, and America was stupid enough to welcome them. But Miami got stuck with them. There were 125,000 of them! They left Mariel Harbor in Cuba in 3000 boats and brought their crime and their drugs with them. They set Cuban progress in Miami back a decade. They're just plain black scum."

I was really surprised by her venomous racism, but I excused her because I knew that the *Marielitos* were blamed for making Miami a drug-infested crime hole. It hurt tourism, and it hurt Gloria's pocketbook. Besides, as I later learned, she had generations of racism bred into her. Cuban whites had ruled Cuba for 400 years. They were the governors, the diplomats, the hotel owners, and the millionaire sugar planters. The masses were blacks descended from imported African slaves. They worked the fields just like my people did with Cesar Chavez in California.

Gloria kept up her racist diatribe as she sipped on her *café cubano*. "So now we've got all of these blacks together with the Puerto Ricans and *Mejicanos*—no offense to you, Teresita—making trouble, getting into drugs and violent crime. You don't see them hustling like we white Cubans who started our own businesses from nothing. There are too many of them who are unskilled workers in a job market that's full. So they just help themselves to whatever they can get by stealing or handouts. You don't see them opening any businesses to take care of themselves like we did.

"Teresita, you should be thankful that you have a job here. Don't ever forget how good I've been to you. You're a good worker, but there are many others just like you who would give their right arm to have your job! Oh wow, look at the time. I've got a ton of things to take care of, and you've got to get back to work. I gotta' go, *adiós!*" With that, she swallowed the last of her coffee and strolled out of the restaurant.

Twenty-three

Yuck! I groaned, as I awoke one morning lying in my own vomit. I had drunk too much booze the night before and gotten sick. Suddenly, through my foggy brain, I remembered having read that Janis Joplin, the rock singer, had died choking on her own vomit in bed. I was afraid that I was headed in the same direction, so I stopped drinking, cold turkey. I still smoked marijuana, but at least I had started to clean up my act.

Then Miguel and I started going out together in February. I didn't go out with any other guys, and soon we were having sex. I never dreamed that I could get pregnant again. I thought that God had punished me for my abortion and made me sterile, just like He probably did to my mother. But then I got pregnant. It was June of 1986, and I was two months pregnant. And this time there would be no abortion. I was just starting to clean up some of the messes in my life, and I wasn't about to make another one. I told Miguel that I was pregnant in the hopes that he would want to marry me. Wishful thinking.

He told me that he got a white girl pregnant at the same time as me. All along, I thought I was the only one. He said he couldn't support two children, and that he'd have to talk to his mother and see what she said.

The next day at work, Gloria came for lunch and asked me to join her for another one of our "talks." She ordered a glass of red wine and toasted me, *"Salud, dinero, y amor"*—health, wealth and love. Then she got right down to business.

"Teresita, Miguel told me your problem. He makes too many problems with the women and leaves me to solve them. So, Teresita, look, you're very young. You're all alone. Your family is up north. You can barely support yourself. As I told you, although you're a good worker, you're lucky to have this job. You can't make it as a single mom. But most important of all, I don't want a mulatto grandchild. I've decided that you should have an abortion. I'll pay for it and make all of the arrangements. I'll be frank with you, Teresita, I want a white grandchild."

"Racism within our own Latino culture?" I gasped. "Who do you think you are?" I finally got up enough nerve to challenge her. "You choose a white grandchild over my brown baby just because of the color of the skin? We're *all* mixed colors—white, brown, and black. Our people's blood is Spanish, Native American, and African. Who said you're pure white? You're not an Anglo! We're all descended from one couple—Adam and Eve.

"What makes you any better than me? You're a Latina just like me! A woman isn't a Latina only in the color of her skin, but in her heart—the *corazón!* I *will* have your brown grandchild!" I threw my napkin on the table, got up and ran to the lady's room where I cried out my shock and anger and renewed my determination to have my baby.

Every day after that, Gloria would come in for lunch and say the same things over and over. After she left, Miguel sounded like her echo, and he repeated all of her persuasive arguments to me. His sisters would come in and say, "Teresita, it's just a fetus. It doesn't have hands or feet or a brain. It doesn't have anything. It's not real yet. It's nothing. It's nothing yet. Yes, Teresita, this is the right thing to do. It's best for the child in the long run. The child would be better off if it wasn't born."

I begged them and said, "There's got to be another way to handle this situation. There's got to be something that we can do together." But they'd just say, "We'll take care of everything. We'll take you to the clinic. We'll pay for it. Everything will be okay!"

"No, it won't!" I pleaded. "I've been through this before. I know. Everything *won't* be okay."

"Well, that's the way it's going to be!" they argued with finality.

I was distraught and depressed and stayed up crying for many nights. I knew that if I had this abortion, I could never make a comeback. I had broken up with Miguel, and I could barely keep up at the restaurant. I had to force myself to go to work every day. But I couldn't afford to lose my job.

Day after day I heard their arguments. There were no other voices. My determination was getting shaky. There was no one to encourage me or to support me. Once again, I felt all alone like the rock at Rock Harbor. Only I wasn't much of a rock. I was weakening. Finally, Gloria gave me an ultimatum, "Either you get the abortion or you're fired."

"Okay," I whispered in defeat.

As I walked home after work that evening, I thought, *I'm alone again with no one to help me. Everything's closing in on me. Maybe I should just go crazy or maybe I already am. That would be the easy way out. Or maybe suicide, but that's too easy. That's just for cowards. It feels like a coffin is closing in on me, and I'm suffocating. Is there a choice to go back to the beginning—back to when Grandma and I had our talks? . . . Back to when Brian and I were just friends and didn't have sex? Back before my abortion, my running away, my Miami Vice, my sex with Miguel . . . Won't someone take me to that place? Where all of my bad choices and their consequences would be made better, and everything would be all right.*

Twenty-four

*C*all us when it's over, and we'll come back and pick you up. Everything will be all right."

Gloria and her daughter had just dropped me off at The Women's Choice Center. It was a Friday morning in July. I never really decided to have an abortion. I just went along like a robot with what was decided for me. I was a single, 18-year-old woman who had just broken up with her boyfriend. I felt so lonely! I felt like I was pushed into a corner and there was no escape, except for the abortion.

They said, "This is the right thing to do! This is the best choice, the right thing to do!" Yet I knew that it was really the *wrong* choice and the wrong thing to do. But I felt, as I did the last time, that I had no other choice.

They handed me the money and left me there on the curb. I walked slowly up the sidewalk and started to notice everything. When I had gone to the Vermont clinic, I was in denial and noticed very little. Now I paid attention, and everything was vivid. This time I knew what an abortion was, and I didn't want to be near this terrible place. I had a hollow, empty feeling in the pit of my stomach. I didn't want to look anyone in the eyes, and I wore sunglasses so that no one would see mine.

There was a group of people praying the Rosary and handing out pro-life information on the sidewalk outside the clinic. One person held a sign that said, *We will help you!* Another held a poster of a beautiful unborn baby sucking his thumb. And another held a sign that said, *The Natural Choice is Life.* That made me feel guilty. My conscience started to bother me.

I thought, *They're praying for my baby and me! Maybe they care. Maybe somebody cares! But how can they help me? I'm being pushed in here against my will! I have no choice!*

Then I noticed a young man and woman walking quickly toward me wearing bright orange vests that said ESCORT. *What's this all about?* I wondered. The Escorts put walkman earphones on me that blared loud rock music into my ears, and a big black raincoat over my head. I suddenly realized, *They don't want me to hear the prayers or see the signs or the information! What are they afraid of? Is this what they call "choice"?*

The Women's Choice Center was just an old house with faded paint on its clapboard siding outside and torn wallpaper on its walls inside. It was filled with the smell of stale air, cheap, used furniture, and what looked like used women. They—actually, *we*—were a gloomy lot. There wasn't a smile in the place. Nobody talked. They all looked straight ahead like statues with blank stares. It wasn't like a doctor's waiting room where patients read or talked to one another. Nonetheless, I smiled at everyone with a phony smile to try to bring some cheer into that unhappy place. But nobody smiled back.

This was the darkest moment of my life. There's a Spanish saying, *Mañana oscura, tarde segura,* which means, "It's always darkest before the dawn." But I didn't see any dawn coming.

When I made the appointment for the abortion, the receptionist said, "We're going to take an ultrasound and give you counseling. We'll give you information, show you a video and carefully explain the procedure to you."

But when I reported to her desk, she just said, "That'll be $350." I handed her the money. The way that she said it, I felt no different than if I were at a butcher's shop paying for meat. She counted my money carefully, gave me a urine cup and "Information Sheet" and said, "Fill this out, give me a sample, and take a seat. I'll call your name when the doctor is ready for you."

I sat down and waited just as if I were waiting with my ticket at a busy deli counter. But at least in a deli shop you take something home with you. I was going to leave someone irreplaceable behind.

The staff saw me sitting there all alone. They could tell I was scared. But they didn't offer me any help. They didn't give me any information whatsoever—no ultrasound, no video, no explanation, no counseling, no nothing! They lied to me! As I continued to sit, waiting hesitantly, my thoughts wandered. . . .

I've already been through one abortion and it caused me nothing but pain. I never felt any relief after it. Why should I hurt myself again? Why should I let these liars abuse me? They just want my money. Those people praying outside don't want any money. They seem to really care. Maybe they could help me. My job can't be the only job in the world. Maybe there's another one waiting for me somewhere. Miguel's family has pushed me too far! What happened to the determined Teresita? Get up your courage, girl! Do what you think you should do! Do the right thing. Make the RIGHT choice, the only choice! Be true to yourself and don't try to please everyone else.

Just then, for some reason, I turned around to the window behind me, and I opened the blinds and looked out. I saw all those people praying out there, and I also saw a life-size image of Our Lady of Guadalupe held by two ladies who were praying the Rosary with a priest. I remembered my mother and grandmother talking about Our Lady of Guadalupe and how she protected Grandma on her walk to Texas. In the Image her hands were folded at her breast in prayer. Her face was full of kindness and compassion. She seemed to be praying just for me and urging me to come out to her. She was pregnant, and so was I.

Suddenly I thought, *Wow! That's La Virgen de Guadalupe. Outside there are people praying, a priest, and La Virgen. Maybe she'll protect me like she did Grandma on her pilgrimage. What am I doing in here? I've gotta' take the risk and trust her. I'm outta' here.*

And with that, I just got up, demanded my money and walked out of that clinic to join the pro-lifers outside.

Dan Lynch

Twenty-five

As I started down the sidewalk toward the Rosary people, the Escort people ran up to me, formed a ring around me, and held their hands in a circle as they yelled, "You don't have to listen to them! Let's go back inside, and we'll talk!"

Then they screamed at the Rosary people, "Leave her alone, shut up, and stop your stupid praying and singing." So I yelled back at the Escort people, "No, you shut up! There's no talking in there. There's only the silence of the dead. I *want* to talk to these people. Now let me through!"

So I broke through their arms, and I fell into the arms of a woman who actually reminded me of an angel. The sun was shining on her blonde hair and fair skin, and light seemed to emanate from her brilliant, bright blue eyes. She gave me a big hug, and I felt like I had been rescued. That hug told me that somebody cared, somebody would help me, and I felt so relieved. I just sobbed and sobbed on her shoulder, saying, "I didn't want to do it. Really, I didn't want to do it. They forced me. I had no help."

She comforted me in her soft and gentle voice. "It's all right; you're safe now. My name's Mary, and we'll help you. What do you need?"

"Food!" I blurted out. "I haven't eaten since I got up. But first . . . I'd like to talk to the priest."

I felt like a little girl who had done something wrong and got caught. I felt guilty. So I made my way over to the priest who was standing alone in the middle of the sidewalk as the escorts scurried back inside the clinic. As I approached him, I noticed that he was young, calm, and showed kindness and compassion in his dark brown eyes.

He said, "Hi, I'm Father John. I'm the Assistant Pastor over at St. Elizabeth's. I'm glad that you came out."

I said, "Father . . . Father, I feel so guilty. I feel so ashamed. I feel so sorry. Father, can I confess to you right here, right now?"

"Sure," he said, "Let's just walk slowly down the sidewalk away from everyone."

So I confessed, "Father, I uh . . . I should have never gone in there. I just felt all alone and like I didn't have any other choice. I really didn't want to do it."

"But you *didn't* do it. You didn't have the abortion. You did the right thing. You stood up for life, and you came out. God's been waiting for you to come home to Him. Hey! You're His child! He loves you. He forgives you. He's a merciful God. Jesus died on the Cross just for you and for the forgiveness of your sins. And look, we have this image of Our Lady of Guadalupe here with us. She's here for you, too. She's been here praying and interceding for you. She's pregnant in that image just as you're pregnant now. She's the Protectress of the Unborn. She watched over you and prayed that you would say 'yes' to life, just like she did."

And then I remembered my great grandmother's *bendición:* "May *La Virgen de Guadalupe* watch over and protect you and your loved ones down to the fourth generation." And here I was carrying the fifth generation in my womb. And her blessing was still in effect on me!

Father said, "God forgives you for thinking about an abortion. It isn't a sin because you didn't want to do it, and you didn't do it! It's in the past now, so you can start anew. Pray a Rosary and go in peace."

"But Father," I said, "I don't know how to say the Rosary."

"Not to worry, the ladies will teach you."

Suddenly, I felt light again. I felt like an incredible burden had been lifted from me. And I walked over to Mary with a big smile on my face and asked, "Could we get something to eat now?"

"Sure," she answered. "Let's eat!"

We walked across the street to a small restaurant and I ordered two hamburgers and a vanilla milkshake. Mary just got a cup of coffee. She sipped her coffee while I waited for my meal.

"Feeling better now?"

"I sure am! Father John was so good. He didn't yell at me at all. He just said that everything would be all right and to pray a Rosary. But I don't know how to pray the Rosary."

"That's easy," Mary said, as she pulled her Rosary beads from her pocket. "Look, there's only three prayers and they're straight out of Scripture—the Our Father, the Hail Mary, and the Glory Be. There are five decades of ten beads each separated by a larger bead. On the large beads we say the Our Father, on the small beads the Hail Marys, and after each decade we say the Glory Be."

"Is that all?"

"Well, that's the vocal part. Then there's the mental part. While we say the prayers, we meditate on a mystery from the life of Christ, such as His birth, His death, and His Resurrection. The prayers are like background music which prevent distractions so that you can concentrate on the mysteries. I recommend you start with the Joyful mysteries.

"The first Joyful Mystery is the Annunciation by the angel Gabriel of Mary's pregnancy, then the Visitation of the pregnant Mary to her elderly pregnant cousin Elizabeth so that Mary could care of her, then the Nativity or birth of Jesus, and after that the Presentation of the Baby Jesus in the Temple. The last one is the Finding of the Child Jesus in the Temple. I can assure you that when you pray these mysteries, you'll find joy in your heart because you said 'yes' to life just like Mary did."

"Huh," I said. "I never knew it was that easy. My mother never taught me, and I never learned it in Catholic school. My grandmother always prayed the beads when she visited us, but I just thought it was an old lady's mumbling prayers. I should have given her a little more *respecto*. Her prayers were the only Spanish I knew until I studied it in high school. I can still hear her praying, *'Santa María, Madre de Dios . . .'*"

My burgers came, and Mary said, "Hey, you haven't even told me your name."

"Teresita, hungry Teresita. This hamburger tastes great."

"Teresita, I'm Mary Sullivan, and I want you to see what your baby looks like."

Then she pulled out a pamphlet which showed a picture of a twelve-week-old baby. He was beautiful. He was sucking his thumb, floating in a golden-hued amniotic sac.

Mary looked me in the eye. "It's a *baby,* Teresita. It isn't just a fetus. He has hands, feet, a brain and brain waves, a heart and a heartbeat. In fact, the baby's heart starts beating even before the mother knows that she is pregnant."

"Miguel's sisters lied to me! They said it was just a blob of tissue. And the clinic told me nothing. I didn't think it was a baby 'till around five months. I didn't know that it was a baby so early. I feel like such a fool, Mary. But I'm happy that you saved my beautiful, thumb-sucking *baby* from being killed."

"Yes, Teresita, it's a baby from the very beginning—from conception." Mary ordered another cup of coffee and started peppering me with questions about my living situation. "I'm here to help you. What do you need?"

"I need everything," I gulped. "I work in a restaurant. The manager is the father of the baby. He and his mother pushed me into this because, if you can believe it, his mother didn't want a brown grandchild! He got a white girl pregnant at the same time as me, so his mother wanted to support her white grandchild. They decided that I would have to have the abortion—either that or be fired. So now that I've decided against the abortion, I can't go back there to work."

"Well, you've come to the right person," she said. "My brother runs a nice family restaurant. He could probably use your help. But before that, we'll hit the social agencies and see what assistance you're entitled to. We'll get you stabilized, and then you can start to work."

"Really?" I said as I slurped the last of my milkshake through the straw. "This is too good to be true. Mary, you didn't just save my baby, you saved me, too."

So just like she said we would, we hit the social agencies, and I got some assistance for my rent and food. We went to her brother's restaurant. It was really nice and clean and catered to families. There was no alcohol served. He had an opening, and he hired me. Things were really falling into place. It seemed like I just had to stand back and let things happen.

As my head hit the pillow that night, I prayed my first prayer in a long time. . . .

God, I think that I believe that You are really there. And that You really care. And that You really are listening to me, after all. I just want to thank You for what You have done to save my baby and me and to put Mary in my path. Your timing is uncanny. When I was ready to say "yes," You already had everything lined up. You prepared the way and put the right people in my path. And Virgen de Guadalupe, thank you for watching over me and protecting me. Thank you for being there when I needed you the most. Thank you, and good night.

Twenty-six

"**M**y mother is on my back," Miguel screamed into my telephone. "If you know what's good for you, you'll get that abortion!" I had sent the abortion money back to him. After he received it, he called me in a rage.

Somehow I found new strength and calmly replied, "I do know what's good for me. That's why I *didn't* get the abortion. And that's why I'm *not* going to get the abortion, no matter what you say. I know it's wrong, you know it's wrong, and choices have consequences. I've made the right choice this time. The *only* choice, actually. I know it's going to be hard for you to accept this, but please don't interfere and don't threaten me. Goodbye, Miguel." And I calmly hung up the phone.

The next day after work, I was approaching the stoop to my apartment when two men jumped out of a car parked on the curbside. One grabbed me from behind and held my arms, while the other one turned me around and kicked me in the stomach. He kept kicking and punching me. Then he stopped and yelled, "If you won't get the abortion, we'll give it to you." I could smell the booze on his breath.

I saw an opening and kicked him in his groin as hard as I could. He howled and the other guy threw me to the ground. I fell down at the feet of the statue of Our Lady of Charity and screamed at the top of my lungs. My landlady opened her door. The thugs jumped in their car and sped off. My landlady helped me into the house and onto her couch and called 911. The Rescue Squad came and took me to the Emergency Room where the doctor gave me an ultrasound to see if the baby was injured. As I waited for the ultrasound results, I prayed. . . .

God, are You punishing me just like my mother used to punish me? I feel like I deserve it. I don't deserve to give birth to this baby since I aborted my first one. I'm not worthy. It was all my fault. But, on the other hand maybe You're just testing my trust in You. God, You know that I have a permanent limp because of my mother's attempted abortion of me. Please don't let my baby die or be hurt. I've gone through so much to have this baby. Please don't let it end now. Holy Virgen de Guadalupe, please protect this baby.

The doctor walked in and glumly said, "Look at this picture of your baby. As you can see, the placenta is torn. This is what feeds the baby and when it's damaged, the baby can't get the nourishment it needs. At this stage of the pregnancy, a torn placenta . . . isn't good. The odds are that your baby won't make it. You'll probably have a miscarriage. I'm sorry."

"NO!" I cried. "I've already given birth to a dead baby. I can't do that again. It can't be! This baby has to live."

"Well, that would take a miracle. Go home now and give yourself complete bed rest for a month, and we'll see what happens."

So, with a heavy heart I went home and went to bed. Mary and her friends brought my meals, my boss gave me a leave of absence, and I prayed. . . .

Dear God, the doctor said it'll take a miracle for my baby to make it. Well, You're in the miracle business. Please give me that miracle. Not for my sake, but for the baby's. I've already given birth to one dead baby; I can't do that again. I think I'll go crazy. Please don't punish me with another dead baby. Virgen de Guadalupe, in your image you're pregnant just like me. You gave birth to a healthy baby. Please let me do the same. I trust in your help. Amen.

And so it went, day after day for the month of August. I lay down and prayed the Rosary for *aguante,* the strength to endure. I didn't hear from Gloria or Miguel because the police warned them to leave me alone. They didn't have enough proof to charge them, but the police scared them enough that they didn't bother me anymore.

Mary and her friends prayed with me, helped me, and hoped for me. They even arranged for a special shower for me at Sunday Mass. I didn't know anything about it. Mary and the girls came over one Sunday afternoon and brought all kinds of gifts for me and my baby—baby clothes, blankets, diapers, and even a crib! They also gave me a nice card with some money in it. Inside the card, there was a handwritten message that expressed their confidence in a healthy birth. This is what they wrote:

We will pray and fast for you, your baby, and a healthy birth. We will join you in your anxiety while you wait in patient hope. We will suffer with you in your birth pains, and then we will rejoice with you for having said "yes" to life and birthing a healthy baby!

Love,
St. Elizabeth's Parish

A month later, we went back to the hospital, and the doctor did another ultrasound. I'll never forget the look on his face as he came back with the results. He was beaming and said, "I told you that it would take a miracle, and it looks like you got one. Look, the place where the placenta was torn has healed. There's no evidence of any permanent damage. The baby is growing normally. I think you're going to have a healthy baby."

"Praise God!" I yelled.

"Yup," the doctor replied. "You can't praise me for this one."

Twenty-seven

*W*hat's *Tepeyac* mean?" I asked Mary. We were standing at the entrance door to Dr. Espinoza's waiting room. Mary had referred me to this pro-life doctor for follow up. He was a Mexican-American, like my mother. We had taken the elevator to the third floor and, as we got out of the elevator, I saw the brass sign. It said, *Tepeyac Mothers' Center.*

"*Tepeyac* is the name of the hill on which Our Lady of Guadalupe appeared on December 12, 1531, in Mexico," Mary said.

"Yes, December 12th! My mother told me. It's also my birthday!"

"That's a good day for a birthday, Teresita. That's the day that the Virgin came to Tepeyac appearing as the pregnant mother of Jesus and said, 'Am I not here who am your Mother? I am your fountain of life!' That's why she is called the 'The Protectress of the Unborn' and that's why Dr. Espinoza named his practice after Tepeyac, for pregnant mothers."

"December 12th is also the day that I aborted my baby," I sadly confessed. But maybe *La Virgen* was even looking over me then, Mary. When I was at the lowest point in my life I'd like to think that, even then, she was praying for my baby and me."

"She was. She's there for us in the good times and in the bad times, just like a good mother should be."

As we entered the waiting room, the first thing I noticed was an image of Our Lady of Guadalupe prominently displayed on the wall. Pregnant mothers sat and watched their children playing with toys on the floor. The receptionist welcomed us with a smile and said, "Please be seated." The room was full of warmth and happy conversation, so different from the cold silence of the abortion clinics I had been in. Dr. Espinoza even came into the waiting room to greet me.

"*Buenos días,* come on in!"

I followed him into his office and noticed the soft blue rug that contrasted with his dark walnut desk. Diplomas and certificates filled the wall behind it. He sat me down in a chair placed alongside his desk and then walked behind it to sit down.

"How can I help you?" he smiled.

"I'm pregnant, and I've just recovered from a torn placenta. I want to be sure everything goes okay. I want the best for my baby."

"Well, you've come to the right place," he said as he waved his hand across the wall papered with his diplomas. "I'm *proud* of my mother and baby care." He emphasized the word *proud* so heavily that I couldn't help but wonder why. Surely he didn't need to brag about himself.

With anxious anticipation, I showed him the before and after ultrasound pictures of my baby. He studied them carefully and said, "This is remarkable—a torn placenta one month and a totally healed placenta the next. You must've had a good doctor. He did a great job."

"Nope," I said. "He didn't do anything. Even he gave credit to *La Virgen*."

"Oh, I see. You're a fan of hers, too. Welcome to Tepeyac. Between the two of us, we'll take good care of the two of you. As you can see from your pictures, the ultrasound tells it all. It's such an amazing invention. Ever since it was invented, we doctors have known that we have *two* patients with a pregnancy, the mother and the unborn child. We also learned without a doubt that life begins at conception."

"I know that now. I just wish that I had known it before."

"Yes, the truth is scientifically shown by the ultrasound. It's such a remarkable invention that it converted the Jewish doctor Bernard Nathanson to belief in the scientific truth that life begins at conception. Before that, he founded the National Abortion Rights Action League and was the director of the largest abortion clinic in the world. He was involved in over 75,000 abortions, and he even aborted his very own child!"

"Oh my God, and I thought I was bad."

"God's mercy is unfathomable, Teresita. He forgives. The worst of us can change for the better, just like your worst ultrasound changed for the better." It almost sounded like he was talking about himself, but then he went on about Dr. Nathanson.

"Dr. Nathanson told the history of abortion in a book called *Aborting America*. He said that he helped the cause to legalize abortion by telling a lot of lies, quoting false statistics, and blaming the Catholic Church for everything. He said that the media believed them all without even checking them out. He's sure come a long way. . . . Now he says that abortion is *never* a necessary medical procedure, and it kills the second patient. I wouldn't be surprised if he becomes a Catholic someday."

Then Dr. Espinoza proceeded to examine me. He assured me, "In my opinion you are going to have a happy, healthy baby. But just to make sure, let's bring this to prayer."

Then he placed his hand over my womb and prayed, "Dear and pregnant Lady of Guadalupe, intercede for Teresita and her child and bring them both to a happy, healthy birth through your Son Jesus. Amen."

After we left his office, Mary and I stopped at a cafe for coffee. While she sipped, I told her what Dr. Espinoza said and I asked her, "What did he mean when he said, 'I'm *proud* of my mother and baby care' and 'The worst of us can change'? I don't know . . . there was something strange in the way he said it."

"Well, he's proud *now* because he used to be an abortionist and he changed to pro-life."

"No way!"

"Yup, he was a big-time abortionist. He actually thought he was helping the Latinas. 'What's best for the women is best!' he used to brag. 'Their choice is my choice!' He'd give them whatever they wanted—pills, contraceptives, IUDs, sterilizations, and abortions. All for the Latinas—until his own Latina ran out of choices."

"What do you mean?"

"Are you sure you want to hear the story?"

"Of course," I said, as I moved forward to the edge of my chair.

"Dr. Espinoza came to the pregnancy care center where I volunteer and gave his testimony. He had it all typed out and gave us all copies. I brought mine with me today. I thought that you'd want to hear it. Here's what he said." Mary began to read.

Medical school taught me that contraception, sterilization and abortion were women's choices that were legal, and that we doctors had to honor them. In ethics courses they never taught us that what's legal isn't always what's right, and that it might even be wrong! They never taught us that some things were *always* wrong. They just taught that if the good outweighed the bad, it was permissible. They never said that you should *never* do anything that had *any* bad in it. And contraception, sterilization, and abortion sure had plenty of bad in them!

Any doctor who really looks at the blueprint for sex knows that sex is for bonding and for babies. It's for bonding married people together in love with an openness to babies for the natural procreation of the human race. Any kind of sex that goes against that is bad *in itself* such as masturbation, premarital sex, artificial contraception, and homosexuality. Because either there's no bonding in marriage, such as with masturbation, premarital sex, and homosexuality or there's no openness to babies, such as with artificial contraception. Those practices also have bad physical and emotional consequences such as sexually transmitted diseases, especially AIDS, unplanned infertility, increased risk for cancer and hemorrhaging, guilt, depression, and anxiety.

"I've had plenty of that," I interrupted.
"I bet you have!" Mary said as she continued reading.

But I did whatever procedures women wanted, all in the name of "Reproductive Freedom" and "Choice." I did them all on a grand scale. But I didn't really feel comfortable doing abortions. All of us doctors knew that we were really killing babies. Ever since ultrasounds were available in 1976, we could see that the baby was alive in the womb. But I felt that I had to honor the women's choices.

My practice was busy and the money was great. But my wife and I were getting old and lonely. We weren't able to have any children, and we were too old to adopt one. So we took in Laura, a troubled 13-year-old Latina as a foster child. Our lives changed overnight. She was a challenge, but she brought joy into our hearts as we shared our lives with one another. She was like my own daughter. Finally, my wife and I had a family. But it ended quickly and suddenly.

One summer when Laura was 16, I received a phone call at the office. It was Monday, July 30, 1978, at 10 a.m. . . . I'll never forget! . . . It was the hospital ER. "Dr Espinoza, I'm sorry," said the doctor, "but your daughter Laura has just been brought in dead on arrival due to hemorrhage from an abortion."

The abortionist had punctured her uterus with his vacuum tube. The clinic didn't even call 911. They didn't want to be embarrassed by an ambulance at the clinic—bad for business, bad image—so they drove her to the ER themselves. Unbelievable!

"Tell me about it!" I said. "The clinics didn't care about me either. But I'm alive, thank God. Poor Laura never had a chance."
Mary kept on reading Dr. Espinoza's story.

My *mamá* always told me that if you run into a problem that you can't handle, go to *La Virgen de Guadalupe*. Well, I couldn't handle Laura's death, so I took my mother's advice literally, and I went to visit the Virgin's miraculous image in Mexico City. I stood before the image of this beautiful pregnant mother and begged for her help. Suddenly, I heard a sweet, gentle voice within my heart. The voice said, *"Why are you hurting my daughters?"* It was the Virgin herself talking to me! Immediately I knew what she was talking about.

Here I was, thinking that I was helping the Latinas with contraception, sterilization, and abortion. But in fact, I was hurting them! They were the Virgin's daughters! As I stood beneath the Virgin's image, I could clearly see the harm. The Latinas came for my services, and all they got in return was encouragement to continue their sexual promiscuity, which resulted in sexually transmitted diseases and pregnancies. Then they'd want their pregnancies ended by abortion or their fertility ended by sterilization. And I would give them whatever they wanted. It was a vast wasteland of sexual diseases and disasters. The Latinas were bearing much of the brunt of the Sexual Revolution. *They* wore the IUDs, *they* took the pills, and *they* suffered from the contraceptive complications, the abortions, and the sterilizations. The men got off scot-free! I was truly hurting the Virgin's daughters, just like she said.

So I came home and began to think. You know, you never realize the value of a life until you lose someone close to you. Life became suddenly very real to me after I lost Laura, and not just from a scientific or medical standpoint. Life quickly became very *precious* to me. I stopped doing contraceptions, sterilizations, and abortions immediately. I could see that they were all anti-life.

I realized, too, that I had been killing someone else's child . . . just like the abortionist killed my Laura! That's when I thought I'd try to help women to make the *right* choices instead of blindly following their uninformed choices against life. That's why I founded the Tepeyac Mothers' Center and dedicated it to the pregnant *Virgen de Guadalupe. Viva la Virgen!*

"So that's Dr. Espinoza's testimony," Mary said as she finished her coffee. "You're in his good hands. Long live the Virgin and long live Teresita's child!" she toasted with her raised coffee cup.

Twenty-eight

*A*ll right, I'm going to deliver this baby now," said Dr. Espinoza. I thought, *Hey, what about me? I thought I was the one delivering this baby*. But I was too polite to say anything to him just then.

It was January 5, 1987, and I was in the delivery room with him. But it wasn't very homey, and it wasn't a very comforting environment. It had big, bright overhead lights with halo-like reflectors around them, antiseptic stainless steel sinks, and a plain white delivery table. They had taken me to the room, placed me on the delivery table, put me on a monitor, and stuck an IV into me. It all seemed a bit invasive and reminded me of my abortion experiences.

As I waited, the pains swept over me like waves in the beautiful rhythm of the ocean. It was like swimming at Nauset Beach with a real bad cramp. When I became bored and impatient with the steady restlessness of the waves of pain, I thought of other kinds of pain that I had experienced, like pain from a swollen infected tooth and from a migraine headache. My birth pain was worse than these, but at least it wasn't constant and it wasn't pointless like them. At least I was accomplishing something, I was gaining something from the pain, I consoled myself.

I thought about fictional accounts that I had read about childbirth— mostly written by men—and I thought, *What do they really know about it? I can just see them in the throes of what I'm experiencing now. Wouldn't they groan and yell for help! And make everyone around them miserable! But here I am doing a nice quiet job.*

Then Dr. Espinoza came in, and the nurse helped to put my feet into the stirrups—more unpleasant memories. I could feel the baby coming in between my labored breathing. He said, "I'm going to give you a painkilling spinal narcotic now."

"No!" I said, surprising even myself. "I want to feel this pain. I want to feel the burning. I want to experience this childbirth."

"Okay, Teresita, it's your choice. I'm just trying to ease your pain." Then he started saying things to me like, "Do this. Don't do that. Stay still . . ." as I tried to get into a comfortable delivery position. He just seemed to want to maintain control. Then he said, "Please take your hand off your stomach," as I tried to help my pushing. That was the last straw.

I gave up my politeness and firmly asked, "Will you please let *me* deliver *my* baby?" He stepped back in surprise, and then he got out some forceps and came toward me with them. I didn't want him to use them so I said, "Please, no forceps!"

Then he put them down and said, "Look Teresita, let's try to cooperate and work together to deliver this baby. Okay?"

"That's what I've been trying to tell you." Now we had a deal, and I asked for his help only when I felt that I really needed it.

The ripples of pain became like tidal waves. It felt like my body was on fire and that I was passing a watermelon. At one point, I felt like I just couldn't take it any longer, and begged Dr. Espinoza for the pain medication he had tried to offer me earlier.

"I'm sorry, Teresita, but you're beyond that point—it won't help you now," he said.

The pain continued, and I fell into almost a mindless, unconscious state—it was the only technique I had to deal with the pain. I just tuned out everyone around me and focused on those contractions. Then, through the burning roar of the waves I heard Dr. Espinoza say, "Push, Teresita!"

Seconds later, I heard a squeal and then the nurse quietly and peacefully said, "It's a girl!" Dr. Espinoza cut the umbilical cord and the nurse checked out my baby and took her over to the sink and washed her. Then she dried her and laid her on my stomach. I was in awe of her. I counted her fingers and toes, kissed her, and held her tiny hands in mine.

When I got back to my room, I put her to my full breast and looked into her eyes. I felt such a strong bond. I felt like she was drawing light out from my eyes. I couldn't believe that I had almost aborted this beautiful child, and I thanked God for her life.

At that point, she only brushed her lips against my breast as if she were too lazy or simply too exhausted to suck, and I said my first words to her. "Hey, little girl, do you think that it's just going to run freely into your mouth? You've gotta' work for it! Here's your start," I said, as I placed my nipple into her mouth. "But now you've got to do your part and suck."

I was filled with awe and thought, *How beautiful and what a privilege it is to be a mother! I pity the woman who's never felt my fear, joy and awe in cooperating with God to bring a child into this world.* I basked in my glory, but at the same time, I thought how much nicer it would have been if I'd had a husband-father to help me and to encourage me. I also vowed that I would never have another hospital birth again. While I was glad everything had come out all right, the experience had been a bit too cold, controlled and sterile for my taste.

Even though I had no husband to share that moment with, at least I was no longer alone. I had my daughter, and we were a family now. She really needed me, and would come to love me like no one else.

My little girl was brown and beautiful. *But what should I name her?* I wondered. I searched my head for female names going through the alphabet, *A, B, C, . . . G . . . Guadalupe!* It popped into my head as clear as a bell. *Of course*, I thought. *Who really helped me to give birth to this healthy girl? Our Lady of Guadalupe! I'll name her "Guadalupe."* So Guadalupe it was. I called her "Lupe" for short, and I could just hear Grandma saying, "Remember, it's pronounced *gwa-da-loo-pay*—it's part of your heritage." I'll have to tell people the same, I thought with a smile—"it's pronounced *loo-pay* and not *loop*."

The next order of business was to get Lupe baptized and to welcome her into the Catholic Church from which my parents and I had fallen away. I didn't want my baby to flounder around in life like I did, like a boat without an anchor in a storm, undisciplined, uncommitted, immoral and confused by so many "choices." I wanted her to know black from white, good from bad. I wanted her to have the stability that I never had. I wanted her to believe, to have the grace necessary to lead a good life, and the guidance of the Church to help her—all things that I had rejected through my bad choices.

I also wanted these things for myself in my new life. So I chose to prepare myself to receive the sacrament of Confirmation that I had rejected as a teenager. *Maybe if I had been confirmed, I never would have gotten into my messes,* I thought. I knew that I would need God's help and the graces that came through this sacrament in order to follow my new way.

The Bishop was coming to St. Elizabeth's on a Sunday in April to confirm the high school kids. So Father John and I planned that I would get confirmed then, and we'd also have the Bishop baptize Lupe. Father asked me if I would give my testimony for the youth after the Mass. I was a little nervous about that since I had never given my testimony before, but I hoped that my Confirmation graces would give me the strength.

I asked Mary and her husband to be Lupe's godparents, and we planned the celebrations to be a reunion of everyone who was there for me on the day that Lupe was supposed to have been aborted.

When the big day came, everyone was there—the Bishop, Father John, Mary and her husband and all of their pro-life friends came to celebrate with us. The Missionary Image of Our Lady of Guadalupe was also there. It was the same image that was at The Women's Choice Center when I almost had the abortion. Mary told me that this image traveled around the country to promote prayer and fasting as the spiritual means to end abortion and bring conversions.

After the Bishop's homily, I stood with Mary and her husband as the Bishop asked us, "Do you reject Satan? And all his works? And all his empty promises?" We responded together, "I do." Then we professed our faith in Jesus Christ and His Church, and the Bishop baptized Lupe into this faith. As I held her, he poured water over her head and said, "I baptize you in the name of the Father, and of the Son, and of the Holy Spirit."

Next, the Bishop asked all of the candidates for Confirmation to stand. He led us in making the same Profession of Faith that we had just made for Lupe. Then Father called each of us by name to come forward to the Bishop. I was the first one. The Bishop dipped his thumb in holy oil and made the Sign of the Cross on my forehead and said, "Teresita, be sealed with the Gift of the Holy Spirit. Peace be with you!"

I responded, "Amen. And also with you."

After we were all confirmed, the Bishop called the whole church to pray. "Let us pray for these sons and daughters of God, confirmed by the gift of the Spirit, that they give witness to Christ by lives built on faith and love."

My chance to give witness came right after the Mass. My Confirmation graces kicked in to give me the courage. I testified about how I had been pushed into the abortion choice. But, because Mary and her friends were there for me with the Missionary Image, I had decided against it, and went to Confession with Father John on the sidewalk, and how I'd now come full circle to have my baby, whom I named "Guadalupe," to be baptized today.

I also urged the youth to seek the truth. I said, "It's not like they say, 'My body, My choice.' Our bodies belong to God as temples of the Holy Spirit, and we should glorify God in our bodies and not blaspheme Him through premarital sex and abortions. There is no such thing as 'safe sex' but only 'sacred sex.' 'Sacred sex' in God's plan is for use only for bonding and babies—to bond a husband and wife together in marriage with an openness to bearing new life. Wake up and don't buy the lies of our culture of death!"

The congregation gave me a standing ovation. I guess I was now a true "soldier of Christ" just like St. Joan of Arc, the heroine of my adolescence. Some people stayed after to talk to me outside the church. A young guy said, "You said it straight, and we appreciate it. We need to hear the truth!"

A woman hugged me and kept saying, "Thank you, thank you . . ." and she kept repeating herself as if in a panic. I began to get concerned so I took her by the shoulders, gently pushed her back, and held her face in my hands. God gave me the words to say to her, and I told her that Our Lord wanted her to hear my testimony for her own healing.

She nodded in agreement and confessed that my story was her story. She hadn't told anyone about her abortion in 15 years. She kept repeating, "I'm so relieved that I can speak it out. I'm going to find Father to hear my confession just like you did." It felt awesome for God to use me to help her.

Another woman remarked afterward, "All we hear and see in the media is that abortion is a woman's choice. We never hear about how the choice is made, or the consequences of that choice. You've told us something that we've never heard before. There are a lot of women out there that need to hear your story. They need to know that there is help and hope for them, that someone cares—that abortion is not really 'pro-choice' but 'no choice.'"

As I left the church, I wondered what they would have thought of me if I had told them about my abortion in Vermont. Then I suddenly realized that I had never even confessed my Vermont abortion. In the confusion on the sidewalk outside of the clinic, I had only confessed that I had made an appointment for an abortion. I didn't even think to tell Father John that I actually had a real abortion in Vermont or about my drugs, booze and sex life. So, when I got home, I gathered up my courage, called Father, and made an appointment to see him the next day.

Twenty-nine

*F*ather, I need to confess—" I said, as I sat down in front of Father John's desk. I had taken Monday off from work, and went to see him at his office.

"But you've already confessed," he interrupted, "and you've been forgiven, just believe that."

"No, Father . . . there's something more. I . . . uh . . . I had an abortion once before. *And* . . . not only that but I . . . uh . . . I led a rotten life afterward."

"Okay, say no more. Let's bring the Holy Spirit into this scene."

So he pulled his seat away from his desk, pulled it into a corner of the room and said, "Here let me help you." Then he pulled my chair over in front of his and said, "Sit down, Teresita . . . relax." His gentle welcome relaxed me, and I felt right at home.

We both sat down facing one another, and he held my hands and said, "Let's call upon the Holy Spirit." He began praying, "Come Holy Spirit of love, mercy and forgiveness. Enter the heart of this child of God who comes to you seeking forgiveness, healing and wholeness. Bring her heart to full repentance, sorrow for her sins and a firm purpose to change her life and to accept and to believe and to know of your love and mercy for her. Teresita, is there anything you'd like to pray?" he asked.

With my eyes closed, I said, "No, Father . . . thank you . . . just let me absorb your prayer in silence."

Then I told him about my sex with Brian, my abortion in Vermont, and the horror that it caused in my life, filling me with guilt and driving me to cover up the voice of my conscience with dancing, drinking, drugs and sexual promiscuity. I told him how sorry I was for these sins and for all the sins of my past life, and that I resolved to follow God's ways and to avoid sin and the near occasions of sin as best I could.

Father said, "Jesus told a story about a prodigal son who left his father and squandered his money on a dissolute life. He wound up taking care of pigs. Then he came to his senses and came home to seek his father's forgiveness. His father saw him coming down the road, ran out to meet him and gave him a big hug and said, 'Let's rejoice because my son who was lost is now found.' Then they had a big family party. And that's what God the Father in heaven is saying to all of his angels now about you, Teresita, and they're having a big party in heaven because you have come home to Him. And in His name, I forgive you. You have to believe that you are forgiven for everything!

"Another time," he continued, "they brought a woman to Jesus who had been caught right in the act of adultery. Jesus said to her, 'Has no one condemned you?' 'No one,' she answered. Then Jesus replied, 'Neither do I condemn you. Now go in peace, but sin no more.'

"So I say to you the same, Teresita. Go in peace, but sin no more."

Then he extended his hands over my head and said, "God, the Father of mercies, through the death and resurrection of His Son has reconciled the world to Himself and sent the Holy Spirit among us for the forgiveness of sins; through the ministry of the Church may God give you pardon and peace." Then he blessed me with the Sign of the Cross with his right hand and said, "I absolve you from your sins in the name of the Father, and of the Son and of the Holy Spirit."

I almost shouted, *"Amen!"*

"Always remember, Teresita, that there's nothing so bad that you can't confide it to the Lord. So don't let your heart ache with lasting regret. He loves you and He'll forgive you, free you and forget your sins. Never dam up your sins. Let the dam break. Here, let me read Psalm 32 to you. It says this a little better than I do:

As long as I kept silent, my bones wasted away;
I groaned all the day.
For day and night your hand was heavy upon me;
my strength withered as in dry summer heat.
Then I declared my sin to you;
my guilt I did not hide.
I said, "I confess my faults to the Lord,"
and you took away the guilt of my sin.
Thus should all your faithful pray
in time of distress.

"And thus should you pray, Teresita. For your penance, pray one Rosary. *And* I want you to volunteer at the crisis pregnancy center on your day off once a week for a month. Hopefully, you can help prevent some other woman from aborting her child and hurting herself like you did."

Then he hugged me, looked me straight in the eyes, and offered this reassuring advice, "Jesus said, 'If the Son frees you, you will be truly free.' Now go in peace and act it!"

I felt newer and freer and cleaner than I'd ever felt before. My insides felt like the cold Nauset surf in spring when it would wash over my body after I'd fallen off my surfboard. I left Father's office with a noticeably new bounce in my step.

Thirty

"*W*e call this place *Mother Cares Life Center*," Mary said, "because Our Lady of Guadalupe, our heavenly mother, cares for unborn babies, and because we provide for a mother's cares for her unborn child. We give free pregnancy tests to see if she's pregnant. If she is, we're here for immediate care. She's often desperate, needs help, and might want to have an abortion because she thinks that's her only choice. We let her know that we're here to help."

I had gone to the church, prayed my Rosary and then dropped in on Mary at the crisis pregnancy center, just as Father John had asked. Mary explained the whole operation to me as she led me through the modest ranch house.

She said, "We try to find out the needs of the mother and meet them ourselves or by referrals to other helpers. In this way, we can get her food, clothing, shelter, health care, and maybe even a job. We show her that there is no reason or need for an abortion. If she can't take responsibility for raising the child, we can help to arrange for an adoption."

I noticed a large image of Our Lady of Guadalupe hanging in the waiting room and interrupted Mary's explanation of the Center: "Why do you have Our Lady of Guadalupe hanging in here? She seems to follow me everywhere that I go."

"The Center is dedicated to Our Lady of Guadalupe because she is pregnant in her image. She's a mother! Here, let me read to you what she said when she appeared to Blessed Juan Diego."

She picked up a holy card and began to read:

I am your Merciful Mother. Here I will show and offer all of my love, my compassion, my help, and my protection. . . . Listen and let it penetrate your heart; do not be troubled or weighed down with grief. Do not fear any illness or vexation, anxiety or pain. Am I not here who am your Mother? Are you not under my shadow and protection? Am I not your fountain of life? What else do you need?

"Isn't that beautiful?" Mary closed her eyes and smiled as if to savor the words. "These are the words that console and give hope to the mothers.

"Our motto is 'We care; we share.' In addition to providing pregnant mothers with their basic needs, we also teach them birth preparation and attempt to meet their emotional needs through counseling.

"As I said, we also provide free pregnancy tests. Unfortunately, that's all most of the women want. They don't want to listen to our counseling when the tests say that they're pregnant. They just hurry out to make the abortion appointment. It's a terrible choice that breaks the natural heart-bond between a mother and a child. It turns the mother's naturally warm heart into a cold heart of stone."

I immediately thought of my mother's coldness toward me and how we never bonded. Now I could see that it probably was a consequence of her choice to abort me.

Mary continued, "But even if the mother forgets her own child, God doesn't forget. So we pray for both the mother and the child. To help us to remember, we often repeat God's words in the verse from Isaiah 49:15:

Can a mother forget her baby,
be without tenderness for the child of her womb?
Even if she forgets,
I will never forget you.

"That's very consoling," I said.

"Yes it is. And if the pregnancy test shows that the woman is not pregnant, we try to encourage the single mothers to be chaste until marriage, but that's a hard row to hoe. Most of them are sexually active with one or more partners—and people wonder why we have social instability? There's just no commitment to each other or to anyone or to anything.

"If the woman is married," Mary went on, "we try to encourage her to use Natural Family Planning, known as NFP, instead of artificial contraception. Through NFP, married couples can regulate the birth of their children through the natural awareness of the woman's bodily fertility signs each month. The fertile time only lasts for about a week and the couple can try for pregnancy if they want a child, or abstain from sex during that time if they have good reasons to avoid pregnancy. It leads to a much happier sexual relationship where both the husband and wife are involved in the family planning decisions."

As Mary led me around, she looked at my leg and said, "I've always wondered about your leg. What happened to you?"

I hesitated, looked down at my leg, and then said, "Let's sit down at the table, and I'll tell you." With much emotional pain, I told her the story about my mother's botched abortion of my twin and my survival with a damaged left hip. She was awestruck.

She said, "God spared your life for a reason! You should tell your story! You're an abortion survivor. There aren't many of you. You can tell the truth about what they call a 'safe procedure.'" Deep in thought, she drummed her fingertips on the tabletop and stared up at the ceiling.

"You know, probably the best way to get this truth out is through a lawsuit. I know a lawyer who's had some experience with abortion malpractice. Would you like me to call him and set up an appointment for you? His name is Mike Reilly, and he's an Irish tiger for his clients."

"I don't know . . . I've never thought about a lawsuit before."

"Well, it's time that you started thinking about it. I'll call him for an appointment and let you know. Okay?"

"Yeah, you're right. I should start thinking about it. That abortionist should pay for my pain."

Thirty-one

M ary told me about your mother's abortion and your survival. Unbelievable! You know, there aren't many abortion survivors."

It was May of 1987. I was at attorney Mike Reilly's office. He had a shock of red hair and seemed larger than life as he came out to greet me in the waiting room. He shook my hand warmly, introduced himself, and led me to his office. I immediately thought, *He's like my Mr. Right, the maverick lawyer that I romanticized about on the Cape. He's in it for the cause and not for the money.*

A no-nonsense kind of guy, Mr. Reilly got right down to business. "Please fill me in on the dates and the details of your experience." Once more, I told my story. When I finished, he said, "I think you've got a claim for the doctor's attempt to kill you, and the permanent injury that he caused you. His defense will be that your mother consented to it, and he could have permanently killed you, if your mother let him finish the job, but because she didn't, you wound up with a permanent limp. So it's all your mother's fault for not letting him finally kill you. Doesn't that sound ridiculously absurd? Welcome to the culture of death."

He paused to let me absorb both the contradiction and the reality.

"And that's just what I'll prove. That defense is absurd. Also, your mother couldn't legally consent because abortion was illegal in 1967. And you certainly didn't consent to wrapping your leg like a necklace around your neck! So you've got a good case, but it's an old one. The statute of limitations for an injury to a minor runs out three years after age 18. So we'll have to bring suit before you're 21."

I hung my head down and said softly, "I . . . uh . . . I also have another case for you."

"What's that?"

Then I told him all about my Vermont incomplete abortion and the birth of my dead baby.

Mr. Reilly exhaled slowly and sat up straighter in his leather desk chair. His empathy was clear, as well as his outrage. "It's similar to the situation with your mother. Their defense will be that you consented to the abortion. But how can you consent to something that you don't know anything about? They didn't inform you. Your consent must be *informed.*" He said the last word very slowly and loudly so that I would be sure to understand him. He let it hang there for a moment and then went on.

"They're supposed to tell you the pros, the cons and the risks of an abortion, so that you can make up your own mind and make a real *informed* choice. They're always talking about choice, but no one wants to give you the actual facts which would convince most people to choose life. They don't want you to choose life because they'd go out of business.

"Remember, Teresita, our choices end when our duty to another begins. So we can't choose to kill another person because we have the duty to respect the other person's life. But they don't remind you of such simple facts. They don't tell you that it's a life, that it's a baby, even though they're nauseated by the site of the dead babies in their dumpsters. They don't tell you all the risks, and they don't show you an ultrasound because they're afraid that you'll see your real live baby—kicking, swimming and alive—and change your mind about the abortion. Talk about nauseating! That kind of deception makes me sick!

"Even if you had really consented to the abortion, they're supposed to do a safe job and not put you at risk like they did. It must have been terrible for you to undergo all that anxiety and physical trauma, wondering if and why you were still pregnant and what you would give birth to. They should pay for that!

"You know, they're just butchers who want your money. They've got a job they're afraid to lose, and they justify it just like the producers putting all the smut out on our TVs. It's good money, it's a living, and people buy it, whether it's good or bad for them. I've got a case now where an abortion facility killed a young girl. They perforated her uterus and killed her. The dirty bastards—excuse my French, Teresita. They didn't even call an ambulance. Bad for business, you know. And they took her to the hospital in a car! If they had treated her earlier, they might have saved her. But they didn't want to embarrass their clinic so they took a slow ride to the hospital without any flashing lights, sirens, emergency personnel, or equipment."

I realized that he was speaking about Dr Espinoza's daughter, Laura, and I said, "Make sure that they pay for that one, too!"

"I will," he said. "The only language that they understand is money, so if we make them pay big, maybe a few of them will stop doing abortions. Or maybe someone will read about it and open their eyes. And maybe then one or two more will be on our side. That's our hope, Teresita, that with girls like you, we can bring out the truth about abortion and maybe get a few abortionists to stop."

As I left his office, I felt confident I was in good hands with Mr. Reilly.

Thirty-two

Through my appointments with Mr. Reilly over the next few months, I got to know him better. One day I asked him, "How did we ever get into this legal abortion mess, Mr. Reilly?"

"Seven men and a pen," he answered.

"What do you mean?"

"Well, before 1973, most of the states had laws making abortion a crime. Then, suddenly and without warning, seven judges of the United States Supreme Court took a pen and wrote that abortion was legal, and all of the states' laws against it were declared unconstitutional. They said a woman's choice for abortion was within *her* constitutionally protected right of privacy. Isn't that ridiculous? Her privacy gets protected but the baby's *life* doesn't!"

I nodded in agreement as he continued. "Despite all of the biological evidence that says that life begins from conception, and the constitutional guarantee of the right to life, the Judges said that the unborn baby has no right to life. The people never got a chance to vote on the abortion issue. The Supreme Court just pulled the rug out from under us and the wool over our eyes. They forced abortion on demand down our throats and millions of dead babies down our sewers. Women have been suffering for it ever since."

"You can say that again," I sighed.

"There's never been a historical precedent for abortion in the entire *world*. It's really national suicide. It's the death of the future of a culture. President Kennedy said that children are our most important natural resource and our best hope for the future. The legalization of abortion has corrupted the principles and the practitioners of medicine, law, and politics. If you don't have the right to life, you don't have any rights."

I sat there a little confused and slowly said, "I really didn't know that life began at conception until Mary told me. I thought there was no right to life until the baby could live outside the womb around 7 months."

"Teresita, in some states, farmers actually have to pay taxes on unborn livestock—that is, any pregnant cow or sheep must legally be reported as two. Why is the government suddenly so 'confused' when it comes to human life? It's a baby from the get go."

"Well, I know that now. But I didn't know that before my abortion. And neither did my friends. We never learned that life begins at conception. No one ever told me that the heart started beating at only 21 days, even before the mother knows she's pregnant. So that's why I was personally opposed to abortion, but I also thought that each woman should be able to make her own choice."

"Sure, and wind up here like you. Right!?"

"Well, we can't impose *our* values on *others* . . . can we?"

"Of course we can, and we do it all the time! What do you think happens if you take a knife and kill someone? It's a crime! Most of the criminal code *imposes* the moral values of Judeo-Christianity on *everyone*. And with good reason. The laws against murder, stealing and perjury are taken right from the Ten Commandments. So were the laws against abortion—'Thou shalt not kill.' You've gotta' wake up and think, girl! You're just mouthing pro-choice propaganda."

"I guess it was instilled in me by the culture," I replied. Well, that sure hit a raw nerve with Mr. Reilly, and he went off. He got up from his desk and started walking back and forth waving his arms as if he were making a closing argument to a jury.

"Look, Teresita, you're just promoting the propaganda slogan of the culture of death—'My body, my choice!' First of all, it's not your body. It's your *baby's* body. And it's not your *choice,* either. You already *made* the choice when you had sex. The baby is not a choice, it's a *consequence* and a human being, one worthy of your reverence and bringing to birth. The so-called 'pro-choice' argument is as old as the pro-slavery argument." There was no holding Mr. Reilly back now.

"In the debates between Abraham Lincoln and Senator Stephen Douglas before the Civil War, the issue was pro-choice for slave masters or pro-liberty for slaves. Douglas was pro-choice and insisted on the principle of freedom of choice—for people to choose slavery or not. But Lincoln insisted that there was a *higher* principle. A person's freedom of choice, he argued, ends as soon as another person's freedom is threatened. Slavery is wrong *in itself*, and no one is free to choose evil.

"Lincoln said, 'If you admit that it is *wrong*, nobody has a *right* to do wrong.' The same principle applies to abortion. The South didn't follow Lincoln's principle because they had too much to lose—too much *money*, too much convenience to lose—and the Civil War soon followed. God help us if we don't follow this principle. The very essence of moral self-government, from the time of the Mayflower Compact until today, demands that we preach the principle for blacks as well as unborn children, both of whom have the self-evident 'inalienable rights' spoken of in the Declaration of Independence—'life, liberty and the pursuit of happiness.'

"What good is a government if it doesn't protect these rights?"

He answered his own question as I tried to think about it. "It's not doing its job! The whole purpose of government, as it states in the Declaration, is *to secure and protect* these rights. And the first right is the right to life. No other rights have any meaning if you don't have life. Can't you *see* that?"

He talked passionately as if he couldn't get his point across, as if I were brainwashed. And I have to admit that my brain did seem drugged by the culture and its propaganda, and that I had never really thought deeply enough about the morality of abortion. The *experience* was bad enough for me, both as an unborn baby and a pregnant mother, and I had tried to bury any *thoughts* about abortion.

But now it was beginning to dawn on me that I had to start *thinking* about the moral implications of abortion for our culture and not just be a mouthpiece of its propaganda. It was becoming clear that the so-called "right" to abortion was based on lies and deceit, and I had a responsibility to think critically and get to the truth.

Mr. Reilly hardly caught his breath as he went on. "Any nation that exalts individual choice over what is morally good, such as the choice for abortion over reverence for another person's life, leaves itself open to becoming a nation where the strong will prevail over the weak. In the long run totalitarianism results. Mother Teresa said, 'The fruit of abortion is nuclear war.'"

"Really?! Well, how will we ever end abortion, Mr. Reilly, before it gets to that?"

"Another American Revolution or Civil War won't do it. We need a *spiritual* revolution. Slavery was a geographical evil—it was confined mainly to the South—but abortion is an unconfined *universal* evil. It's like slavery was a localized skin cancer but abortion a widely metastasized carcinoma spread throughout the body. You can remove a skin cancer, but cancer spread throughout the body often requires a transplant at the very core—the bone marrow. We need a total transplant from our culture of death to a culture of life. Hearts must be melted so that life will be revered. If not, God help us. His merciful remedy will likely be worse than we can imagine—worse than the Civil War that ended slavery. . . ."

He looked at me and must have noticed my wide eyes and open mouth. He then smiled politely, and said, "Sorry, Teresita, I got carried away."

"It's okay, Mr. Reilly. You're helping me to understand how bad the abortion situation really is."

He made a fist with his right hand and started punching it into the open palm of his left. "There's a moral fault line in America and its name is *abortion!* You know how an earthquake occurs around a fault line on the earth's surface? Well, we have social disorder occurring along this moral fault line of abortion. Just like an earthquake, it's emanating and rippling out in all directions, manifesting itself in different ways and reaching different parts of society—but it all begins at that line. It just can't go on Teresita. Lincoln said, 'We can't stay half-slave and half-free,' and Mike Reilly says, 'We can't stay half-pro-choice and half-pro-life.' Something's gotta' give. Mark my words, Teresita. There's going to be a moral earthquake along the abortion fault line."

"Is there anything I can do to help people wake up?"

"Yes, there is. Listen. . . ." he began. "We've got to do our part to try and stop the killing. I want you to write your life's story so you know it cold. Write it all down. Because the abortionists' lawyers will ask you questions and interrogate you before trial in examinations called depositions. They'll ask about your family heritage, family life, and upbringing. They'll try to wear you out, embarrass you and humiliate you so that you'll get discouraged and drop your case.

"Write it all down, Teresita. They'll show you no mercy! They'll do their best to shame you and overwhelm you. They won't leave any stone unturned and neither should you in your story. They'll try to scare you into dropping your case. They'll ask you all about your abortion experiences and even questions that aren't relevant, especially about your sex life. They'll try to destroy you. So make sure you write it all down first and get comfortable with it. Okay?"

Again, I slowly nodded my head in silent agreement.

"Believe me, Teresita, you're stronger than they are. You can out-write, out-talk, and out-last them. I see it in your eyes. I see your determination for justice. You can do it!"

"Listen, Mr. Reilly," I finally said, " I bear the permanent scars of abortion in my body and in my soul. I know what I'm talking about, and I'm not afraid of any lawyer's questions!"

And so I began to write the story of my life.

Thirty-three

A year went by, and I got the basic story written down. But Mr. Reilly couldn't locate the California doctor who performed the illegal abortion on my mother. Too many years had passed. Records and staff had disappeared. So we gave up on that case and brought a lawsuit against my Vermont abortionist. As I reached the fourth anniversary of my incomplete abortion in October of 1988, I was reviewing the case with Mr. Reilly when I suddenly realized that I still didn't know what a P.A. was. So I asked Mr. Reilly, and he explained that it stood for a Physician's Assistant.

"Assistant?" I said angrily. "You mean they're not even qualified physicians? I thought that she was a doctor! She had a white dress on and everything. She sure looked like a doctor! When you entrust yourself to a medical person, you assume that you're in competent, trained hands. They never told me that she was only an *assistant.* Maybe if I had known that, I wouldn't have had the abortion."

"Looks are deceiving, Teresita. In Vermont anything goes. It's the most liberal state for abortion. You don't even have to be a doctor to perform one. It's hard to believe, but it's true."

"Can you find out more about that?"

"Sure, I can take the P.A.'s deposition."

"What's that?" I asked.

"Don't you remember? A deposition is a pretrial oral examination of a witness under oath where you ask all kinds of questions about the case or the witness's background. That's what they're going to do to you, and that's why I asked you to begin writing down your story."

"Oh yeah, but I forgot the legal name. Would it be possible to take her deposition before they take mine?"

"Sure, I'll schedule it right away. Actually, this goes to the heart of our claim that you never gave your *informed* consent to the abortion. I'll bring the transcript of the P.A.'s deposition back from Vermont for you to read."

When Mr. Reilly returned from Vermont, he called me in for an appointment. As usual, he personally came to his waiting room to greet me with his warm handshake and smiling face. I really felt comfortable with him. He escorted me into his office, sat me down, picked up the typed transcript of the deposition, waved it triumphantly and said, "We've got them on the run, Teresita! *Ms.* Samantha Jones, Physician's Assistant, is lying through her teeth. She's trying to make it look like she was qualified for her dirty job, and that you knew what you were getting into. But it's all a bunch of bull, and I'll tear her up when she gets on the witness stand. You should've seen her at the deposition. I sat directly across from her at the conference table in her lawyer's office. I looked directly into her eyes and questioned her. She never looked me in the eye but just sat there, looking at her lawyer, impatiently tapping her fingers on the table."

Mr. Reilly told me all about his trip to Vermont, his visit and tour of the abortion clinic, and his deposition of the P.A. He even agreed with me that the entrance tower looked like a witch's hat sitting on the building. "A witch's hat for a witch's business," he said disgustedly. "Here, take this transcript home and read it . . . but not at bedtime. It'll give you nightmares. Like the P.A., I also give unqualified medical advice," he smiled as he led me to the door.

I couldn't wait. When I got home, I sat right down and read the transcript:

Mr. Reilly: Ms. Jones, please tell us what medical school you graduated from.

Ms. Jones: I didn't attend any medical school.

Mr. Reilly: You didn't? Well, tell us what college you graduated from.

Ms. Jones: I didn't go to college.

Mr. Reilly: No college? Well how about a community college? Did you graduate from there?

Ms. Jones: No. But I went to Burlington Community College for one and a half years before I dropped out.

Mr. Reilly: What degrees have you received?

Ms. Jones: I got a high school diploma from Burlington High School.

Mr. Reilly: That's it?

Ms. Jones: That's it.

Mr. Reilly: Please tell me, Ms. Jones, how you came to be a Physician's Assistant.

Ms. Jones: I apprenticed. The physician at the Feminine Health Clinic taught me how to be her assistant.

Mr. Reilly: You mean that you were an apprentice like a plumber's apprentice?

Ms. Jones: Well, you could call it that, but I also read medicine and did procedures for a couple of years.

Mr. Reilly: And where did the physician teach you?

Ms. Jones: At the clinic.

Mr. Reilly: So the clinic was your school, and the abortion doctor was your teacher.

Ms. Jones: Yes.

Mr. Reilly: What did she teach you?

Ms. Jones: Why, how to do abortions, of course!

Mr. Reilly: Did you learn how to cure people? How to care for them? Especially emergency care?

Ms. Jones: Well, I was taught how to handle a patient's panic. Some women are frightened about the procedure.

Mr. Reilly: You call a 16-year-old girl a woman?

Ms. Jones: The law says they don't need parental notification or consent. So, yes, they're women. They're free to make their own choice.

Mr. Reilly: But is it an *informed* choice?

Ms. Jones: What do you mean?

Mr. Reilly: Did you *inform* Teresita of all of her options and the risks and consequences of the choice for an abortion?

Ms. Jones: Well . . . not really. But, she signed a Consent Form.

Mr. Reilly: May I see it?

Ms. Jones: It's not in her file.

Mr. Reilly: Why not? Wouldn't that be something important enough to keep on file?

Ms. Jones: Yes, but somebody misfiled it, and it's lost.

Mr. Reilly: Do you expect a jury to believe that? The truth is, there never was a Consent Form, was there, Ms. Jones? How can you remember a Consent Form that's four years old?

Ms. Jones: I have an excellent memory.

Mr. Reilly: Well, do you remember questioning Teresita about her medical history to see if she had any medical problems?

Ms. Jones: No.

Mr. Reilly: How about her psychological condition? Wasn't she in a state of fear and uncertainty?

Ms. Jones: We didn't get into that, but I reassured her. I reassure all the patients. I was trained to do that.

Mr. Reilly: Then she probably wasn't in any psychological condition to have an abortion performed on her, was she?

Ms. Jones: That's not my call. I'm a P.A., not a psychologist.

Mr. Reilly: Did you inform Tersesita of the option of giving birth and either keeping the baby or putting it up for adoption?

Ms. Jones: Of course not! She was there to have an abortion, wasn't she?

Mr. Reilly: That's what we're trying to find out, Ms. Jones! Did you tell this 16-year-old girl that you might perforate her uterus, which could result in a hysterectomy and sterility? That you might puncture her bowels, which could result in death from peritonitis or a permanent colostomy? That you might damage her cervix causing her future miscarriages? That you might cause a blood clot from her womb to enter her bloodstream and kill her? That you might kill her psychologically through post-abortion traumatic stress syndrome?

Ms. Jones: I didn't have to tell her any of that since she signed the Consent Form.

Mr. Reilly: Which has conveniently disappeared. What did your physician teach you to do if any of the things that I've just described happened?

Ms. Jones: To call an ambulance.

Mr. Reilly: So that a *real* doctor in a *real* medical facility could treat her for your botched job. Is that what you're telling me?

Ms. Jones: We're not trained or equipped for those kinds of things at our facility. And under the law, we don't have to be.

Mr. Reilly: Well, let's forget about these other possibilities for a moment. Did you tell her about the possibility and danger of what actually happened to her? That you might fail to complete the abortion, which would necessitate a later saline abortion and the birth of a dead baby?

Ms. Jones: Who says it was incomplete?

Mr. Reilly: A *real* physician at the Green Mountain Hospital, that's who. Did you try to notify Teresita's parents who knew her much better than you did and might have warned her about the dangers— which you didn't do—and might have encouraged her to carry the baby to birth and raise it herself or place it for adoption?

Ms. Jones: Legally, you don't have to do that in Vermont.

Mr. Reilly: Well what *do* you have to do in Vermont to be assured of what you call "a safe and legal abortion"?

Ms. Jones: You have to have at least a P.A., like me, and you have to get the patient's consent.

Mr. Reilly: Which you never got, Ms. Jones. And with a P.A. like you, who needs a real doctor, right? I think you've said it all. No further questions.

Thirty-four

I feel deceived! They didn't explain that she was only an *assistant,*" I told Mr. Reilly as I leaned forward in my seat, staring at the deposition in my lap. I had rushed to his office first thing the next morning, my heart pounding, and my adrenalin level high. "I can't believe that she wasn't a doctor. That explains why the procedure hurt so badly. She probably didn't know what she was doing!"

As I said those words, I suddenly stopped talking and reflected on them for a moment. Then I went on.

"You know, now that I think about it, she really *didn't* know what she was doing. She must have thought that she was really helping me carry out my choice to be free of my baby and an unwanted pregnancy. She really didn't know what she was doing. Didn't Jesus say about those who crucified Him, 'Father, forgive them for they *don't know what they're doing'?*"

"If she didn't know what she was doing, she *should've* known, and they should pay, Teresita. From your pain, they shouldn't gain."

Then I blurted out, "I don't think that I want to pursue this lawsuit, Mr. Reilly. What good will the money do?"

"Hey, what do you mean? Don't be so impulsive! I've been working on this case for a year and a half now, and you've got it all written down. I say let's go forward. The money we get will teach them a lesson, and maybe there will be one less abortionist or at least they'll be more careful next time."

"I don't want their dirty money. It's blood money. They can keep it. And I don't want them to be more careful, Mr. Reilly. I just don't want there to *be* a next time! Please make them an offer to settle for enough to cover your expenses, and the medical bills for me and Lupe. I'll give anything leftover to the Mother Cares Center."

"Well," he said, "if you insist. If you're going to get out, now's the time to do it before they take your deposition and get you all upset. I'm sorry,

Teresita, that you don't want to go all the way with this, but I can understand. You know, now that I think of it, maybe there *is* something else that you can do. They're getting away with murder up there in Vermont, and it's just not right! If you could help prevent just one mother from going through what you went through, if you could save just one baby from what your baby went through, would you do it?"

"Do what?"

"Rescue a mother and her baby."

"What do you mean? How could I rescue a mother and a baby?"

"Do you know what the Bible says about rescuing?"

"No, I don't."

He pulled down his Bible and opened it to a tagged page. "Here's what it says in the Book of Proverbs, Chapter 24, verse 11, 'Rescue those who are being dragged to death, and from those tottering to execution withdraw not.'

"What that says to me, Teresita, is that God calls some of us to rescue the babies who are being dragged to death at the abortion clinics. We're called to be the voice for the voiceless unborn and the last line of defense for the defenseless. We're also called to be the last hope for the mother. To be there for her, to tell her the truth about what abortion does to her baby and to her own body and soul, and to meet her needs so that she can bear her baby. You know, Teresita, you've been there! You were in need, and nobody was there for you or your baby in Vermont."

". . . Nobody . . . how can I help?"

"You can place your body peacefully and nonviolently between the abortionist and the mother who's about to enter the abortion clinic. In other words, you could block the entranceways."

"But wouldn't that be illegal?"

"It shouldn't be, but it is. It's a *necessary* trespass that is justifiable in the law for any other reason. For example, if a baby was in a burning house you could justifiably trespass to save it because it's necessary. But the courts don't buy that for abortion, because it's not 'politically correct.' But we have to be willing to take some risks in life to do the right thing, to stand in the face of evil, even if it is illegal. And there are many brave people who are willing to do the right thing and get arrested for rescuing even just one mother and baby.

"Just because it's illegal," he went on, "doesn't make it wrong, and just because something is legal doesn't make it right. Abortion is legal. But it's not right, it's wrong. Rescues are illegal. But they're not wrong, they're right. It was illegal for blacks to sit in white restaurants during the Civil Rights Movement. But they did the right thing. They trespassed and got arrested. So, do you want to be like them and do the right thing, Teresita?"

"What is the right thing?" I questioned.

"As I said, you could do a Rescue. They're completely nonviolent. You just sit there with the other Rescuers in the hope that the mother will see your witness and change her mind and not go into the clinic to kill her baby."

"If they had been there for me, I never would have entered that Vermont clinic. I definitely would have turned around and left."

The Rescue concept appealed to my sense of justice for the oppressed which was instilled in me by my mother's cause for the oppressed migrant farm workers. Unborn babies are the most oppressed minority in history, I reasoned. Millions of them were being killed each year throughout the world. The idea also appealed to my sense of compassion for the mothers going in for their abortions. They had no idea what they were getting themselves into.

"What specifically can I do to help, Mr. Reilly?"

"Well, I help as a lawyer in the Rescue Movement. Rescuers get together from all over a region and go as a group to an abortion clinic before it opens. They pray, sing hymns, and sit down. They lock arms to prevent the mother's entry to the clinic and to prevent the abortionist from having access to her. They block the doors, block the stairs, block the sidewalks.

"When the police come to arrest them, they act like the helpless babies to be a witness for them. They make their bodies go limp and get manhandled by the police, just like the babies get manhandled in their abortion.

"I represent those who get arrested, and I raise the 'necessity defense'— that the trespass is a necessity to save the lives of the unborn children, and that it's a necessity to intervene to try to stop the mother from entering the clinic. But the judges don't let the defense in. They say abortion is legal, so you can't stop it. We try to make sure the Rescuers get treated fairly and are not hurt. We also try to be an influence on the conscience of the judges, police, and jail keepers.

"We're fighting a losing battle legally, but morally we're on the high ground. It's the same old story. The English pushed my Irish ancestors off their good farmland, and the California farmers pushed your Mexican ancestors onto bad land—pesticide poisoned farmland. Now your generation of young women is being pushed to the abortion clinics by the whole culture of death!"

"The *same* old story. . . . "

"We have a few lawyers in the East who help one another on Rescue cases. I heard that they're planning a Rescue in November at the same Vermont clinic where you had your abortion. It's cold up there, Teresita, but so are the hearts of the abortionists. Maybe you could help to soften them and show that someone really cares for the unborn and their mothers."

"Yeah, maybe this is my chance to make up for what I did by going into that Vermont abortion clinic. Maybe I could prevent some other mothers from making the same mistake that I made."

The Rescue concept also appealed to my sense of *coraje*—the righteous anger of Martin Luther King, Jr., of Cesar Chavez, and of my mother in her early days. I remembered that Cesar said, "Migrant workers are human beings with inherent dignity as children of God." How much more did this apply to unborn babies! Cesar would be proud of me.

"When is the Rescue?" I asked.

"Four days from now."

"That doesn't give me much time. . . . "

"It's better not to think about it too much, Teresita. You might chicken out. Go with your gut. If you think that this is the right thing for you to do now, if you think that God is calling you, say 'yes.' The car is leaving tomorrow. I'll make the arrangements for you. They're driving straight up to Vermont, changing drivers, and sleeping on the go. They'll get there the night before the rescue."

"I don't know, Mr. Reilly. . . . "

"Look, Teresita, when are you ever again going to get the chance to go back to the same clinic that hurt you and try to prevent them from hurting another mother? Isn't that the right thing to do?"

"I don't know how long I'd be gone. I'd miss my daughter. I'd have to take time off from work, and I really need the money. . . . I guess you're right, but I don't feel too courageous about it. As a matter of fact, it all sounds a bit . . . frightening."

"It *is* frightening, Teresita. And the truth is, you may not be ready yet. But sometimes in life, we're called to take risks without counting the cost. Bad things happen when good people do nothing."

"I know, and I've done nothing. Somebody's got to do it, but . . . God help me! I'll do it, Mr. Reilly. I'll go."

I felt a sense of satisfaction as I made my first choice to do something good in an effort to make up for all of my bad choices.

Thirty-five

*W*ell, here I am," I told the young man and older woman, "all packed and ready to go. I've brought my sleeping bag, a change of clothes, and my toothbrush." It was early the next morning. I had dropped Lupe off at Mary's house where the other Rescuers picked me up.

"Good job," said the young man. "We travel light and we travel long. Mike Reilly sent us. My name's Tom and she's Ann."

"Hi, I'm Teresita. If I seem a little nervous, it's because I'm new at this. Thanks for taking me, Tom and Ann."

"No problem. You're helping us. Thank you for thinking of the babies and sharing the driving. Don't be nervous. We'll explain everything to you along the way. We've got a long nonstop drive ahead of us, so let's get started."

For the next two days, we drove nonstop to Burlington, switching off drivers and sleeping in the backseat of the car as we drove. We didn't have much money to buy meals, so we just snacked along the way.

On the third day, we reported to the Community Evangelical Church in Vermont. It hosted the Rescuers. We left our baggage on the floor of the church and went downstairs to the cafeteria to eat. Finally, we got a decent meal that they provided for us on the night before the Rescue.

After our meal, the leader gave us an introductory talk. He was tall and dark with bulging muscles and short, cropped hair. Everyone quieted down to listen. He spoke slowly, loudly and clearly.

"My name is Richard Thornton, I'm an ex-Marine. Their motto is 'Semper Fidelis'—or, 'semper fi,' we say—which means 'Always Faithful.' That's going to be our motto also. Always faithful to the Rescue Principles.

"You see this card that I'm holding?" he continued. "This is the Rescuer's Pledge. When I'm finished talking, you have to sign this Pledge if you want to Rescue with us tomorrow morning. Basically, you will pledge to follow the Rescue Principles.

"These are the principles. You must be totally peaceful and nonviolent in word and deed. You must follow my instructions without questioning them. You must be polite and non-argumentative with police or abortion supporters. You must be loving, forgiving and gentle. And you must all act as one unit with each member committed to the others. It's one for all and all for one. Finally, you must be totally non-cooperative with the police."

That last one sounded pretty illegal and scary to me. So I politely raised my hand and Richard recognized me.

"I know we're not supposed to question your leadership, but I need to question your last principle. I'm sorry, this is my first time. What does it mean to be 'totally non-cooperative'? Are we going to resist arrest?"

"No. I just told you that we are totally peaceful and nonviolent. So how do we square that with total non-cooperation? Easy. We don't cooperate with them, but we do it in a peaceful and nonviolent way." He smiled.

"If the police ask you what you're doing, you say that you're justifiably trespassing to save the lives of unborn babies. That's all you ever say. If they ask you if you're going to leave the abortion property, you remain silent. If they order you to get up and leave, you simply stay there. If they say that you're under arrest and to come with them, you don't. If they want to arrest you, they'll have to carry you. So, you go limp with no resistance but also with no cooperation. If the police or anyone asks your name, you say 'Unborn Baby' because you are a living witness for the unborn. What they do to you with their pulling and shoving is what they do to the unborn babies. Only they die. You don't have that risk. Understand?"

I silently nodded my head.

Richard went on, just like Mr. Reilly with his serious exhortations. "You are the last line of defense between the mother and the abortionist. You are the last hope for the mother and her unborn child. Act like an unborn child who has no voice and no defense and is helpless. Act helpless, totally passive and non-resistant, and go limp when the police come to arrest you. You absorb the pain of being handcuffed and the humiliation of being carried, just like the unborn baby has to endure the pain of the abortion. You will do this in reparation to make up for what the abortionist does to the unborn baby.

"And remember, Jesus said, 'There's no greater love than to lay down your life for your friends.' The unborn children are your friends, and you're laying down your lives and bodies for them. Don't give your real names. Remember, you will identify with the unborn babies and become living witnesses for them. So again, when the police or judge asks your name, say 'Unborn Baby' even if it sounds ridiculous. Don't cave in to their threats of jail. Don't be afraid, take courage, be strong!"

Then we all signed the Rescuer's Pledge, held a brief prayer meeting and went upstairs to get some sleep. We slept in our sleeping bags on the bare floor. It wasn't very comfortable without a pillow. My body ached from all the pressure points as I lay on the floor with nothing to cushion myself.

Richard woke us up at five o'clock the next morning and told us not to eat or drink anything and to go to the bathroom. This was because we wouldn't have another chance until later that day, and he didn't want us to be in agony for want of a bathroom

It was November of 1988, and it was cold. There was frost on the windshields of our cars as we came out into the dark parking lot of the church. And here I was from Florida with only a light coat. Fortunately, someone gave me a sweatshirt for a little more warmth. Then we packed ourselves into the back of a rented U-Haul truck, and someone drove us to the clinic. We all jumped out of the back of the truck like you see the Marines jumping out of landing ships in the movies. We ran up to the clinic's steps and sidewalk, sat down on the cold concrete and blocked the entranceway. We prayed silently in the dark. The truck drove off.

As it got light, I noticed that the clinic still had its dead-blood color and the conical roof over the entrance that looked like a witch's hat, just as I remembered it. Then I saw something that I hadn't noticed on my previous visit. There was a Catholic grammar school located directly across the street. *How ironic,* I thought, *one side of the street educates children, while the other side kills them. . . .*

When the first of the clinic personnel arrived around eight, we were singing and praying aloud. They demanded that we get off their property. "You have no right to do this. You're trespassing. It's illegal. We're calling the cops." We remained silent. There were about twenty of us.

Around nine, a dozen abortion supporters arrived. Their faces were contorted in anger, and they yelled and screamed at us. They carried blasphemous signs such as "Abort Jesus!" We said nothing. We just maintained our composure in prayer and hymn singing. It was another hour before the police arrived. They came in about five police cars flashing their blue and red lights. The TV vans came with them. You'd have thought that a mass murder had occurred.

A big sergeant walked right up to me first. I was trembling. *Why is he coming to me first? He must sense that I'm a rookie. I can't remember the principles! What will I say or do?* My heart was banging in my chest, and I felt like I was going to wet my pants.

"What are you doing here?" he screamed at me. I just sobbed.

"Get off this sidewalk! You're trespassing!"

"No . . . no . . . I'm not," I stammered. "I'm here to help these women who want to get an abortion. They don't know what they're getting into. I think I'm doing the right thing."

"Well lady, I'm telling you that you're dong the *wrong* thing. Now get up and get out!"

I finally remembered the principles to shut up and stay put. I folded my arms in front of me, closed my eyes and bowed my head in prayer.

"If you don't leave now, I'm going to arrest you for trespassing," the officer continued, "and you can tell it to Judge Titus!" *Tell it to Judge Titus . . . tell it to Judge Titus,* echoed through my head, and I prayed that I'd have the courage to do so.

At that moment, another cop got behind me. He grabbed my arms, pulled them behind my back, and pushed me flat to the sidewalk. He put his knee into my back with all of his weight and cuffed me. He pulled the nylon straps as tight as he could. The pain went right to the top of my head. Then he grabbed my legs, the sergeant put me in a headlock and they carried me to the cruiser. They shoved me into the backseat.

When people saw it on TV, everything looked all nice and gentle, as if the police had just gently picked me up and carried me to the car. But they didn't see my face shoved down in the dirt, the knee in my back and the tight cuffing. They had no idea of the excruciating pain in my wrists that felt like they would fall off for lack of circulation. The TV reporter said that because I was "disruptive," I had to be politely carried by "two of Burlington's finest" to their car. So much for truth in the media.

As they carried me to the car, the abortion supporters chanted, "Don't let her stay! Throw her away!"

Yeah, I thought, *just like the unborn babies. This is what the aborted babies must feel. They are at peace, and then someone suddenly attacks them and throws them away. But at least I understand what's going on. They don't have a clue. They just get sucked up, chopped up, burned, and killed.*

The cruiser drove directly to the police garage where I was dumped onto the concrete floor. I lay there as the rest of the Rescuers were dumped near me over the course of the next two hours. As more were dumped, we started singing and praying. Finally when they all had arrived, the police loosened the cuffs. I don't think that I could have stood it much longer.

Later, they took us to Judge Abraham Titus. He was a black Catholic, so I thought that he'd sympathize with us and dismiss the cases in the interest of justice. Wishful thinking! As soon as he started disparaging us for wasting his time and clogging up his court calendar, I knew that we were in for trouble. Since he was a black Catholic, I realized that he overcompensated to show that he had no unfair sympathy for me, a brown Catholic. He was harshly impartial to assure his reelection by the liberal and so-called socially progressive Vermonters. I anxiously waited and wondered what he would do to me as I was called forward to his bench.

Thirty-six

"Y ou with the dark black hair, get up here!"

I pointed to myself with a questioning face and asked, "Me?"

"Yes, *you*, come forward," Judge Titus ordered impatiently. "What's your name?"

"Unborn Baby."

"What do you mean, 'Unborn Baby'? State your real name—now!"

"The babies that you allow to be killed are nameless. So I remain nameless to remind you of them."

His face twisted in anger and he yelled, "I don't allow anyone to be killed! What's your name, young lady?"

I simply smiled at him.

Then he quickly read the charge to me and promptly added, "I'm going to find you in Contempt for not giving your name. I sentence you to ten days in jail."

I was shocked! I had never heard of anything like this happening in America. He found me in Contempt for merely being silent! I always thought that Contempt was when you insulted the judge by saying something nasty. I hardly said anything, and I was found guilty without a trial or anything. It seemed like we were in China or more like in *Alice in Wonderland* when the Queen said, "Off with their heads, *then* we'll have the trial!"

Judge Titus, noticeably irritated, asked if I had anything to say before he executed the sentence. As I stood before him, I felt like Jesus must have felt before Pontius Pilot. Judge Titus was sitting on his bench, which was eight feet higher than the floor level. So I was looking up into his all-controlling, all-powerful smirk. He looked over his half-glasses and down his nose at me and said, "Well, young lady, what have you got to say for yourself?"

His voice boomed throughout the courtroom. He was speaking through a microphone, although I was only five feet away. It was ridiculous. I could have heard him if he had spoken to me in a whisper. It was like the Wizard of Oz showing off his false powers behind a pompous, noisy smoke screen. So, I thought that I'd act like Dorothy's little dog Toto and run around the screen to expose his humanity by appealing to his heart with my pre-sentence talk. All of the other Rescuers said that it was a very moving argument. They even got the Court Reporter to make a transcript of it. As my heart began pounding and my breathing quickened, I began.

"They passed a law that all male babies had to be killed. A mother broke the law, gave birth to her son, and floated him away down the river. Another woman broke the law and rescued that baby. That woman was the Pharaoh's daughter. Would you have put her in jail for rescuing Moses?

"They passed another law that said you couldn't rescue an escaped black slave. Harriet 'Moses' Tubman rescued hundreds of slaves and gave them food, clothing, and shelter. She led them through the Underground Railway to freedom in the North. Would you have put 'Moses' Tubman in jail?

"They passed laws in the South that said blacks couldn't eat in white restaurants. Martin Luther King, Jr., broke the law and trespassed by trying to eat in a white restaurant. Would you have put Martin Luther King, Jr. in jail?"

With a newfound strength I firmly concluded.

"And do you want to put me in jail for rescuing unborn babies just like Pharaoh's daughter rescued a born baby? Do you want to put me in jail for rescuing unborn babies just like 'Moses' Tubman rescued helpless, enslaved men and women? Do you want to put me in jail for trespassing just as Martin Luther King, Jr., trespassed to defy injustice? How am I any different than the Pharaoh's daughter? How am I any different than 'Moses' Tubman? How am I any different than Martin Luther King, Jr.?"

The judge interrupted me and snarled, "You're not them, and this isn't Egypt or the Deep South. You're in *Vermont* and abortion is *legal* here. You can't stop it. And you're not going to jail for trespassing. You're going to jail for *Contempt*."

"Your Honor," I started crying. "With all due respect, I think that *you* are the one who is in contempt! You're in contempt of our unborn brothers and sisters in humanity. We're not talking about trespassing. We're talking about *life and death!* And God said to *rescue* those who are being dragged to death. These mothers entering the abortion clinics, whether they know it or not, are dragging their unborn children to death by an abortionist, and

131

we're there to stop the abortionists and to help the mothers. Can't you see that? How can I be in Contempt for doing the right thing?"

"All I can see is that you trespassed on their property, and you're in Contempt of this Court because you didn't identify yourself."

I pressed on. "If I walked by your house yesterday while you were here in court, and I saw it was on fire and heard your baby son yelling for help, could I trespass and run in there and rescue him? Or would you file a trespass complaint against me and find me in Contempt if I remained silent and anonymous because I didn't want any reward?"

"We're not talking about my family. Don't get personal with me."

I could see I was getting nowhere near his heart, so I let out all the stops and went for the jugular.

"Your Honor, I am an abortion survivor. I know what I'm talking about. I have a permanent limp from a botched abortion upon my mother, which killed my twin and left me permanently disabled. That same clinic I was at today, gave me a botched abortion without explaining anything to me. Then they sent me to have my baby chemically poisoned—Judge, please listen! They burned him. . . . He was *burned alive* in my womb because of their botched abortion, done by a Physician's Assistant who wasn't even a doctor!

"I speak for those whose voices have been silenced by abortion. I speak for the voiceless. I defend the unborn who have no one to defend them. I speak for the defenseless, and I'm willing to suffer in reparation for their death. I forgive you for your contempt of them, for your hard heart, and for your desire to please your constituents rather than to please God."

Then I crumpled to the floor and remained there like a helpless unborn child. Judge Titus yelled, "Get up off my courtroom floor!" But I remained still and silent. One of the other Rescuers yelled to the Judge, "Now you see how you treat helpless unborn children with your unjust laws! She's a living witness of an unborn child, Judge!"

"Take her away!" Judge Titus yelled in disgust. The Court officers picked me up and dragged me out of the courtroom and off to jail.

Thirty-seven

"You can do this in one of two ways," said one of the deputy sheriffs as they carried me to their car. He leaned me against the opened rear door of their bright white car and said, "One, you get in yourself nice and peaceful-like, or two, we shove you in. Which will it be?"

I dropped to the ground, responding, "You're no different than the Nazi soldiers who put the Jews in the boxcars on their way to the death camps. Can't you see that? You're not just doing your duty. You're part of the transportation system of the culture of death that kills innocent unborn babies and jails their Rescuers."

"All I can see is that you're resisting. Do you want to get charged with that, too? Just shut up and get in the car." And with that, he shoved me into the backseat.

They brought me straight to the Chittenden County Correctional Center. I guess they didn't have penitentiaries or prisons in Vermont. Just nice-sounding "correctional centers" to correct and not to punish so-called criminals like me. They took me past the high chain-link fence topped with razor wire, past the welcome sign, and into the bleak block-building. The steel entrance door clanged and locked shut behind me with a terrifying sense of finality.

I called Mary and apologized for my unexpected absence. She said not to worry, that she'd be happy to have Lupe. But I was pained by our separation. It was my first and last phone call from the jail.

After I got there, they started to bring in other female Rescuers, including Ann. I learned that seven others had followed my example, including Richard and Tom. They didn't give their names, and were sentenced by Judge Titus to serve ten days. Upon our arrival, we were strip-searched. They wanted to be sure that we weren't bringing in any drugs or weapons. Then they gave us day-glow orange jumpsuits to dress in. We looked like a bunch of Halloween candies. They not only stripped us of our clothes, but they stripped us of our dignity as well. I guess they also wanted to be sure they could spot us if we escaped.

The other female prisoners were in for crimes like drug sales and child abuse. It seemed odd that they were all white. I learned that there were very few blacks or Hispanics in Vermont. Judge Titus and some college professors were the exceptions. I was the only brown-skinned person there. The other girls looked rough, with scraggly hair and tattoos on their bodies. Some of them had lost custody of their children to the Welfare Department. On our first day, we tried to minister to them. We told them that God loved them no matter what they had done, and He'd forgive them if they'd just turn to Him in sorrow for their actions and ask for His help. Our words fell on deaf ears. So we started singing joyful hymns to try to give them some hope.

By the end of the day, my anger at the judicial system was peaking. Here I was in jail because I didn't give the Judge my name. I was in prison for my beliefs and not for what I had done. I felt like a political prisoner of conscience, so I decided to act like one. I wouldn't cooperate with any of their rules. But I'd react to the guards with love and respect. In this way, I thought that I could give witness for the helpless aborted children and offer my sufferings to God for them. I refused to cooperate with a judicial sentence that supported the structure of the abortion industry by preventing rescues of those who were about to be killed.

The guards said, "No obedience, no privileges." So they locked me in my cell. When they came to release me for meals, I wouldn't budge. I decided that if they wanted to move me, they could carry me. They didn't; I stayed in my cell. I prayed and fasted, and they no longer had any power over me. They placed me under 24-hour cell lockdown—in solitary confinement. I had no recreation, no telephone, no TV, radio or movies, and no visitors. But I was no longer their prisoner. I was free!

I remembered a sixteenth century poem I memorized in high school by Richard Lovelace, "To Althea from Prison":

Stone walls do not a prison make,
Nor iron bars a cage.
Minds innocent and quiet,
Take that for a hermitage.

So I decided that my cell would be my hermitage. My cell—with its heavy steel door and its narrow slat covered with iron mesh through which I could only see other cells. My cell—without windows and with obscene, graffiti-covered, concrete block walls. My cell—with one light bulb, one porcelain toilet, one roll of toilet paper, and one iron cot. But I could barely sleep because of the constant noise. One day in the early morning, I hunkered down and wrote a poem. I named it "In the Cold, Hard Dawn":

> Chill jail cell whose paint has cracked
> All shirts save one stripped from my back.
> Corridors echo with babies' wails
> Which haunt the halls of our nation's jails.
>
> Angels hover over cells
> As praise and worship music swells
> In antiphons of song and prayer
> From the Christians gathered there.
>
> Iron bars a cage do make
> Incarcerated for the babies' sake.
> Who'd have thought our land so free
> Would legalize a killing industry?
>
> Marked for death by choice or deformed,
> The "abortion cure" will be performed.
> I pray for my nation so far gone,
> From my prison cell in the cold, hard dawn.

The cold dawn came hard because I didn't sleep at night. Even worse, I wasn't given library privileges. But a kind, older guard slipped me a Dorothy Day anthology and some articles and books by her. As he handed me the package, he said with a wink, "Here, you might enjoy the story of another Christian jailbird."

I was amazed to learn that Dorothy Day, like me, had an abortion. It was in 1919 when she was a genuine forerunner-hippie in New York City. Like me, she ran around drinking and partying. Like me, she got pregnant and was pushed into an abortion. Like me, her boyfriend dumped her right afterward. He left her an icy note which said, "You are only one of God knows how many millions of women who go through the same thing. Don't build up any hopes. It is best, in fact, that you forget me."

So she did. Soon after that, she began to live with another man. Then a few years later she dramatically converted to Catholicism against his objections. She received God's forgiveness for her past and began to live a new life. The beauty of nature had brought her back to God. Like me, she lived by the ocean and she fished, clammed, and rejoiced in the sun, the moon, and the stars, the water, and the sea breezes. "How can there be no God," she wrote, "when there are all of these beautiful things?"

Like me, she was later an unmarried mother. And like me, she also made the Catholic baptism of her daughter her first order of business. She wrote, "I knew I was not going to have her floundering as I had done, undisciplined, and amoral. I felt it was the greatest thing I could do for my child."

Like me, she struggled as a single parent to raise her daughter. Later she opened houses of hospitality for the poor, the hungry, the homeless, and for pregnant mothers.

I was also amazed to learn that, like my mother, Dorothy Day also marched with Cesar Chavez and, like me, she was sent to jail. She was jailed in 1973 at the age of 75 for picketing with Chavez and the United Farm Workers in California. When she was in jail, she wrote a prayer in the front of her Bible to Pope John XXIII:

Dear Pope John—please, yourself a *campesino*, watch over the United Farm Workers. Raise up more and more leader-servants throughout the country to stand with Cesar Chavez in this nonviolent struggle with Mammon, in all the rural districts of North and South, in cotton fields, beet fields, potato fields, in our orchards and vineyards, our orange groves—wherever men, women, and children work on the land. Help make a new order wherein justice flourishes, and, as Peter Maurin, himself a peasant, said so simply, "where it is easier to be good."

Dorothy Day was my kind of woman. She wrote a book about St. Therese of Lisieux. I learned that Therese was called "Little Teresa" in contrast to St. Teresa of Avila who was called "Big Teresa." My name, Teresita, means "Little Teresa." My mom told me that she had been a great admirer of Dorothy Day in the sixties. She had read her book *Therese* and learned that Dorothy named her daughter Tamar Teresa after St. Therese. So Mom did the same for me, and I was given the Spanish name for Little Teresa—*Teresita!* St. Therese wrote, directed and acted the lead role in a play in her convent about St. Joan of Arc, my adolescent heroine. Dorothy Day, St. Therese and I seemed to have a lot in common.

St. Therese realized that she didn't have any great talents, so she figured that her best way to serve God would be simply to love Him and her neighbor. She called this her "Little Way" to God—doing her ordinary daily duties with love and without complaint, and offering up her disappointments, annoyances, and sufferings to God in reparation for all the evil in the world. She figured that this was the quickest way to God. It was the late nineteenth century, and the elevator had just been invented. It was a quick way to get to the top floor. So she called her "Little Way" her elevator to God, and she got to Him very quickly. She died at the age of 24 from tuberculosis, without complaint and with resignation to God's will. I took St. Therese and Dorothy Day as my role models.

Meanwhile, I spent my time reading, praying, and fasting on bread and water, remembering Jesus' words, "This kind does not leave except by prayer and fasting." I wanted the evil of abortion to leave, and I was trying to do my little bit to help. It wasn't that hard to fast, and I felt better when the other Rescuers told me that the prison food was terrible.

However, the loneliness was agonizing. I had no companionship but the cold, hard dawn. I missed my daughter Lupe, and I worried about her. I prayed that she was doing fine with Mary. So my loneliness and the noise became my daily offerings to God, my "little way." The noise in prison was maddening! Radios and TVs blaring, cell doors slamming, prisoners crying, arguing, cursing, or screaming. I couldn't escape the cigarette smoke that hung oppressively in the air.

A prison experience amplifies an inmate's feelings of hostilities, fear, and loneliness. This was especially so with the lesbian prisoners. They would switch partners constantly, causing jealousies and envy and nightly noises of sexual moans and jealous bickering. It was all beginning to get to me, but my ten-day sentence soon passed. The prosecutor decided to drop the trespass charge, and I was released. I was a free woman, and I left with Tom and Ann for Florida.

Thirty-eight

O ver the next two days, we drove home to Florida the same way that we came up—nonstop while sleeping in the car. When we arrived, I reported everything to Mr. Reilly, and he congratulated me on my courage.

He said, "You got screwed by the judge, but I knew you were a tough, determined girl. You wanted justice for the innocent, right? Well, who's more innocent than unborn children? It makes all other causes pale in comparison—even your parents' causes for civil rights and migrant farmers—because we're talking about the cause of life itself. If there's no life, no other cause has any meaning whatsoever. I bet you can't wait for your next rescue!"

After I got home, I thought about his words. But then I decided that I couldn't commit myself to the Rescue Movement. My first duty was to my baby. I didn't want Lupe and I to have a non-bonded relationship like I had with my mother, and I didn't want my daughter to suffer because of my outside involvements or psychological baggage. I had already been through that with my mother. The more I thought about it, the more I realized I should write to my mother and try to get some kind of a relationship going again. After all, it had been almost four years since I ran away, and I hadn't heard from either of my parents since. So, that evening I sat down at the kitchen table and started writing.

Dear Mom,

Hi Mom. It's me, Teresita. It's been four hard years for me down here in Miami. I'm sorry I ran away and I'm sorry I haven't written or called. Life's been hard. I'm a single working mom. But I have a beautiful daughter—

your granddaughter! Her name is Lupe. I named her after Our Lady of Guadalupe. Remember when you told me the story? That was a happy memory for me. Now I can pass it on to my daughter some day.

She's almost two years old. Whenever I look at her peacefully asleep in her crib, I think, Where there's life, there's hope! She's the joy and the hope of my life. She was a perfect baby. She hardly ever cried, even when her diapers were wet or dirty. At four months, she started babbling and acted as if she were carrying on a conversation with me. At six months, she was crawling and at eleven months, she just got up and started walking. She'd walk off and then come back as if she'd been on a big adventure. And she'd tell me all about it. She'll talk you deaf if you let her. She's very outgoing.

After she was a year old, I started showing her a holy card of Our Lady of Guadalupe. I always explain how she is watching over us. Just like your grandmother prayed for your mother when she left Mexico, and for you and me and down to Lupe—the fifth generation!

She reacts to the picture as if she recognizes Our Lady—really recognizes her as her eyes follow the picture. She can't tell you exactly, but she seems to know and feel Our Lady inside herself. It's like she has Our Lady's spirit in her. I can see that when she grows up, she'll definitely be out there talking to everyone about Our Lady and carrying on the message.

I thank God for my beautiful daughter. My life would be so empty without her. She brings me so much hope. Hope for a peaceful future. Hope for reconciliation with you. Hope that I'll find a good husband and a father for her.

When I get down in the dumps and sit on my couch staring into space with tears streaming down my face, Lupe comes to me, climbs up on my lap and looks into my eyes with her little smiling face. She starts running her fingers through my hair, and says, "It's okay, Mommy." I look at her, and the tears stop. My eyes light up, my heart warms, the corners of my mouth break into a genuine smile, and I shake my head in agreement with her saying, "Yes, Lupe everything's going to be okay."

At times, I feel such overwhelming sadness that her father, and you and Dad, her grandparents, don't know the joy of her. You're missing something that can be so beautiful in your lives. Maybe you could write or call or maybe even come down sometime to see her. I hope so.

Love,
Teresita

As I finished my letter, I reflected some more on my relationship with Lupe. Once again, I remembered Hawthorne's novel, *The Scarlet Letter.* Hester, the novel's heroine, had a daughter named Pearl who was born out of wedlock, just like my Lupe. Pearl was the joy of Hester's life, just as Lupe was to me. Hester named her daughter "Pearl" because she likened her to the precious pearl that Jesus talked about in chapter 13 of Matthew's Gospel— the one that was so valuable that the merchant who found it went and sold all his possessions in order to buy it. Like Hester with her Pearl, I gave my all for my Lupe.

Eventually Lupe and I settled into a routine. Lupe would go to Mary's for daycare each day, and I'd be off to work at the restaurant. I felt guilty about always using Mary as a free babysitter. I had thought that I was taking advantage of her, and one day I apologized to her. But she reassured me and told me that she had the time and didn't need any money. She said that she and her husband couldn't have any children, that he had a good job and supported her so that she didn't have to work, and she felt like Lupe's second mother since she had helped to save her from abortion and helped me to give birth to her. I didn't ask her then why she couldn't have children, but one day I would learn her horrific story.

The other Rescuers kept going back to that same clinic in Vermont rescuing, closing it down for many hours, preventing many abortions, and being vilified by the media as "women haters, baby lovers, and terrorists."

Judge Titus kept sentencing them to jail. Finally, they weren't even bringing the Rescuers to court to face the charges. The cops just picked them up off the sidewalk and brought them straight to jail. It wound up that they had 90 Rescuers in jail in Vermont for 90 days. They were the largest group imprisoned for the longest time in the history of America. But you'll never read about it in the history books. Martin Luther King, Jr., received more press for spending merely a weekend in jail in the sixties.

When I got some free time, I'd write letters to Judge Titus in Vermont because he continued to hammer the Rescuers up there with unjust jail sentences. I hoped to appeal to his conscience to do the right thing and simply give the Rescuers probation and let them go. But like the mighty Pharaoh with the Jews in Egypt, he was too stubborn. Nothing changed. He wouldn't let them go.

My mother never answered my letter.

Thirty-nine

"Mommy, why did you kill me? I would have been a good boy." The little boy raised his tiny arms to me in sorrow and tears began to run down his cheeks. I heard his cry over and over and over again.

I hadn't slept well in jail because of the nightly chaos, but my sleeping difficulties worsened when I got home. I started having nightmares again of babies screaming over the noise of a loud vacuum machine. I saw thousands of dismembered babies passing before my eyes wailing against a blood-red background. One night a single baby boy came to me from a lush green garden with flowers of every color; and a beautiful blue sky overhead. He walked toward me down a garden path dressed in a white gown. He looked right into my eyes with a quizzical and confused look and began his plaintiff cry, "Mommy, why did you kill me? I would have been a good boy."

I woke up in a cold sweat and stared at the ceiling. The total reality and impact of my abortion came crashing down on me. I thought, *Yes, I know God has forgiven me. But I don't feel forgiven. I still feel guilty. What did I do? What did I "really" do? I really killed my own flesh and blood. An innocent baby boy who never had a chance to even see the light of day. And he would've been a good boy! He said so himself. What have I missed? What have I done? I'm so sorry little boy, my son, who doesn't even have a name.*

Maybe I've never actually dealt with the guilt and the grief. Maybe I just stuffed down all the memories of the abortion. Maybe I've never dealt with the abortion on the deepest level of my being. Maybe that's made everything worse.

I lay there with these thoughts running through my mind for the rest of the night. And I resolved to deal with my abortion on a deeper level. But I didn't know how. The next day was Easter Sunday and I forced myself to get out of bed and take Lupe to Mass. I was feeling low and needed a change so I went to a different church. On the way out, I noticed a beautiful quilt hanging on the back wall of the vestibule. It was multicolored with embroidered patches and wording. I went closer for a better look.

A sign under it said, *The Quilt of Love.* My eyes were drawn to the center patch that showed an image of the Holy Family—Joseph, Mary, and Baby Jesus. It said, "Life Begins in Love and Grows in a Family." I thought, *My baby boy's life didn't!* Just as I was thinking that, I saw another image. It showed a pair of arms and said, "Ann, I'm sorry that my arms never hugged you. Love, Mom." I didn't understand what this was all about until I saw another image. It showed a baby's smiling face and said, "John, you never had a chance to smile. Please forgive me. Love, Mom."

Then I realized that these were messages from mothers who were naming their aborted babies and seeking their forgiveness. There was a poster next to the quilt that gave contact information and said:

Have you had an abortion? Name your baby and seek his/her forgiveness.

Since it was Sunday, I thought I'd take Lupe over to Mary's and find out if she knew anything more about The Quilt of Love. She told me that she did but that she hadn't mentioned it to me before since she didn't think I was ready for it.

"But now that I see you're making the first move," she said, " I guess it's time. The first step in the healing process for a mother who's aborted her baby is to recognize that she aborted a real person—that she really killed her own baby and shouldn't blame anyone else but herself. The mother is personally responsible for her baby's death."

I winced at that. The truth hurts but it must be acknowledged. It won't allow itself to be denied. It won't let you deny it without suffering serious disorders like my drinking, drug abuse, and sexual promiscuity. They were all cover-ups to deny the truth.

Mary explained that The Quilt of Love was a quilt with individual patches for aborted babies. The mothers make patches for their aborted babies and send them to a national center where they are sewn into a quilt. The quilts then travel around the country like mobile memorials and are hung in churches like the one that I saw. Mothers finger the quilts lovingly over the names on the patches just like they do at the Vietnam Memorial Wall in Washington, DC.

Mary continued. "You can make your own personal patch for *your* baby. You should name your baby and put the name on the patch with the date of the abortion and a short message to your baby. Have you ever thought of naming your baby?"

"Yes," I said. "When I prayed to him for forgiveness once, his name popped into my prayer, and I said spontaneously, 'Dear Luke, please forgive me.'"

After I told her the date of my abortion, Mary said, "Now you can write something like, 'Dear Luke, I'm sorry for December 12, 1984. Please hold God's hand until I can join you. Love, Mom.' How's that sound?"

"So true. . . ." I replied with a downcast face.

So I went to the library and got some books on embroidery, learned how to do it, and embroidered the patch with the message exactly as Mary had suggested. I cried many tears of sorrow as I embroidered Luke's patch. Once again, I thought of Hester Prynne from *The Scarlet Letter.* I thought that we shared the same emotions—we both felt guilty and shamed, but free through forgiveness. Hester had to embroider and wear a scarlet-colored letter "A" which stood for "Adulteress" because she had a child out of wedlock in Puritan New England. She embroidered her letter up in Salem, Massachusetts near my home on the Cape almost 350 years before me. I thought of her, and with each stitch I felt more freedom. It was very therapeutic.

When I finished the patch, I sent it to the national headquarters of The Quilt of Love, and they added it to a quilt. When the quilt was finished with other anonymous patches, the organizers asked me to receive the quilt at my parish church and display it.

When the quilt arrived in May, I hung it in the back of our church. Women would walk up to it and touch it reverently in tears. Many mothers were moved by the quilt and inspired to come out of their denial and admit that they had really killed their babies. Many of them phoned me and poured out their stories. "Where do we go from here?" they asked. "If I really killed my baby, how can I ever be forgiven? How can I forgive myself? How can I be healed?"

I gave them my ear and some simple words and advice—go to confession, have faith and hope—but I felt overwhelmed and powerless to help them. As the weeks went by, I wondered if I were really healed myself.

Forty

ARE YOU HURTING FROM AN ABORTION?
There is healing and hope! Be reconciled to your child.
Come to a RACHEL MOTHERS RETREAT
Hear others who were hurting and were healed.
June 8, 1989, 9 a.m.
Holiday Inn, 1300 Sunset Highway, Miami.

I had received this flier in the mail in late May. I hung it on my bulletin board and made plans to attend the retreat. I looked forward to the day when I might receive healing and hope.

Once again, I turned to Mary for more information. She told me about the Rachel Mothers. She explained that they were named after Rachel of the Old Testament who was the wife of the Patriarch Jacob. Mary said, "She became the matriarch of the Jewish people. She died in childbirth at Ramah. The prophet Jeremiah later saw Rachel as a figure coming through history and weeping for her children, her descendants who were led into captivity in Babylon. He said, 'In Ramah is heard the sound of moaning, of bitter weeping! Rachel mourns her children, she refuses to be consoled because her children are no more.'

"Then Matthew brings this figure forward into the New Testament and applies Rachel's weeping to the slaughter of the Holy Innocents—the children who were killed by King Herod. Today Rachel is a symbol of a mother who has lost her child by abortion. But she gives her hope. Jeremiah went on to say, 'Cease your cries of mourning; wipe the tears from your eyes. The sorrow you have shown shall have its reward. . . . There is hope for your future.'

"Teresita," she said, "there's hope for *your* future. You now seem ready for a Rachel Mothers Retreat because you're weeping now but don't know where to go from here. The Rachel Mothers are there for you and all mother victims of abortion who admit the need for healing and are ready to be totally honest and vulnerable before God and each other."

I wondered whether Mary was wrong about me. *Am I really ready to be so vulnerable?*

Mary explained that the Rachel Mothers sponsor weekend retreats where abortion victims minister to each other under the spiritual guidance of a priest. So I called the phone number and made my reservation. I arrived in fear and trembling at the motel where the retreat was scheduled. I didn't know what to expect.

Twenty mother-victims of abortion like me showed up! I was amazed. We met in a conference room, drank coffee, ate too many donuts, and small-talked during the opening social hour. Then we heard the first talk. A mother gave witness to her experience. She stood bravely in front of all of us without any notes and began her tearful, gut-wrenching testimony.

"My name is Kelly, and I had an abortion," she said in her firm but gentle voice. "I was eighteen years old, too old to remain a virgin but too young to get married—or so I thought. My boyfriend and I were seniors in high school and were sexually active. We even practiced so-called 'safe sex' and used condoms. Well, it was unsafe sex for me because I got pregnant. He was from a good Catholic family. I didn't want to embarrass him or his family, so I never even told him that I was pregnant. I wanted to save him from it. Besides, we were getting ready to go to college. There was no way that we could have the baby and go to college, too. I just thought of myself, wanted to keep my boyfriend and not the baby, and go on to college. Nobody told me that there were plenty of good people waiting to adopt babies. So I went down to our local abortion center and got the abortion. They never told me anything about physical or psychological risks or any other options. They just said, 'Everything will be fine!' "

I noticed that a lot of heads were shaking as if they had been told the same thing. Kelly dropped her voice and continued.

"But everything wasn't fine. While I was driving home, I was in a daze, I felt worthless and just wanted to drive my car into a tree and end it all. Somehow, I made it home. But I never made it to college. The main reasons for the abortion—keeping my boyfriend and going on to college—never materialized. My boyfriend left me, and I was just too disturbed to go on to college. So I buried the abortion experience deep inside me with anger, sorrow, and activity. I tried to keep busy all the time. I cleaned and re-cleaned my apartment, exercised furiously, and ran marathons. But I couldn't run away from my problem. I tried to bury it in a mistaken attempt to protect myself from spiritual and emotional pain. But the more I buried it, the more spiritual and emotional pain I suffered.

"My emotions were in a tumult. I had self-hatred, intense grief and sadness, anger and rage, bouts of depression, suicidal urges, nightmares, panic attacks, and flashbacks. I left my baby and a good part of myself behind me the day that I left that abortion clinic."

Just like me, I thought as I hung my head.

"Of course, there was no grieving for my dead baby," Kelly went on. "There was no acknowledgment that this was even a real baby. No wake, no funeral, no cards, no support of friends. It was a big secret and nobody knew. I had constant temptations to commit suicide. I felt that was the only way out, the only way that I could stop the pain."

Many faces winced at her words, in obvious sympathy with Kelly.

"On the contrary, the truth was that the only way to resolve the pain was to admit it and face up to it like any other pain. I knew that I was stronger than the pain, but I had nobody that I could confide in. I was too ashamed and didn't trust anyone.

"I held my pain deep down inside of me. But it was like holding a beach ball under water. You can't do it for very long. Eventually, the pain, like the ball, pops up to the surface.

"I knew that I had to talk to someone to bring all of my pain to the surface, so I could process my emotions. But there was no one there for me. I didn't treat the wound inside, and it just festered. I walked around with a wounded heart."

A tear squeezed out of Kelly's eye as she paused to renew her strength.

"Then a friend told me about these Rachel Mothers Retreats. She said, 'You know I just read an article about post-abortion trauma. It said that women could suffer for years from an abortion with fear, anxiety, and worry. But Our Lady of Guadalupe said, "Let nothing depress you or alter your heart or your countenance. Have no fears or anxieties. Am I not here who am your Mother?"'

"My friend told me that her church was going to sponsor a Rachel Mothers Retreat for healing and hope for post-abortive mothers. She said, 'What happened was terribly wrong. But don't give in to discouragement and don't lose hope. Try rather to understand what happened and face it honestly.'

"So that's what I resolved to do. I would go to the Rachel Mothers Retreat and face what happened *honestly!*"

"Tell it like it is, Sister!" someone yelled as Kelly continued her testimony and I anxiously waited to hear how she faced the reality of her abortion.

"At that time I was a freelance journalist, a stringer for the Associated Press. It was ten years after my abortion. Catholics were having conferences about Mary around the country, and thousands of people were going to them. One was held here in Miami so I went to report on it. There was a large image of Mary there known as The Missionary Image of Our Lady of Guadalupe. She was the one who my friend said gave the message of hope. A speaker named Dan from Vermont explained the whole story about the Image and how she appeared in sixteenth-century Mexico and ended the human sacrifice of the Aztecs and how she could do the same thing today and end abortion—our modern-day human sacrifice. I thought, *That's ridiculous! How can an image do anything?* So I made an appointment to interview Dan later that day.

"I said to him, right up front, 'What can an *image* do?'

"He said right back, 'It's not just an image. Our Lady of Guadalupe is spiritually present with this Image and works through it to save mothers from abortion.'

"I countered, 'How can Our Lady of Guadalupe stop abortions?'"

She stopped mine, I happily remembered as Kelly continued her story.

"'That's easy,' Dan said, 'She'll melt the hearts of mothers, and they will reverence the life within them and bring it forth rather than kill it. She'll simply melt cold hearts.'

"Well, that struck me to the depth of my cold heart! For some reason, I felt that Dan was someone I could trust even though I didn't know him. I felt that he would listen and understand. I also had an inspiration that this was the time to unburden myself of my abortion. It was now or never. So I just blurted out to him, 'I had an abortion ten years ago, and you're the first person that I've ever told. I named my baby John and asked him for his forgiveness.'

"I couldn't believe that I had just shared with a total stranger something that I had kept buried inside of me for ten years. But Dan radiated compassion, peace, and acceptance in allowing me to share this with him. When he said, 'Our Lady will melt hearts,' I felt mine melting, and I had an intense longing to finally let somebody know. It was like I had spent ten years squelching a scream for help, but finally I had to let it out. I felt that if I did, I would finally get the help that I needed to be free of the burden that I carried for so long. It just seemed to be drawn out of me. I think that through Dan, God placed His mercy in my heart to fill up the empty place left by my abortion.

"Dan looked me straight in the eye and said, 'Your son forgives you and is living with God. But have you asked God for forgiveness?'

"'No,'" I said, "'I was too ashamed.'"

"Dan said, 'Wait right here, I'll be right back. I'm going to go and get a priest.'"

I remembered my own Confession with Father John as Kelly told about hers. She continued her story.

"I started shaking. It seemed okay to tell Dan. But to tell a priest?

"He quickly brought back the priest and left us alone, and I had my Confession. Finally, I faced my abortion honestly. I had killed my own baby and needed to ask for God's forgiveness and love. I received it in the Sacrament of Penance, and then I received my first Communion in ten years at a special healing Mass at the conference that night. A month later, I attended a Rachel Mothers Retreat and the rest is history. I was home free!

"So now I speak to you out of my own painful experience as a defender of life. Maybe God is calling you to do the same. Think about it."

With that, Kelly finished her talk to tearful and heartwarming applause. Her closing line stirred my romantic ideals, and I could imagine myself becoming a speaker at these retreats as a defender of life.

Then Kelly pointed to a large image of Our Lady of Guadalupe. She said, "This is the same Image that was at my conference. It's called the Missionary Image of Our Lady of Guadalupe. It travels around the country to bring conversions and end abortions. Twenty abortion centers have closed shortly after visits of the Missionary Image to them, many mothers have changed their minds about abortions at the centers after seeing the Image, and many have been healed of post-abortion traumatic stress syndrome. I invite you all to come and venerate it and ask Our Lady's help to heal you of your abortions. Please come up."

As I started forward, I realized that this was also the same Image that was at the clinic when I went in for my abortion and the one that was at Lupe's baptism. Now I was more curious about this Image. I went up to it, put my hand on Our Lady's womb in the Image and begged her to give me another chance—to help me to get pregnant again the right way, in a committed marriage relationship. Her womb felt warm and a heat flash went through my hand and arm into my own womb! I took this as a sign from Our Lady that I would get married and that I would get pregnant for the third time.

At lunchtime, I sought Kelly out, and we sat down together to soup and a sandwich. I told her about my abortion and how I ran away to Florida and almost had another abortion. I explained how my baby had been saved by the Missionary Image and the pro-lifers. I asked her for more information about the Missionary Image. She said, "Teresita, you could become a Guardian of the Image yourself!"

"What's that?" I asked.

"A Guardian is a host for a Visitation of the Image who forms a Team to plan a Visitation in coordination with the pastors. The Image goes wherever our Mother's love is needed—to churches, homes, prisons, hospitals, schools, and nursing homes. You should write to Dan's headquarters in Vermont to volunteer as a Guardian, and his staff will train you and explain your duties." I instantly made a mental note to do this.

Forty-one

"You will come to understand that nothing is definitely lost, and you will also be able to ask forgiveness from your child, who is now living in the Lord." We were at the afternoon session of the Rachel Mothers Retreat. A priest was explaining that we mother-survivors of abortion needed not only God's forgiveness which most of us had received in the Sacrament of Reconciliation, but we also needed our baby's forgiveness. It was certainly a relief for me to know that my baby would forgive me and that he was now living in the Lord!

Then the priest said, "Let's use some guided imagery. Imagine that you are alone in your room, you're crying over the loss of your aborted baby. You're feeling sorry for yourself. But now Jesus comes into the scene. He is tall and dark skinned, with chestnut brown hair falling over His white tunic. He slowly walks over to you and gently pulls your head to His chest. You can hear His heartbeat as He softly assures you, 'It's okay, you are sorry for what you did, and I forgive you. Your baby is living with Me, and he also wants to forgive you. Do you want his forgiveness? Do you want My mother to bring him to you?'"

The priest continued, "Then Mary walks in carrying the baby across her breast. She has long, dark brown hair falling over her blue gown. She says, 'Isn't he beautiful? Here, would you like to hold him?' She places him in your arms and gently suggests, 'Perhaps you could tell him you're sorry.' You tearfully say, 'I'm sorry, please forgive me.' And your baby returns your sorrow with a happy smile."

I was sobbing uncontrollably as the whole scene passed through my mind's eye. It all seemed so real. I don't think that it was just my imagination. I really think that Mary brought my baby Luke to me. I saw his blue eyes—just like mine—and his rosy cheeks. He smiled at me, and I received his forgiveness. I really felt it.

Then the priest said, "To confirm your sorrow and desire for your baby's forgiveness, I suggest that each of you sits down this afternoon and writes a letter to your baby. Remember to give your baby a name! That child is a real person, more alive than you and I, united with God in Heaven. Just let the letter come from your heart. And remember, no one will see it except your baby."

I went straight to my room and sat down at the desk with my pencil and paper. I had already named my baby. The words came fast and furious. They were baptized in my tears that fell on the white paper.

Dear Luke,

A few years ago I made a choice, a real bad choice. I broke my bond with you and decided that you would not share my life. I deprived you of a life of joy and happiness. I deprived you of my mother's milk, of my reading to you, of singing songs together, going to the parks and playgrounds, and running through the fields. I'll miss all of your birthdays, Christmases and graduations.

I'm so very sorry for my weakness and my bad choice. I know that there is no excuse for what I did, but I want you to understand. I didn't hate you. I was young, there didn't seem to be anybody to help me, and there didn't seem to be any other choice. I was still in high school. I felt terrified of telling my parents, and abortion seemed like such a quick and easy way out. Your father wouldn't even acknowledge you were his. I felt so alone and used. I never let myself think about what I was doing. It was just an act of desperation. I'm so sorry. Please forgive me.

I've never really forgotten you, and I've always loved you. But I buried your memory deep inside of me. Now it's come to the forefront, and I acknowledge you and ask for your forgiveness. I ask you to accept my love. Although I can't hold you in my arms, I can hold you in my heart, and I always will. Please love me as I love you. I know that you are living with the Lord and you are happy forever where there's no pain or suffering.

May your tears for me be tears of joy and love and not of sorrow. Please pray for me in our re-established bond of love. Thank you for loving me. Thank you for praying for me. Please help me to arrive where you are, in the Father's embrace with our dear Lady and her Son, Jesus, beside us forever.

Love,
Mom

Later that day, as I reflected on Kelly's talk, I began to understand why I had suffered from crying spells, drug and alcohol abuse, sexual promiscuity, nightmares, and my emotional roller coaster of anger, grief, sorrow, and emotional numbness. I had buried all the pain from the abortion very deeply inside of me in a mistaken attempt to protect myself. The spiritual and emotional trauma was just too much to confront honestly. But now I understood that the more I buried it, the more spiritual and emotional pain I suffered. So the only way of resolving my crisis, the only way to truly heal, was to face it like any other pain.

I learned by facing the pain, you can conquer it because the truth inside each of us is stronger than any pain. By denying that my baby was real and that I had killed him, I soothed my conscience, but it was just a coping mechanism that didn't work. I was only numbing the symptoms, not healing the wound. After the abortion I had no one to talk to, but that's just what you have to do in order to bring things to the surface and process all of your emotions. Otherwise, they remain buried where they just fester and get worse.

Not only did I lose my baby in that abortion; I also lost a part of myself. But now I was no longer alone. I had thought I was the only person to ever suffer from the symptoms of post-abortion traumatic stress syndrome until I attended the Rachel Mothers Retreat. I thought I was weak or crazy or something. But when I met the other mothers who suffered just like I did, I felt strength and courage. I no longer felt alone. There were other women who had gone through the same symptoms and the same problems as me. I could share my pain, which in itself helped me tremendously to cope and to heal. We talked and cried and understood each other as no one else could. We had all gone down the same path. And we talked about our babies as real children whose loss we could mourn and whose life with Jesus we could celebrate with the hope that one day we would be able to rejoin them.

I had learned that to have an abortion, a mother must sever the natural bond that exists between her and her baby. So in order to recover, she must re-establish that bond by acknowledging the child and asking for its forgiveness and for God's forgiveness. Then she can be reconciled with the child and with God.

Now I realized why my mother had acted so strangely and unnaturally toward me. She tried to abort me, and she had cut off our natural bond, which she never attempted to re-establish with me. I constantly reminded her of the abortion and of my twin whom she did abort. Now I could recall without fear my nightmare memory of my twin's abortion. I looked at it with the eyes of an adult with understanding and not as an unborn child. I confronted it, and I was no longer afraid. I believe that God gave me that nightmare so that I could spread the message of its reality—the injustice, the pain, and the dismemberment of a real abortion. The nightmares of my twin's abortion stopped and so did the nightmares of my Luke's abortion. Now I could meet that memory, which I had tried so hard to stuff and forget, with a message not of "forgotten" but "forgiven."

Now I also understood how my very presence must've pricked my mother's conscience and made her feel guilty. I was a walking assault on her conscience. She just didn't want to deal with her abortion or with me. So she'd have her "spells" and yell at me, pull my earlobe or hit me for no apparent reason. It was all so clear now. Her whole adult life was dominated by post-abortion traumatic stress syndrome! So I prayed, "Father, forgive her. She doesn't know what she is doing." I'm sure that He did, and I forgave Mom also.

I ended the retreat with my heart worn out from tears of sorrow and joy. Now not only had I been forgiven by God and my son, but I had forgiven my mother and myself. My wound from the abortion was no longer a running sore. It was now a healed scar—a testimony of what I had survived.

Forty-two

I feel like I have a new heart and a new spirit," I told Mary a few days later over coffee.

"That's what happens when you honestly face the reality of your abortion," she said. "And if you can face that reality, you can face others with that truth."

"Like how?"

"Like by giving your testimony at a Rachel Mothers Retreat."

"No way. . . . I'm not ready for that."

"Of course you are. You gave it at church after Lupe's Baptism and your Confirmation."

"I must've had a special grace to do that. Besides, I didn't tell them anything about my real abortion in Vermont."

"You've still got that same grace. You can do it, Teresita!"

"I don't know. . . ."

"Let me set it up for you. Think about it."

Just then, Kelly's words from her testimony came echoing into my mind. *So now I speak to you out of my own painful experience as a defender of life. Maybe God is calling you to do the same. Think about it.*

"Well . . . I guess . . . all right Mary. I'll go home and think about it. I'll let you know."

When I got home, I sat down in my rocking chair and thought about it. After a while, I slowly turned my head to my bookshelf and noticed the spine of my tattered copy of *The Scarlet Letter.* I realized how many times that novel had come to my mind recently, and how uncanny it was that when I first read it years ago, I never could have guessed I would connect so deeply with its plot.

I remembered the story pretty well since I had read it at least three times. The setting was in 17th century Puritan New England. The novel's heroine, Hester Prynne, had her sin of adultery in the woods publicly revealed in the town square. According to the town's punishment, she had to wear a scarlet letter "A" on her bosom, which stood for "Adulteress." But she admitted her guilt, grew through her suffering, and found peace through her reconciliation with God and her acts of mercy toward her neighbors.

In startling contrast, I remembered that the Reverend Arthur Dimmesdale, her minister-lover, was tortured by secret guilt and could not make peace with himself or with God. His guilt even manifested itself physically, and it literally killed him.

I followed an interior urge, got up, took the book off the shelf, and thumbed to a page with its top corner turned down. The heading said, "Chapter XXIV, Conclusion." My eyes glanced down the page to a part that I had hi-lited years ago, and without thinking, I began to read it aloud:

> Among many morals which press upon us from the poor minister's miserable experience, we put only this into a sentence: "Be true! Be true! Be true!" Show freely to the world, if not your worst, yet some trait whereby the worst may be inferred!

I put my head down for a moment of silence. The quote had spoken to me. I took it as a message from God. I resolved then and there that my guilt could no longer—and would no longer—be secret. I would be true. I would freely show my worst. I would give my testimony.

Two months later, I stood trembling before twenty-three women at a Rachel Mothers Retreat. I looked out at the faces staring back at me. Some hard and cynical. *Will they listen? Will they accept me and be with me?* After one deep breath, I began. "My name's Teresita, and I had an abortion."

I told them all about the botched abortion by the P.A., the completed abortion at the Green Mountain Hospital, my running away from the Cape, my life of Miami Vice, Miguel's pressure to abort Lupe and his goons attempt to beat her out of me. I told them about my rescue by Mary and the pro-lifers, God's forgiveness through Father John's Confession, my suffering from post-abortion traumatic stress syndrome, and my healing through The Quilt of Love and the Rachel Mothers Retreat. I covered a lot of ground.

Then I said, "I'm here because of a challenge made to me by a girl named Kelly at my retreat. She said, 'Maybe God is calling you to become a defender of life and to speak to others out of your own painful experience.'

"And I say to you, as she said to me, 'Think about it.' I saw quizzical looks on a few faces. I continued, "Has any of this made any difference in my life? . . . I want to shout it from the rooftops and say, 'Yes!'"

"Things just got progressively better for me. Gone forever were the blues and the bad days and nights. No more memories of hangovers, dirty dancing or the men with whom I lain. I felt like I had just taken a shower, only better—I was clean on the outside *and* on the inside. All of the bad that I had absorbed like a sponge had now been squeezed out of me.

"I felt like I began to live again. Everyday and everything was beautiful! I began to do the things that I used to enjoy back home on the Cape. I took long walks and went kite flying on the Miami beaches and made visits to the library, museums, and the Seaquarium. Seeing the fish suspended in the water reminded me of the peace and joy of swimming, so I took it up again. I felt so free and protected in the water, like free-floating in the womb. I snorkeled and swam the backstroke on my back, letting the water flow over me and my mask, and looking through it to the sun and the clear blue sky. I felt like I was being washed clean. The whole scene was symbolic for me. It was like God was speaking to me through nature. The blue sky was Mary's mantle that surrounded the sun of Jesus that basked me in the rays of the Father's love and washed me with the water of the Holy Spirit."

I almost started sobbing and my voice started to crack. So I reached to the shelf beneath the lectern and brought a glass of water to my lips. I composed myself and continued.

"I ate less and exercised more. I drank lots of water and ate mainly fruits and vegetables, fish and low-fat meat. I lost a lot of weight. I got my high school equivalency diploma and began to take courses at our community college at night.

"As soon as I started studying, I gave up the television. I used to have it on all the time. The TV characters seemed to keep me company. I got involved in their lives and thought of them as real people and not just as actors in fantasies. I'd sit on my couch with my remote, and when I got bored, I'd surf from one channel to another. There always had to be some fast action, or I'd switch the channel. I never focused on anything because the TV always diffused my attention. There was just too much happening at once—too much noise, too many images, and too many concepts that were abruptly and fleetingly delivered. I wasn't thinking objectively anymore but just absorbing images and emotions.

"It began to drain my life, especially the news. Trying to keep up on what was happening just made me agitated. Besides, there wasn't any good news. All the bad news just made me feel depressed and too helpless to help anyone else.

"Finally, I tried life without TV. I turned it off. Immediately, I began to feel calmer and more focused. I started to think more objectively and to put things in their proper perspective."

A lot of heads were nodding in agreement with me. Other faces looked incredulous, like they couldn't believe I had actually made such a bold move as to permanently turn off the TV.

"I began to feel good about myself again and felt a deep joy and simple gratitude for the gift of life. Since God and my son had forgiven me, and I had forgiven myself and my mother, I became more compassionate toward others and was very careful not to judge. I knew where I had come from and how much I had needed forgiveness and compassion. I remembered the words of Jesus, 'Judge not lest you be judged' and, 'Forgive your enemies.'

"In the meantime, I was enjoying life. I began to listen to classical music that soothed my nerves and reminded me of my piano playing days. I was more observant of nature—the smell of the air, its feel on my cheeks, the sounds of the birds and their comings and goings, the beauty of the trees and flowers and their multitude of shapes and colors, sunrises and sunsets, and the sparkling stars of night. What a world and what a universe of awe and wonder! And what contentment to be able to meditate on the great God who created it all out of love for us!"

I started to get emotional again so I held the lectern with my hands to steady myself. Then I went on.

"I began to study the Catholic Catechism and to read the Bible, poetry, and good literature. I could see myself in the interior lives of the characters, and I began to understand the universality of the human experience. I truly was not alone. We were all brothers and sisters in Christ who died for us all so that we might have eternal life with Him. I began to say often, 'Hallelujah, praise God!' And I meant it. I went to church every Sunday and stopped often on the way home from work to make visits to Jesus really present in the Blessed Sacrament.

"Miami life had always seemed too fast for me, like a rat race of getting and spending and running on all cylinders. The cultural environment seemed totally toxic—toxic tourism, media, and entertainment. All glitz, frivolity, noise, business, and action. I needed more light and love, the true, the good, and the beautiful. I needed to slow down and calm down. So I started meditating on the peace of Christ. I'd just go to my meditation corner in my apartment, light a candle, sit in my rocking chair, and start breathing in deeply and out slowly. It brought back happy memories of watching my grandmother as she rocked peacefully in her rocking chair.

"I made up an acronym to help me to pray—'PACT,' for Praise, Adoration, Contrition and Thanksgiving. I'd talk to God in my own words from my heart, praising Him for His gifts, especially the gift of life. And I'd give Him the glory for any good that I'd accomplished, adoring His goodness and holiness, expressing my sorrow for my sins and thanking Him for His help to be a better person and mother.

"My interior thoughts and imaginations began to quiet down as I thanked God for His love for me and focused on the silence and stillness. Soon I wouldn't be aware of anything—no interior confusion, jumbled thoughts, ideas, or distractions—only a great internal silence and peace. I would come out of it after 15 minutes or so and be at peace, sometimes for the whole day. I smiled at my restaurant customers and walked more slowly and calmly but did my work even more quickly and efficiently. It seemed that the slower I went, the quicker and more efficiently things got done. God was in control. I had let go and let God."

Many of the women were smiling at me now. I thought that they were with me and that I had better wrap it up before I lost them. I leaned toward them with an inviting voice.

"So if that kind of a life sounds good to you, here's my way for getting to it through my post-abortion healing formula. I call it the seven pillars for post-abortion healing. Here they are." And I read from my paper:

1. God said, "Thou shalt not kill." Jesus said, "You shall know the truth and the truth shall set you free!" (Jn 8:32).

2. The truth is that your abortion was a sin.

3. You disobeyed God and killed your unborn child.

4. But, God loves you! He is merciful and wants to forgive you, free you and grant you peace. Your child prays for you and also wants this for you.

5. You must confess to God (preferably through a priest, minister, rabbi or friend) that you sinned, say that you are sorry, ask forgiveness from God and promise that with His help, you'll never do it again.

6. Then say the same thing to your dead child. You should give him or her a name, tell him or her that you are sorry for being responsible for the death, ask forgiveness, and pray that your child's soul is saved and living with God in everlasting life.

7. Accept and believe in the forgiveness of God and your child, your reconciliation with them and your healing. Now forgive yourself. The truth has set you free!

I held up my seven pillars and said, "I've made copies of these for you. You can pick them up now if you'd like to. Thank you for your attention. And always remember that there's hope for healing."

I walked down the aisle to the beat of heavy applause and received many hugs during the coffee break that followed.

A young woman came up to me and said, "Thank you for sharing, do you remember me?"

"Well, you look familiar but—"

"I'm the girl you talked about who wore the bright orange vest and escorted you into the clinic."

"Wha . . . What are you doing here?"

"I had an abortion just like you and I thought that I had to protect the 'right of choice' for women like you so I promoted abortion with a vengeance. But now I realize that it was simply to justify myself and soothe my conscience. Seeing all of those pro-lifers praying outside the clinic had the same effect on me as it did on you.

"After seeing pro-choicers screaming and yelling their slogans week after week, the peace of the pro-lifers' prayer presence had an effect on me. I quit and, to make a long story short, here I am seeking the same healing that you've received. In the meantime I joined the Centurions."

"The Centurions?" I asked.

"Yes, they're former abortion employees—nurses, receptionists, escorts like me and even some doctors! Your own doctor, Dr. Esponoza, is one of us."

"He's a good one. Why are you called Centurions?"

"A centurion was a commander of a group of 100 men, called a century, in the Roman army. The most famous centurion was one of the soldier-executioners of Jesus. To assure that He was dead on the cross, he thrust his lance through His heart. The blood of Jesus fell on him and he was converted and exclaimed, 'Truly, this was the Son of God.'

"Like him, the blood of the innocent unborn babies is on our hands, we've been converted and we say, like he did, 'Truly these were the children of God.'"

"Hopefully, there will be more and more of you," I said. "I'll spread the word that there's hope and help for former abortionists. Thanks for telling me about the Centurions."

As I lay in bed that night, I reflected on the testimony I gave, especially my challenge to forgive your enemies. I thought, *Practice what you preach, girl! What about your own family and ex-friends? You, too, need to forgive, especially Dad, Brian, Miguel and Gloria, but that's going to take some doing. The best approach in relationships should be total honesty. As I've been totally honest with myself, now I should be totally honest with them. But how? When? Especially since we're so estranged?* I filed these thoughts in the back of my brain to await further revelation or inspiration

My life went on. Being a single working mom was hard, but I persevered with the spirit of *aguante* that my grandmother had seen in me. I had to get up early in the morning to feed and clothe Lupe and myself and get ready for work. Then I'd drop her off at Mary's and pick her up after work, get home to clean the house, wash clothes, and prepare dinner. It never seemed to end. But I didn't complain. I loved being with Lupe. I just needed more peace.

But I wanted this peace all of the time, day after day, not just when I prayed. I wanted to be at peace like Mary. I wondered how she kept her peace. I envied her. I made a mental note to ask her the secret of her peace someday.

Forty-three

Now that I had cleaned up my own act, it seemed that I should be doing something to help others. I remembered all the help that Mary and the pro-lifers had given me, and I wanted to do my part. So I went back to the Mother Cares Center for Life. It was December of 1989, and I had just turned 22. Jane, the bubbly new hostess, received me and offered to give me a tour. Since I'd already been there a few times before, I knew the basics, but I didn't want to spoil her enthusiasm. So I let her give me the tour.

As she led me around the simple ranch house she said, "My name's Jane and our center is dedicated to Our Lady of Guadalupe because she is pregnant in her image and is our heavenly mother. She is a mother who cares for her children on earth, especially mothers and their unborn children. That's why we call this place 'Mother Cares' and *we* care, too, and try to provide for their needs.

"We're here for mothers who are in a crisis pregnancy because of pressure to abort from parents, boyfriends, or husbands, or because they are young and scared or poor or homeless. We're here to help them through their pregnancy and to provide whatever they need to make it. We also provide friendly advice to those who think they've made up their minds to abort. We tell them of the risks to their body, mind, emotions and soul. It helps to have someone who's been there to talk to these mothers."

"I'll do that!" I blurted out. "I've been there. I had an abortion, and I can tell them the horror that follows afterward. Nobody ever told me before I had it. I never made a real informed choice. So maybe I can help someone by telling them the truth before they make their choice."

Jane smiled and said, "That's our hope, and you sure can help. Like Jesus said, 'The truth will set you free!'"

"Yes," I sighed regretfully, "Free to be me and what God wanted me to be. If only I had known then what I know now."

So I began to volunteer at Mother Cares Center for Life on Saturday mornings. I went with great romantic ideas of saving many mothers and babies. But it seemed like most of the girls just wanted free pregnancy tests. If the tests showed that they were pregnant, they just said, "Well, I guess I have no choice but to get an abortion," and they'd be out the door before I could tell them the truth. If the tests showed that they were not pregnant, they just sighed with relief and said, "See you next time."

"Wait!" I yelled as they left. "There shouldn't be a next time. Stop your unmarried sexual activity! Be chaste! Wait till marriage! Don't let him use you! Don't be a condom depository!" It all fell on deaf ears. I got very discouraged. I never got to counsel anyone because none of these victims of sexual promiscuity seemed to care.

So I tried to help in another way. I began to give my testimony at a few more Rachel Mothers Retreats. These mothers cared! They'd suffered from their abortion experiences. They wanted healing and hope, and they listened. This work was much more satisfying to me, but it was emotionally draining. I needed some spiritual support. I needed rest and peace. I needed my friend Mary.

Mary's calmness and inner peace had always attracted me. I wanted what she had, and now seemed to be the right time to ask her how I could get it. So one day I went over to her house for a little talk. She had just finished her house cleaning so she had some time. She offered me a cup of coffee and we sat at her kitchen table.

I said, "Mary I feel like you've been a guardian angel for me, always there for me in my hour of need."

"Well, I try to be. That's what friends are for, aren't they?"

"Yeah, but you seem to go above and beyond the call of duty. I really appreciate your friendship. Not everyone has the ability to listen like you do, without preconceptions and prejudgments. Most people just think about how they're going to respond without even listening to what's being said. Or they just want to give their own advice or talk about themselves. I'm so thankful for your listening to my feelings and needs. It was almost like you knew just where I was coming from, as if you had conquered the same problems as me. Like you were victorious."

"Teresita, you have to understand that post-abortive healing takes time, patience and perseverance." Her voice, as always, was calm and soothing. She went on.

"In our fast food, throwaway culture, it's difficult to maintain the stamina to complete the process. It's filled with ups and downs, accomplishments and disappointments. But you've got to hang in there and keep telling yourself, *I will be healed!* And you need a friend to keep reminding you."

"And you do a good job of that!"

"Just talking about it like we're doing now helps. It helps you to sort all of your mixed-up emotions and form some kind of definite plan of action. Talking is like a safety release valve on a propane gas tank. When your bottled-up emotions are ready to blow, the safety valve of talking prevents an explosion. So keep on talking! That's why I'm always here for you. When I was in need, no one was there for me."

"How could you have ever been in need? You seem to have it all together. Mary, I uh . . . I've never said this, but I envy your peace. I want it. I want to know how you manage to keep it always, day after day."

She simply said, "I stared into the mouth of hell, and I didn't blink."

"What do you mean by that?" I asked in confusion as I shifted in my seat.

"It means you have to face evil honestly for what it is, look it in the eye, not deny it and bury it, but absorb it with forgiveness."

"Yeah, I did that with my abortion. What can be worse than that?"

"Being raped by your father and enduring a *forced* abortion."

I recoiled in horror with my hand over my mouth. I thought that I had it bad with my dad, but you never know what's really bad until you walk in someone else's shoes like Mary's. I sat there in stunned silence and listened to her story.

"My father had an incestuous relationship with me when I was between nine and twelve. I thought that this was normal, that this was how fathers and daughters loved one another. This is what I innocently thought until I got my period at 13. I went to see the school nurse and asked her what I should do when my father came for me if I was wearing a sanitary napkin. Naturally, she was horrified. It was in the days before child abuse sensitivity and laws, so she simply told me not to let him do it anymore. She said that it was wrong.

"Well, soon after my father came for me as was his habit. I said no. He ignored me and had his way. I squirmed and said that the nurse said that it was wrong. But how does a 13-year-old daughter fight her father? I can still hear him purring, 'You're Daddy's little girl!'

"Well, Daddy's little girl got pregnant, and I told my mother everything. She defended him and said that I must have teased him on. It was all my fault. Can you believe it? My own mother!

"Then my father took me to a motel. He and another man stripped me and lay me down on the bed while a woman started to give me an abortion.

She just smiled and said, 'Father knows best.' They claim that it is a woman's choice, but this was my father's choice. I didn't consent to anything!

"I tried to get off the bed. But she injected me with a muscle relaxant to keep me from struggling. I continued to scream that I didn't want an abortion. She told me, 'Shut up and quit your yelling!' Eventually, my baby was brutally killed.

"Afterward, the woman said, 'The abortion will solve your problem,' when it was never really a problem in the first place. She said, 'Your father knows what's best,' when my father was only concerned about his reputation. She said, 'You made the right decision,' when I was never given a choice. More importantly, where was my baby's choice?

"I grieve every day for my baby. I have struggled to forget the abuse and the abortion. I can't do either. All I think of is, I should have done more, fought more, struggled more for the life of my baby.

"My situation may not be common, but I know it's not unique either. The emotions and problems I've had to deal with because of my abortion *are* common. The trauma of the incestuous rape and abuse were only intensified by the forced abortion. The guilt of knowing my baby is dead is something I will have to live with for the rest of my life.

"I was violated and betrayed over and over by my father, whom God created to love and protect me. I was humiliated, hurt, and . . . yes, violated again by the abortionist. I ran away from home, lived on the streets and with friends until the social welfare workers found me. I told them everything, and they placed me in a foster home. That's why I've taken such an interest in you, Teresita. Because you were a runaway, and like me, you've suffered from your abortion.

"And I love your daughter! I can't have any children. The abortionist did her dirty job too thoroughly. She rammed her instruments up my vagina and damaged the cervix muscle. Then she scraped the insides of my womb so hard that she scarred the wall of my uterus so that a baby can't stay implanted there. Because of the scarred wall and the weakened cervix muscle, I miscarried all of my pregnancies."

"I've had six miscarriages! So I have to use natural family planning. My husband and I have to avoid sex during my fertile times to avoid getting pregnant since I'm not able to carry a baby to term, and I can't go through the grief and sorrow of another miscarriage. I'd lose my mind. So I've lost seven babies—one by abortion and six by miscarriage."

"Oh, Mary!" I sympathized. "How horrible!"

"The only way that I've managed to survive all of this is by honestly admitting the horrific evil of it and absorbing it with forgiveness for my parents and the abortionist and with prayers for God's forgiveness of them. I think that I received a special grace from God to be able to do this through a special healing Mass that I attended for mother victims of abortion. That was the last step in my post-abortion healing and forgiveness. Maybe it can be your last step, too, Teresita. Remember, you haven't forgiven Brian and Miguel."

My stomach churned at the mention of their names. It would be a while before I'd be able to think about them.

"There's one of those healing Masses coming here soon, and I think you should go and ask for the special graces of forgiveness and inner peace. There's a priest with a national post-abortion healing ministry coming to Miami to celebrate the Mass on January 22, 1990, the anniversary of the Supreme Court decision which legalized abortion in America."

"Well, that's an ironic coincidence!" I said. "A healing Mass on the very day that has caused millions of deaths for unborn babies and wounds for their mothers."

"Teresita, there are no coincidences with God. We have our free will to do evil, and God permits this, but He works all things together for the good, despite the evil plans of men. He throws these evil plans into confusion and ultimately brings good out of the worst."

"Well, I certainly hope so, and I'd really like to go to that Mass." As I got up to leave I said, "Once again, Mary, thank you for being my friend."

January 22nd came, and I eagerly went with Mary to the Mass of Healing and Reconciliation. All the prayers and readings dealt with forgiveness, healing, and hope. The entrance song was sung by a small choir, which imitated the voices of our aborted children. They chanted, "Hear, O Lord, the sound of our voices. Take head to our pleading. Forgive our parents. Though their sins be like scarlet, make them white as snow. Hear, O Lord, and gift them with rest and peace."

I started crying and silently prayed, *Yes Lord, give me Your rest and peace. I know that You have forgiven me, Luke has forgiven me, and I have forgiven my mother and myself. But I need to forgive Brian and Miguel, and I need Your rest and your peace. The peace that passes all understanding and only comes as a gift from You.*

As if in answer to my silent prayer, the priest then prayed for God's mercy for us. He chanted as if he were Jesus Himself, "I see your tears, I hear your prayers. I forgive you, and I will grant you my rest and peace."

We sung in response, "Lord, have mercy!"

He chanted, "I pour out my mercy and my grace. Have no fear! I am your comfort and rest."

We chanted, "Christ, have mercy!"

The Gospel reading was from Luke. It was about the sinful woman who washed the feet of Jesus with her tears and wiped them with her hair. *What self-abasement and humility!* I thought. Jesus told her, "Your sins are forgiven because of your great love. Your faith has been your salvation, now go in peace."

I felt as if Jesus was saying those words just for me. I imagined Him gently placing His hand on my head and giving me the same blessing. Peace flooded my heart. It was as if warm blood flowed from my heart throughout my body and I was aglow with pure love. This love was inflamed after I received Jesus in Holy Communion. I resolved to forgive Brian and Miguel, if and when the circumstances presented themselves. I felt like I floated out of the church on a cloud as the recessional song was sung, "Let there be peace on earth, and let it begin with me."

As I left the church I thought, *I've reached the final step in my healing process. What a long road! Now I can see how I was healed by God with the help of Mary. Neither of them gave up on me. I hope that all of this pain was not in vain, and I can help other hurting women whom God might bring into my life. He brought me Mary, and He brought me through the isolation, the desperate times, the unreality and the guilt, fear and shame. He cares about me. I'm not alone as I thought I was that day at Rock Harbor after the abortion. He's formed me in His gentle hands like a potter who forms the clay and molds it according to his own pattern. He'll never reject this pot and throw it away. Jesus, I trust in You. I'm sorry for all of the things I said to You at Rock Harbor.*

With that profession of trust, I felt a great burden being lifted from me. I knew that I had been heard.

Forty-four

*W*here to now, Lord? After I got home, I sipped on a nice hot cup of chamomile tea with honey to calm me. I stared out the window. Then I remembered what Kelly said to me at the Rachel Mothers Retreat. "You can be a Guardian of the Missionary Image." So I got the address for their center in Vermont and wrote them a letter to ask them how to do this. *Maybe there is something good that can come out of Vermont after all,* I thought.

A couple of days later, a nice lady called me from the Missionary Image center and told me that I had to form a Team to plan the visit and that she would send me a Guardian Training Manual and a video to guide us. After they arrived in the mail, I watched the video and read the manual. They explained that the mission was to melt hearts, bring conversions, end abortion, and heal mother victims of abortion.

I had no idea of all of the signs, wonders, conversions, healings, and closed abortion centers that were associated with Visitations of the Missionary Image. I felt like Mary's cousin Elizabeth who said at her Visitation in the Gospel of Luke, "How is it that I should be honored with a visit from the Mother of my Lord?" We scheduled the Visitation for early October.

I formed my Team: me as Guardian, Mary for Liturgies, and some friends of hers for Publicity and Financing. Starting in July, we met every week for three months and planned visits to churches, schools, hospitals, prisons, and abortion centers. The plan was that Mary would give talks to explain Our Lady of Guadalupe and the Missionary Image, and I would give my testimony about how she saved me from an abortion and from a miscarriage and gave me hope for new life at the Rachel Mothers Retreat. Everything was shaping up, and we eagerly awaited the arrival of the Image in October.

Federal Express delivered to my apartment the six-foot by four-foot Image folded in half in a large case. I answered the knock of the Federal Express man who stood on my doorstep with a flock of birds flying around his head. He looked perplexed and said, "What have you got in here? A year's supply of bird food?"

"No," I answered, "It's an image of Mary, the mother of Jesus."

"Well," he said, "she must be very special because these birds followed me all the way from my truck! Sign here."

I wheeled the case into my apartment and opened it up. Immediately I smelled a waft of sweet roses from the case that filled the whole room. It must have been like that when Juan Diego opened his cloak for the Bishop and the roses fell leaving Our Lady's image on his cloak. I set up the Image in its full size supported by a pole in the back like on a picture frame. When I looked into her eyes, I felt them penetrating mine, and I said, "I'm going to take you as my mother. Please establish the bond with me that my earthly mother and I never had."

The lady next door had seen all the birds, so she came over to see what was going on. I showed her the Image and explained its mission. Soon word spread throughout the neighborhood, and people started streaming through my apartment to pray and venerate the Image.

They'd place their hands reverently on Our Lady's heart and beg her for special favors—for healings, for marital and family unity, for jobs, for peace in the world. Soon they started writing out petitions and dropping them at Our Lady's feet. They'd leave in tears and say, "Thank you for bringing her and sharing her with us." They acted like it was really Our Lady and not just an image—just like Kelly had been told when she was at the Marian Conference.

Our Visitation began on October 12, 1990, the last day of Hispanic Heritage Month, known to most Americans as Columbus Day but to Hispanic-Americans as *El Día de la Raza,* "The Day of the Race." It marks Christopher Columbus's first voyage and so-called "discovery" of the New World. It also marks the Spanish and Indian encounter that resulted in the *mestizo* Hispanic people. It was the day of the beginning of *my* race.

In Miami, Little Havana always celebrated this day with a big parade through the streets. So I got permission to carry the Missionary Image in the parade. It was awesome. We took turns carrying the Image, and people would come off the sidewalks to touch it in prayer. They also threw flower petals at it from the bouquets that they held. They showed it in the newspapers and on TV. I felt great pride for my race and for Our Lady of Guadalupe, the mother of our race. I remembered that she told Juan Diego,

"I am of your own kind. I am your merciful mother and the mother of all of you united in this land." We felt a great sense of unity and peace. It was a happy day. The happiness overshadowed the dark memory that this day was also the sixth anniversary of my incomplete abortion in Burlington.

We took the Image to ten churches, two schools, a nursing home, a hospital, and a women's prison. Our Lady melted hearts everywhere she went. Almost everyone who venerated the Image was touched in one way or another. Some were given an inner strength to deal with their problems and adversities; some received confirmation of their prayer requests; some were led to Confession; and some were miraculously healed. We gave away thousands of brochures, Rosaries, holy cards, and medals of Our Lady of Guadalupe.

We took her to junior high school students in a Catholic school. We set the Image up in the auditorium, and all of the classes came in for veneration. One of the girls touched the pregnant womb on the Image and said that she felt the heartbeat of the Baby Jesus. Her classmates started laughing until the teacher also felt it. Then the teacher began to doubt and told the students that it must've been their imagination.

However, one of the students was bright enough to suggest that the teacher get the school nurse to examine the Image. So the teacher went and got the nurse who came back with her stethoscope and, with some embarrassment, placed it over Our Lady's womb. Then her eyes lit up, and she announced to us all, "Ohhh . . . I hear a baby's heartbeat!"

Then she stood up and said, "There's no doubt about it, I just heard the heartbeat of an unborn child." Everyone started excitedly asking questions of her. "What does it mean?" someone yelled.

"Well," the nurse hesitatingly replied, "A baby's heart beats even before the mother knows that she's pregnant. I think that this is a sign from God that life begins at conception and what you hear about abortion as a 'woman's choice over her own body' is just a big lie. It's a choice over *another* person's body, a choice to kill.

"The unborn baby has different DNA from its mother from the moment of conception. The baby's entire genetic code is established at conception. It's all there like a wound-up audiotape and just remains to play itself out over the baby's lifetime. Don't pay attention to all the propaganda you hear, especially, 'My body, My choice.' It's not your body, and nobody has a right to choose to kill the innocent. Don't be like the fools in Nazi Germany who believed the propaganda that their leaders spread with their slogan, 'If you tell a Big Lie often enough, everyone will believe it.'" Then she slowly walked out of the room deep in thought, her head bowed.

We also took the Image to a hospital where a four-year-old girl named Ann lay dying from bronchiolitis obliterans, a rare lung disease. I brought the Image to Ann's hospital room on the day before her father, the Chief of Surgery, predicted she would die. He had given up all medical hope and wanted to prepare his family to accept Ann's death. So he built a small coffin together with her brother and sisters. But Ann's mother had more hope. She read that the Image was in town, and she called me to take it to her daughter.

When we got to her room, Ann's mom lifted her up to the Image, and she tenderly touched and kissed it. The next day when her dad went into her room expecting to find his dead daughter, he was shocked when he found her wide awake. She asked him for McDonald's chicken nuggets and a vanilla shake. He later said that her healing was totally and medically unexplainable. But he was a doctor and not big on giving Our Lady credit for miracles. Her mother and I said that it was a miracle.

At one of the churches, a woman started sobbing as she prayed in front of the Image. I gently asked her, "May I pray with you?"

She said, "I've never confessed my two abortions. I've felt a ripping torment, hurt and devastation beyond description for killing my babies. Now I feel that Our Lady is drawing me to herself. She is so beautiful. Her face is filled with tenderness and compassion. She seems so loving, understanding, and forgiving."

"Yes," I said "and she's gently leading you to her Son in the sacrament of Reconciliation. Father's waiting now in the confessional. He's there for you." She left for her Confession with a big smile on her face.

On the next to last day, we went to The Women's Choice Center from which Mary rescued me. We went to maintain a Peaceful Prayer Presence. We prayed for an end to abortion and for the conversions of the abortionists, their staff, and all who supported abortion. We prayed for the mothers to choose life. We knew that the battle against abortion was not a mere political battle, but more of a spiritual battle for the minds and the hearts of the people. So we used the spiritual weapons of prayer and fasting. We recalled that Jesus said, "This kind can be cast out only by prayer and fasting." To us, "this kind" meant the demons of abortion. We took Jesus at His word, and Mary and I fasted on bread and water for the whole day.

To me, these abortion centers were the Calvaries of the modern world. The innocent Jesus was crucified on Calvary while the passers-by jeered and His Mother stood in prayer at the foot of the Cross. That's why we brought the Image to stand in prayer with us while the innocent unborn children were crucified at The Women's Choice Center on a Cross of "Choice" and the passers-by on the sidewalk jeered at us.

We brought the Image front and center on the sidewalk facing the entrance door. It was near noon on a Friday morning, and young pregnant girls were streaming to the clinic for their abortions. We started praying the Rosary and handing out pamphlets on the dangers of abortion and our willingness to help the mothers. I talked to one mother and told her all about my abortion. She said, "If it's like that, I don't want any part of it. They told me that it wasn't a baby." And she walked away. It gave me some consolation that God could use my horrible experiences to save another mother and unborn baby from abortion.

As we prayed, the sun seemed to get bigger and then a huge blue aureole cloud surrounded it that in turn was surrounded by a large round rainbow. I had read that when the Missionary Image left Mexico, this identical phenomenon happened and that this was how Our Lady of Guadalupe originally appeared to Juan Diego—emerging from a light more brilliant than the sun surrounded by a round rainbow. We took this as a sign from Our Lady that she was with us in the Image.

The media reported it as a solar phenomenon caused by ice crystals in the sky. But we knew that God can use natural means to bring a supernatural message, just like He left Noah a rainbow as a sign of hope. The solar rainbow message to us from Our Lady was, "Thank you for responding to my call. Keep up the good work. Don't lose hope!"

As I knelt in prayer on the hard pavement, someone came running out of the clinic up to me and hung two coat hangers around my neck. I felt like Jesus might have felt when they placed the crown of thorns on His head. Then someone else walked by, spat at me and threw condoms at the Image while cars drove by, honked their horns, jeered and gave us the finger. We didn't feel very welcome, but I just hoped that maybe there would be somebody in the clinic like myself who needed help. At least we were there for her and in prayer for all the supporters of abortion who seemed to hate us so unnaturally. We prayed, sang hymns, and left without any apparent results. However, about two months after we left, the clinic closed. They announced that it was for lack of business. But that was just another lie.

They closed in answer to our prayers. We later found out that the abortionist was on the run from New York where his license had been suspended. He had fraudulently obtained a Florida license and was exposed by one of his patients. He had perforated her uterus. So much for safe, legal abortions. I thought that the coat hangers belonged on his head and not on mine.

Our closing Mass was held in the morning at the Hispanic parish of St. James. St. James is the patron saint of Spain. Spanish soldiers always invoked him in war with their battle cry of *Santiago!* We were met at the church entrance by many adults holding lighted candles, children holding roses, and an honor guard of the Knights of Columbus in full ceremonial regalia with plumed hats, capes, and swords. Three times they shouted, *Santiago!* and then they led a procession of the children and the Image to the altar accompanied by the Hispanic choir and guitars. They sang to Our Lady very lovingly, *Buenos Días Paloma Blanca*—"Good Morning, White Dove."

When the procession arrived at the altar, the pastor incensed the Image as a sign of reverence. All the children placed their roses in vases around the Image. Then, many of both the old and the young crawled on their knees from the concrete steps outside of the church and up the aisle to the Image where Our Lady awaited their veneration and petitions.

After the Mass, the Image was processed out very slowly while the congregation threw rose petals at her and the choir sang, *Adiós, Madre Mía*—"Goodbye, My Mother." Tears filled the eyes of the congregation as they shouted out, "Come back to us! Don't forget us!"

I was inspired right then and there to sit down and write a "Thank You" prayer. I wrote it out and dropped it in the prayer basket:

Thank you, Mother, for helping me to say "Yes" to bring you here to be with your people. Thank you for the Team who gave up their time to help me to bring you to so many churches and the other places where your mother's love was so needed. Thank you for providing a free van and all of the free roses and for gentlemen police officers who freed up city streets for us and enabled us to parade and to peacefully pray at the abortion center. Thank you for healing the little girl and for answering the people's prayers and giving them hope. And thank you, dear Lady, for Lupe. Amen.

Forty-five

*A*fter the Image left, I crashed from exhaustion. It was all I could do just to get to work every day. Other than that, I took good care of Lupe and slept. It was about a week before I got my energy back and things began to return to normal. Thanksgiving was coming in a month, so I thought it was about time to get my house in order. I cleaned from stem to stern, as my nautical father used to say. It was like what we called "spring cleaning" back home on the Cape, only here in Miami we had no spring or any change of seasons. It was fall up home, and we'd be putting away the lawn furniture and boats and getting ready for the long winter.

The only way that I could tell that the seasons were changing in Miami was to see the sun moving south on the horizon each day. On the Cape, it was simply sunny or not sunny for me on any day of the year. But now I had begun to take notice of things and not take everything for granted, including sunshine. I noticed that from the Spring Equinox around March 21st, when the sun rose in the middle of the eastern horizon, it moved a little north each day. Then it would reach its northernmost point at the Summer Solstice around June 21st, the longest sunlight of the year, and then start south again until it reached the Fall Equinox around September 21st, and eventually its southernmost point at the Winter Solstice around December 21st, the shortest sunlight of the year. Then the sun would start the cycle to the north all over again. As the song from the musical *Fiddler on the Roof* said:

> *Sunrise, sunset, swiftly flow the years. One season following another, laden with happiness and tears.*

There was more happiness than tears for me now as I got into the rhythm of nature and began my spring cleaning in November of 1990.

I vacuumed the rugs, scrubbed the floors, waxed the woodwork, dusted the walls and ceilings, and cleaned the windows. I threw out old newspapers and magazines and a lot of other miscellaneous junk that I had accumulated in the five years that I had been in Miami.

For some reason, I began to wonder about Miguel. He was often on my mind as I cleaned. At first I angrily dismissed any thought of him. But then I remembered the resolution I had made at the healing Mass to forgive him . . . "if and when the circumstances presented themselves." The more his memory came up, the more compassionate I felt toward him.

The key for me was to recognize my feelings and honestly express them. In the beginning, I was tempted to write to him to tell him how much I hated him for what he and his goons had done to me in their attempt to have Lupe aborted. But now I began to put myself in his place. I followed the old Indian saying, "Don't judge a man until you've walked a mile in his moccasins." So I figuratively put on Miguel's moccasins and went for a walk in them.

He was the son of a domineering mother—a white Supremacist, racist, Cuban refugee—and a father who was a workaholic restaurant owner. Both of them started in Miami with nothing. By putting work first, they had succeeded materially and realized the Great American Dream of rags to riches. Miguel was their only son. He was made in their mold, and after his father died he focused obsessively on his goal of taking over the family restaurant. He was willing to do anything to please his mother. I wondered how he slept at night—probably no better than I used to. I actually started feeling sorry for him.

My passion *against* him was mysteriously transformed into compassion *for* him. I even began to pray for him remembering Jesus' words, "Pray for those who hurt you." It was hard at first, but like any other good thing in life, it got easier the more that I did it. I wondered what had happened to Miguel over the last four years. I was soon to find out.

Forty-six

After Christmas, I went back to the Mother Cares Center for a visit on one of my days off. It was December 28th, the Feast of the Holy Innocents. This Feast was in memory of the innocent children who were killed in Bethlehem by King Herod in an attempt to kill the Baby Jesus. It was always a special day at Mother Cares Center because we saw ourselves as trying to stop the killing by abortion of innocent children. It was near lunchtime, and I decided to join the volunteers for lunch. It had been a while since I had stopped by, and I just wanted to catch up on the news with the girls. As I entered the house, I noticed a man mowing the lawn. I hadn't seen him around before so I asked the receptionist, "Who's the guy mowing the lawn?"

"Some new guy—a volunteer. We prayed a Novena to St. Joseph for some male help around here and bingo! On the ninth and last day of our prayers, he showed up and said he felt called to help, and he needed to do this for himself. So now he comes a couple of days a week for handyman stuff and grunt work like taking out the garbage and filing. He's been a God-send."

Just then, he came in behind me, and I heard him say to the receptionist, "Don't worry, I'm not quitting, I just need a glass of water." That voice! It sounded just like Miguel, but the guy was in the bathroom before I could see who it was.

"What's his name?" I asked.

"Miguel."

He came out of the bathroom and recognized me immediately. I could see his white Cuban face get much whiter. "Teresita, I, uh, I've been wanting to talk to you." I just glared at him as he looked back at me speechless with his mouth hanging open.

"You tried to kill my baby, get out of my face! We don't have anything to talk about."

"Teresita . . . please . . . I . . . uh . . . I've been wanting to meet you, but I didn't know how to go about it."

"You could have written, you could have called," I icily replied.

"I didn't know how to do it. I felt paralyzed. Listen, Teresita, please don't beat up on me. Can we go out for lunch?"

"*Lunch?*" I screamed. "After almost five years, all of a sudden, we'll just go out for lunch?"

"Yes," he said. "I'm really sorry for what I did to you. I was a jerk, but I've changed and I want to tell you my story. Maybe God set up this unexpected meeting just so that you and I could have lunch together."

God? I thought. I had never heard Miguel mention the name of God before, and here he was not just recognizing God's existence but His actual involvement in human affairs. He was giving the living God credit for bringing us together. That was enough for me. I felt as if I had to accept. My anger subsided.

"Okay Miguel, I'll go with you, but I'm still very hurt."

"So am I," he mysteriously replied.

I didn't want to go to a private or intimate place with him, and I certainly didn't want to go to his mother's restaurant. I suggested that we go somewhere close so Miguel could go to work after our lunch. So I said, "Let's get something to take out and eat it in Maximo Gomez Park."

"Sounds fine to me," he said. "Let's go."

I used to eat my lunch there on my days off when I worked at Gloria's. It was a small corner park about 25 yards square also called "Domino Park." It was always filled by elderly macho men playing dominoes. The inside wall was covered with murals of male Cuban heroes. The other three sides were surrounded by a high wrought iron fence. The message was clear: "Only elderly men enter here!" There was a tradition that the park was only for the use of elderly men to sit and passionately play dominoes while smoking Cuban cigars and drinking Cuban coffee. But my feminist tendencies led me to continually challenge the tradition, much to the dismay of the men.

I left the Mother Cares Center with Miguel with some trepidation, not knowing what to expect. We went down to the *Calle Ocho* to "Little Havana To Go." I noticed a bilingual sign on the door as we entered:

Abrimos a las 11:00 a.m. . . . . Hora Cubana!—
We open at 11:00 a.m. . . . . Cuban Time!

We got there just before noon. They had just opened—on Cuban time. We bought some cokes and sandwiches, and went to Maximo Gomez, the park on the corner next door.

We entered the park and sat at a corner table under a shade tree. The men stopped playing their dominoes. They were too polite to say anything, but they glared at me for a full minute before returning to their games.

Miguel made small talk about his mother's restaurant, and I told him about the one where I now worked. As I slowly opened and ate my sandwich, Miguel just sat there with his sandwich unopened staring at the domino players. I waited for him to break the awkward silence.

"Well, Teresita, I heard that you had your baby—"

"No, I had *our* baby. What did you think? That I was a killer like you?"

"Oh, Teresita, come on . . . please don't say that. What did you name it?"

"She is not an 'it,' she is *your* daughter, and I named her 'Guadalupe.' I call her 'Lupe' for short."

"Hey, is she named after Our Lady of Guadalupe?"

"Of course, what do you think she's named after? The French island in the Caribbean?"

"Please Teresita, I'm just trying to establish some common ground . . . I know all about Our Lady of Guadalupe, but that would take me ahead of my story. . . . " He took a deep breath and nervously began. "Teresita, I know that you don't think much of me after what I tried to do to you and your, uh, *our* Lupe. But I'm going to try to open myself up to you. I hope you understand that's a hard thing for me to do, you know, the macho Cuban thing and all . . . but I'm going to tell you a story that I hope you'll believe."

I stared at him, my alternating emotions of anger and pain flashing from my eyes. I said, "I hope that I believe it, too. You've got a lot of explaining to do."

"Well, it's like this. I'm really sorry for everything that I did to you. It wasn't just a bad plan, it was an *evil* plan."

He said "evil" very slowly with an accent on the first syllable. I was surprised to hear him make his own moral judgment. He never talked before as if his acts were good or evil. They were just simply choices.

"It was an evil plan concocted by my mother out of her Cuban pride to have a white grandchild. She's as proud as they come. She was at the top in Cuba, down in Miami as a refugee, and now back up again. She doesn't want any reminders of being low on the totem poll like she was in her refugee days. The black *Marielito* refugees really hardened her racial prejudices.

"Then I got two women pregnant which exasperated her. She was determined that if she were going to have a grandchild, it would be white. She wouldn't suffer the embarrassment of having a mulatto grandchild, and you and I were the victims of her determination."

"Wait a minute," I interrupted, "how were you a victim of anything? *I* was the victim! I was pushed to the abortion center! Your thugs beat me up in an attempt to make me miscarry my baby. Don't give me any of your 'victim' crap!"

"Well, maybe 'victim' isn't the right word. I guess I've always thought of myself as a victim of her dominance, but now I'm beginning to see that I was just a coward, cowering to her demands in fear that if I didn't, I would incur her wrath and lose my chance at owning her restaurant.

"I'm not proud of myself, but let me go on, Teresita. I'm sure that you remember Sally, my other girlfriend. She gave birth to a white son. She named him William. I called him Billy. Billy and I bonded from the beginning. When I fed him his bottle and looked into his bright blue eyes, they seemed to connect with mine.

"Sally and I soon broke up, but she let me visit Billy, and I'd even babysit for him when she went out with her other boyfriends. I was the one who saw his first walk! This one night I just knelt on the floor and kept encouraging him as he held on to a chair, 'Come on, Billy, come to Daddy! It's all right, I'll hold you.' And I kept holding out my arms and bringing them together to show him that he'd be safe. Finally, he wobbled right into my arms! What a moment—"

"Well," I said quietly, looking down at my food so he wouldn't see tears welling up in my eyes, "you should have been there for Lupe's first walk into my arms."

"Yeah, you're right Teresita. I know I wasn't there for either of you. Please don't pour on the guilt right now. The point I'm trying to make is that Billy and I were close."

"I see your point very clearly, Miguel. You don't have to rub it in—"

"Easy Teresita. One night, when Billy was almost three years old, I wasn't able to babysit. Sally got one of her boyfriends to watch him while she went out with another guy—she was some mother, that Sally! The babysitter was an alcoholic who didn't know the first thing about babies, but he knew where he could get some free booze for babysitting. He didn't know why Billy kept crying and crying . . . but Billy was just tired and hungry. Nobody had fed him!

"The more Billy cried, the angrier the guy got. I think he got frustrated 'cause he couldn't stop the crying. Finally, the guy reached his breaking point—which didn't take much, he was pretty drunk by that time. He snapped. He picked Billy up and shook him . . . he shook him and shook him . . . and then Billy stopped crying. He was dead. That guy killed my little boy. . . . Billy was only hungry . . . only hungry, Teresita." Miguel was sobbing uncontrollably. His whole body was shaking. I could see the genuine and intense pain in his eyes, and I started crying with him.

"Oh, Miguel, how awful," I sobbed. "I'm so sorry. I had no idea."

"I'm not looking for sympathy, Teresita. I'm looking for understanding. Please hear me out. My life went into a tailspin. I cried out to a God who I didn't even believe in, 'Why, why did you allow my innocent and beautiful boy to be killed?' I didn't receive any answer.

"Then I started having nightmares of dead babies. One night Billy came into the middle of them, and I screamed out, 'Why was he killed?' Then I heard a sweet feminine voice answer me, 'Why do you ask only about your son? You tried to do the same thing twice to your daughter.' I woke up in a cold sweat. I knew that she was talking about Lupe, but I didn't have a clue what I should do."

"For starters, you should've recognized that Lupe was *our* daughter not just my daughter. So tell me, what did you do?"

"The next day, I was walking down the street when I passed a Catholic church. It had an image of Mary on the outside wall next to the entrance. I later learned that it was the image of Our Lady of Guadalupe, the same one that you named *our* daughter after. So you see, we have something in common. I looked at that image, and I melted right there on that street. I felt compelled to kneel down, and slowly I felt myself being gently pushed down into a kneeling position—right there on the public sidewalk."

"Proud Miguel on his knees in public. That's hard to believe."

"I told you that this was going to be hard to believe. But it gets better. I got up off the pavement and went right into that church and knelt in a pew. I felt such peace, and I just started praying spontaneously. I prayed, 'God, please take Billy to heaven. I really miss him, and I'm really sorry for trying to abort Teresita's baby.'"

"Our baby," I interrupted again. "Did you uh . . . really pray that way, Miguel?" I asked in disbelief.

"Yes, everything just tumbled out of me. I *was* sorry for trying to abort *our* baby. I prayed for forgiveness. Then I heard that same feminine voice inside my heart say, 'Seek forgiveness and reconciliation.'

"Just then I noticed a priest walk into the church. He started to pick up hymnals that were left all over the pew seats. He carefully picked them up and placed them in the racks on the backs of the seats—all very neat and tidy. It was like a prophetic vision for me, and I had this urge to pick up the messes in my life and get neat and tidy myself. So I asked him if he'd hear my Confession. He did. I was forgiven. I got a fresh start.

"I began to appreciate life much more, since a part of my life was gone with Billy. I also felt that I had to make up in some way for what I tried to do to you and Lupe. So I started to volunteer at Mother Cares Life Center. I was the only man they had, so there was plenty of work for me to do. That's where I learned all about Our Lady of Guadalupe. I also started to pray more and began to realize that the voice that I heard must've been that of Our Lady of Guadalupe. When she said, 'Seek forgiveness and reconciliation,' she didn't mean just with God, she also meant with you and Lupe. So Teresita, I'm here to tell you that I'm truly sorry, and I ask your forgiveness."

"It's not just that simple for me, Miguel. I forgive you in my head, but my heart still has some holes in it. It'll take time. I don't hate you . . . I'm just in pain, and this has come as a complete surprise."

"That's all right, Teresita, take all the time you need. Would you like to see me again?"

"Well, I think I probably should. After all, you *are* Lupe's father. Why don't you come over to my apartment on Saturday afternoon to meet her?"

"Okay," he said, "Let's go now. I've got to go to work at the restaurant."

We left the Park, and Miguel left his sandwich behind. He hadn't even touched it.

Forty-seven

Miguel dropped me off at Mary's house where Lupe was waiting. I thanked Mary, and she gave us a ride home. All the while, I was trying to process my meeting with Miguel. When I got home, I put Lupe in her crib for a nap, sat down in my rocking chair, and began some deep breathing exercises in an attempt to sort things out. I needed at least a dozen deep breaths to settle down. But a flash of anger caught up with me after only two. I felt very angry . . . with *myself*.

How could I sit there saying nothing and listening to his story and not even hinting at mine? I don't believe I did it! What a fool! I struggled through his pressure to have an abortion, his thugs who beat me to make the abortion happen, and his absence as a father for four and a half years. I did everything alone. I gave birth to Lupe, I nursed her and worked hard to feed, clothe, and shelter her. He never even asked about her or lifted a finger to help.

My anger and resentment were building up, and I wanted to get them off my chest. So I got out my writing paper and pen, sat down at the kitchen table and wrote a letter to Miguel:

Dear Miguel,

I'm upset! I just got back from our lunch and started thinking that I never got a word in edgewise to tell you my story. How much I hated you for what you tried to do to me with the abortion and the beating by your thugs. I struggled all alone without the slightest concern or help from you.

You and your white Cuban mother made my life miserable. But the girl that you both tried to kill made it beautiful. You missed so much—celebrating the beauty of life with courage and trust in God instead of running from it in cowardly fear of a domineering mother. It's about time you've finally showed some change and some movement forward. God is giving you a second chance with Lupe, and I guess I'm willing to join Him. I hope that you don't blow it.

In spite of my feelings of anger and resentment toward you, I'm thankful that you showed some courage and asked me out to lunch. It wasn't Miami's finest restaurant, but it was something. At least you tried, and it must've been hard for you. I forgive you from my heart now, in spite of my mixed emotions. I've made a conscious decision that no matter how or what I feel, I forgive you. I just had to get my feelings off my chest. Hope you understand. I'm mailing this now so that you'll receive it before our meeting here on Saturday. It's hard for me to say it, but I'm really looking forward to seeing you on Saturday—for Lupe's sake, of course.

Hurriedly,
Teresita

I folded the letter, placed it in an envelope, licked it, sealed it, addressed it, and stamped it. I got up, walked quickly to the corner mailbox and deposited it. I walked back home feeling much relieved. But by the time I got back to my rocking chair, I was having second thoughts.

I wonder what he'll think. Maybe I was too hard on him. But he deserved it, didn't he? He'll think I'm just a bitch. I should've waited until I settled down. I was too impulsive. Just like Mom always said. I should act less out of passion and more from compassion. *Best to accentuate the positive. Maybe he'll actually understand and be sympathetic.*

Saturday was coming too quickly. I cleaned and tidied the house, bought some fresh flowers and special Cuban coffee and snacks, and even a new outfit for Lupe. I took her out for lunch on Saturday, and we got ice cream cones with sprinkles for dessert as we walked home from the *Calle Ocho*. Then I took a luxurious hot bath and anxiously awaited Miguel's arrival.

Just before 3 p.m. I heard a firm knock on the door. I quickly combed my hair, brushed myself off, and walked with Lupe to the door. It was Miguel, and he looked handsome with a navy blue V-neck sweater, khaki pants, and black loafers that matched his freshly cut black hair and dark eyes.

I stood there staring at him as he said, "Hi, hope I'm not too early. Aren't you going to let me in?" I guess I was a little dazzled.

"Sure, Miguel, this is your daughter, Lupe. Lupe, this is your . . . uh . . . Daddy."

"Hi, Lupe," he said, as he brushed past her into the house.

Immediately I could see that he'd need some time to get to know her, so I just left her with him and said, "I'll get you a cup of coffee. Play with Lupe." And off I went to the kitchen. When I came back with the coffee, Miguel was sitting on the sofa with Lupe on his lap twirling his curly black hair. "She seems to be quite an affectionate little girl," he said.

"Yes, she was made to love. She's the joy of my life. I hope that you get to know her."

"So do I. Listen, Teresita, I . . . uh, I received your letter. Everything you said is true. All I can say is I'm sorry, and please forgive me. I don't have any excuses. I was weak and wrong, and you were right and strong. I'm just happy for you that you have the joy of Lupe in your life."

"She can be a joy in your life, too."

"What do you mean?"

"Well . . . you can spend some time with her, you know, get to know her—develop a relationship with her. After all, you're her *father.*"

"You wouldn't mind?"

"No, I wouldn't mind. I think that I've got to let the past go, Miguel. Let go of all the resentment and move forward and trust in the goodness of life."

"Would you trust me with Lupe?"

"Like how?"

"Like could I take her places?"

"Sure, but I should go along—for her sake of course—to make sure she'll be okay."

"Well, how about tomorrow? Would you like to go to the Seaquarium?"

"That would be great. I love to watch fish swim."

"So how about I pick you both up after lunch?"

"Fine." And with that, he said he had to get to work and he left. It was a short visit, but it was the beginning of what I hoped would be some kind of bond between Miguel and Lupe.

Forty-eight

Swooosh! went the stream of water from the blowhole of Dottie, the Killer Whale. All three of us were drenched. She swam by us on her back, waved her tail at us, flipped over and blew out a 20-foot stream of water. Miguel, Lupe and I laughed like three little kids as we sat near the pool at the Seaquarium.

On my days off over the next few months, we made many other day trips together, enjoying Miami's sights and sounds. We rode the Metromover, a train on an elevated rail, and got a terrific "aerial" view of downtown Miami. Then we got off, walked down Flagler Street, downtown's main artery, explored the shops and ended at the Metro-Dade Cultural Plaza with its flowing pools of water and grand tiled courtyard. There we got a cold drink before we went on browsing.

We also went to the library, the Historical Museum, and the Fine Arts Center. I loved these places because of my interest in history, sociology, and the arts.

One day we walked down to the Miami River and had lunch at an outdoor eatery right on the water. There we watched the oil tankers and freighters that plied the waters between Florida, the Caribbean, and Latin America. After lunch, we strolled down the Miami Riverside Walk to its end near Biscayne Bay. All of this water reminded me of my home on Cape Cod.

Some late afternoons we went to Bayside Marketplace and strolled through its acres of shops and kiosks with their Latino woodcarvings, leather goods, and crafts. Once we had our picture taken with our arms full of live parrots. Lupe loved to watch the jugglers, dancers, and mimes. We'd pick out a restaurant for dinner, and one evening we went to nearby Bayfront Park for an outdoor concert.

I did more in those few months than I had in the six years that I'd been in Miami. It seemed like I was on a whirlwind tourist tour. But it was good for Lupe. She was getting to know her father, and so was I.

One weekend we drove down to Miami Beach and checked out the huge Caribbean luxury cruise ships at the Port of Miami. We continued on down Ocean Drive to view the beautiful ocean and the golden-beige sand beach. We passed the different structures in the Art Deco District with their pale pink, aqua, and green colors. After lunch, we went down the road to the South Florida Art Center where all of the local artists shared gallery space. Then we had a leisurely drive home.

On our way home in the car from Miami Beach, Miguel said, "Teresita, I've been thinking. I'd like to be a full-time father for Lupe."

My breath caught in my throat! Immediately I thought that the last few months of Miguel's good behavior had just been a setup by him to get custody of Lupe.

He said, "What do you think?"

I sat there stunned, thinking that he and his mother missed Billy so much that now they were going to make a play for custody of Lupe with their high priced lawyers. So I went into panic mode.

"Who the hell do you think you are—asking for custody of Lupe? I'm her mother! I have custody, I've always had custody, and I always *will* have custody. How dare you threaten me with a custody suit. You're not even listed on her birth certificate as the father."

"Whoa, Teresita," he said firmly as he slowed down the car. "I'm not threatening you with a custody suit. I want custody *with* you."

"I'm not making any custody deals," I interrupted. "You can keep visiting us just like you've been doing."

"Teresita," he said softly, "please, just *listen* to me. I want to be Lupe's full-time father and your full-time husband. I love you. Will you marry me?"

"Marry you? My God, I never had a clue . . . it never entered my mind. You've caught me completely off-guard."

"Maybe that's the trouble, Teresita. You're always *on* guard and filled with mistrust." As he pulled up to the curb he said, "Trust me. This is for real. I love you and Lupe, and I want us to be a family."

I grabbed Lupe and said, "I don't know what to do. I'll have to sleep on it, Miguel. Thanks for a nice day. We'll talk." Then I ran into my apartment, put Lupe down for her nap, and flopped onto my bed in total confusion. My mind eventually settled into prayer. . . .

Lord, how could I have been so blind? I thought that our dates were all for Lupe. I kept thinking, "For Lupe, of course." But it was also for me. I wonder if I even know myself. I need a man in my life, but I've never admitted it to myself. I've been so lonely for adult male conversation and attention, and Miguel sure filled the bill for that. He's been so good to us, and to me I should say. Taking me all over to give me breaks from my humdrum working single-mom life, being kind, patient, and considerate, and asking for nothing in return. I thought if he were interested in me, he'd be after my body. But he's been the perfect gentleman.

Now that I look back over the last few months, I can see the little loving attentions—the "pleases and thank yous," the gentle touches and chaste, brother-like kisses. He loves me! He wants to marry me. I can only believe that You're working here, Lord. Now it looks like a divine set-up to make a family out of a relationship that his mother planned to destroy. Life bursts forth from the death trap, and only You could have pulled it off, Lord. I love You, and I think that I love Miguel, and I sense Your love for me through him. I'm going to marry him, so if it's not Your will, please stop me. But if it is, than let's go full steam ahead.

Forty-nine

I 'm sorry that I surprised you with my proposal," Miguel said when he called me later that night. "I hadn't intended to say anything to you, but we had such a nice day, and I felt such warmth radiating from you on the ride home. I was just kind of moved to let it all out. I just had to honestly express myself without thinking if it was the right time or place. I know it wasn't very romantic, so I'd like to make up for it and take you out to dinner tomorrow night. Maybe you could get Mary to babysit."

"Thank you, Miguel, I'd like that very much."

So he picked up Lupe and me the next evening. We took Lupe to Mary's and off I went alone for my very first real date with the man who had asked me to become his wife. It seemed a little backward to start dating a man with whom I'd had only a sexual relationship in the past, but it was okay with me to move forward like this.

He took me down to the Bayside Marketplace where we used to walk. I hoped his idea of a romantic dinner wasn't at one of the tourists' international cuisine cafeterias in the Food Court. I hesitantly asked him, "Where are we going?"

"Well, you seem to like the water and boats, so I thought you might enjoy something fit for a Queen—an evening dinner and dance cruise on the 'Queen of Miami.'"

He took me to the largest boat I'd ever been on, a hundred foot, three-decked yacht. It had an air-conditioned lower deck with large windows to dine at while viewing the city's skyline, and an outdoor dance floor on the upper deck to dance on while viewing the stars. We sat down to a luscious dinner with candles and wine and danced under the stars to waltzes. No samba or meringue, just nice slow dances where you could even carry on a conversation. No getting drunk in order to have a good time. I had learned to drink moderately and responsibly—two glasses of wine tops, but usually one was perfect. It was a wonderfully romantic evening.

After one of our dances, he took me to the boat's rail, and we stared at the skyline and the stars above. He said, "I know it sounds corny, but you really light up my life, like the stars do the night. I was depressed after Billy was killed, but then I bumped into you at the Mother Cares Center and light came into my darkness. I acted like Lupe was the only attraction for me because what I did to you was horrible, and I didn't know how to begin a relationship with you. It was easier to act as if Lupe was the only reason for me to take you out. But then the pressure for the truth to come out became too great, and I just let it out in the car, all unplanned and unprogrammed. But now I want to say to you straight out, *I love you,* Teresita! Will you marry me?"

I simply said, "Yes." Then I added, "But I also want to say that it's not just for Lupe's sake. I love you for yourself. I've seen the change in you, Miguel. I believe it's real, and I believe you love me and want to marry me. I also believe that God has made all this possible."

Then I really got poetic. "When all seems hopeless in our shipwrecked lives, God finds a way to save us. He's the Great Salvager of shipwrecks and brings us to a safe harbor. It seems like He's saved the two of us from a stormy sea and salvaged us for each other in the harbor of marriage. We're not flotsam and jetsam from a shipwreck. God's going to make something beautiful out of us, I'm sure. I want to be your wife!"

"Wow, where did that come from?" With that, he turned to me and, for the first time since our sexual relationship five years before, he put his arms around me and gently kissed me on the lips. I warmed to his touch, but then got a hold of myself and said, "Miguel, there's a few things that I want understood. I want our relationship to be based on something better than sex. I want us to practice mutual charity, communication, commitment, and chastity. We'll call it 'The Four C's.' In other words, we get to know each other spiritually, intellectually, and emotionally, but not physically . . . not until we're married."

"That's fine with me, Teresita. I've learned the hard way that sex is no way to start a relationship. There's no commitment. People just use each other for their own pleasure. Premarital sex just covers up problems that should be dealt with honestly and non-physically in a real relationship. What would you like to do, so we can get to know one another better?"

"Well, I miss surfing. It's been years since I've had an athletic outlet. The surf's not as good down here compared to up home on the Cape, but maybe you could take me windsurfing. I've never done that before."

So the next Saturday afternoon he took me to Key Biscayne. It's a small island paradise just minutes from downtown. It's one of the hundreds of coral rock barrier islands lying off the southern end of Miami. The calm bay waters and constant breezes make it a perfect windsurfing spot. We rented sailboards and took off from the beach, perpendicular to the wind, for the fastest start. Miguel floundered around near the shore trying to get his balance. For me, this was easier than surfing because there was no rough surf, and I didn't have to continually adjust my balance on the board. I just stood on the board, held the sail firmly, and let the wind do all of the work.

Turning around, however, proved to be another matter. It was harder since I had to switch the direction of the sail, against the wind, in order to head back toward shore. Like Miguel, I began to lose my balance and tip over, but eventually I managed to wobble back near the shore. I didn't want to show Miguel up. So we both fooled around, having fun in the shallows, falling off our boards like a couple of tourists. By the end of the day, I had taught him how to balance and to let the wind do the rest. He learned very quickly.

A month later he took me to John Pennekamp Coral Reef State Park at Key Largo, the first of the islands that lead to land's end at Key West. I remembered with regret the last land's end that I visited at Provincetown when Brian abandoned me in my hour of need. Now I felt secure with Miguel and hoped that our day there would erase the memory of my insecurity with Brian.

The Park has the largest coral reef in the Western Hemisphere. When we got there, I noticed a snorkeling rental shop. I told Miguel how I used to go snorkeling on Pleasant Bay, Cape Cod, and how I'd love to go right there on the reef. He said that he wasn't a very good swimmer and had never been snorkeling before. I didn't want to push him or cause him any embarrassment, but the attendant assured him that novices were welcome. So we rented some equipment and took a boat ride out to the reef. When we got there, the Captain handed Miguel a snorkeler's life vest. This enabled him to just float on the water surface without really swimming. We had a great time.

The water was a beautiful, clear aquamarine color. You could see 20 feet to the bottom. We held hands and floated over the reef pointing out to each other the beautiful multicolored fish. There were red, blue and multicolored parrotfish; black, gray and green angelfish; and yellow grunts, jacks and snappers. Transparent purple sea fans waved from the reef back and forth in the current seemingly cheering on the passing parade of fish.

This is such a beautiful sight. Thank You, Lord, for the beauty of Your creation. These fish all swim as one. They aren't even aware of their different colors. They are in perfect harmony with their water world. Help all of us people of color to be like these fish—unaware of our different colors and living in harmony in our world.

That evening I reflected on the growth of our relationship. I felt secure and happy with Miguel. I could trust him. I wanted to make the gift of myself to him. I looked forward to our marriage when we would swim as one through life just as we had done that day on the reef.

But there was one more thing I knew I had to do before Miguel and I could move forward together in our new life. I waited for just the right moment, but I can't say I was looking forward to it.

Fifty

"M iguel, there's something that I have to tell you," I said one night as we sat in the car outside my apartment. We had just returned from another nice dinner at the Bayside Marketplace. Lupe was asleep in the back seat.

"Qué, mi amor?" Miguel replied with a smile, in his most romantic Spanish.

"It's about my past on the Cape and my coming to Miami . . . I was a teen runaway and —"

"What were you running away from?"

"Well, that's what I'm about to tell you. I—"

"Were your parents abusive or what?"

"Miguel, please stop interrupting. I need to tell you this, and I need for you to just listen. Okay?"

"Okay, go on."

And so, I made my confession to Miguel. I told him everything, step by step. How I got pregnant after I had sex with Brian at the beach party . . . His devastating attitude in our talk at McMillan's Wharf and how he wouldn't help me to make a responsible choice . . . How he only promised to pay for an abortion—

"An abortion?! You had an abortion? Oh, Teresita, I'm so sorry." He turned to me and gently pulled my head onto his left shoulder.

I started crying softly. I was overcome with relief and gratitude for his compassion. Then I struggled to continue. "It gets worse, Miguel."

"Shhhhh, shhhhhh . . . It's okay, it's okay." He rubbed my back with his left hand and the back of my head with his right.

"No, it's not okay, and I want you to know."

I told him through my tears how the P.A. botched the abortion, and I went home still pregnant. How Julie and I went back to Vermont to finish the abortion. But instead, how I gave birth to a dead baby boy who was burned alive. Miguel started sobbing. I could feel his heart and breast throbbing into my face on his shoulder.

"Teresita, I don't want to hear any more."

"I have to tell you. . . . My breasts filled with milk for my baby who was dead. I was supposed to be a mother for him, Miguel!"

"You've made up for it with Lupe."

"There is no making up for it. There's only God's merciful forgiveness, healing and hope. And that's what I have for our marriage, our future—hope that our pasts are forgiven and behind us only because God loves us, hope that you'll understand my passion for motherhood and children, hope that you'll share my passion and support me in my hopes."

"I do, Teresita, I do," he said softly. And that was Miguel's promise to me, one that he meant with all of his heart.

Fifty-one

"Teresita, do you take Miguel for your lawful husband, to have and to hold, from this day forward, for better, for worse, for richer, for poorer, in sickness and in health, until death do you part?" As Father John spoke these words, I searched Miguel's dark eyes and handsome face.

"I *do!*" I said loudly and firmly.

Father John went on, "You have declared your consent before the Church. May the Lord in His goodness strengthen your consent and fill you both with His blessings. What God has joined, men must not divide."

"Amen," we responded. We were married! It was June 21, 1991. It was a small wedding. Mary was my bridesmaid, Lupe the flower girl, and an old friend of Miguel's was best man. A few pro-lifers came to support us. Gloria, Miguel's mother, observed the ceremony with a sullen expression and an apparent lack of enthusiasm.

"You may kiss the bride," Father John told Miguel. It was the first of many that I received that day. Our celibacy period was over, and we could celebrate our love in total sexuality—spiritually, emotionally, and physically. The seven lonely years I had spent in Florida were finally coming to an end forever. I was no longer a single part, but a part of a new whole. I truly felt that we two had become one flesh, just like it said in the Bible. And from now on, I smiled to myself, it was all right to go forth and multiply as God commanded.

We settled into a nice ranch-style home that we bought before the wedding. It was located just outside the hustle and bustle of the city. Miguel stayed on at the restaurant while I quit my job and stayed at home. What a luxury to stay home all day and enjoy our daughter. I was able to get more housework done and take my time to prepare good and wholesome meals for Miguel. My only regret was that I didn't know how to prepare any of his favorite Cuban dishes—the ones his mother had made for him. He hired a night manager for the restaurant, and we started to have a regular family schedule that included family breakfasts and dinners.

Miguel adopted Lupe and he was officially listed as her father on a new birth certificate. She started kindergarten in the fall, and once again, I was home alone in the mornings. I didn't want to return to work because it wasn't necessary, and I wanted to be there for Lupe when she got home. Now I had the leisure to enjoy her company, and I was free of worry and anxieties. Miguel provided well for us, and I had more time on my hands.

I enjoyed the simple routine of an ordinary housemother and wife. I found dignity in my everyday work and in doing everything the best that I could, following the Little Way of St. Therese of Lisieux. I even had the time to do some more embroidery on napkins, doilies, and dresses for Lupe. I remembered how to do it from the patch that I made for Luke on The Quilt of Love. I found the stillness and the methodical motions very soothing. I also began to pray more. I made a little prayer corner in our bedroom. I continued with my daily meditations, but now I started them with the daily Rosary in the morning after Lupe got on the school bus.

One morning I was meditating on Our Lady as a widowed mother. Joseph, her husband, had died and Jesus had gone off to His public ministry leaving Mary all alone. Suddenly I thought, *Gloria is a widowed mother just like Mary, and her only son has married me leaving her all alone. But, unlike Mary who accepted everything, Gloria hasn't and she's resentful. She's lost her only son to me and Billy, her chosen grandchild, to death. She's been festering in her own bitterness and has never called or come to see us. She only sees Miguel at the restaurant.*

Right then and there I began to pray for her happiness. I surprised myself, and thanked God for my compassion toward her.

I remembered that my grandmother had told me that Our Lady of Guadalupe appeared in Mexico as a *mestiza*—a brown mixture of Spanish and Indian. They called her *La Morenita*—"The Little Brown Girl." This resulted in reconciliation between the Spanish and the Indians, and their subsequent intermarriage formed the Mexican people, *la Raza,* a new race of brown people. So I figured that *La Morenita* would be a good one to pray with for reconciliation between Gloria and me, a white *cubana* and a brown *latina* coming together for the sake of Lupe, my *morenita.*

I also remembered that my friend Mary once told me that anytime I needed something big, I should pray a novena, or "nine days" of prayers. Our Lady and the apostles prayed the first novena after Jesus ascended into heaven. On the ninth day, the Holy Spirit came upon them as tongues of fire, and they were changed from fearful men into courageous ones who then went out into the streets and preached. Three thousand people changed their hearts on that first Pentecost day and believed that Jesus Christ was truly the living Son of God.

So, I decided to pray a novena of Rosaries to Our Lady of Guadalupe for reconciliation between Gloria and me. I didn't tell Miguel. On the evening of the ninth day, right after dinner, the phone rang. Miguel answered it and looked very surprised. "Yes," he said, "she's right here. Just a minute Mom." And then, covering the receiver with his hand, he held out the phone to me and said, "It's my mother. She wants to talk to *you*." He shrugged his shoulders as if to say he didn't have a clue and proceeded to pass me the phone.

"Hi, Teresita. I just wondered how my son's making it without my home-cooked Cuban food?"

"Oh, he's surviving," I cautiously replied.

"How would you like it if I taught you some of my Cuban cooking?"

"Well . . . I'd like that, Gloria. I'd really like that. Maybe you could come over on Sunday and show me how to make something special. Miguel really misses your meals and uh, we've got a lot of catching up to do."

So she came over for what was to become a family ritual of Sunday afternoon dinners. She'd teach me how to prepare Cuban meals and then play with Lupe after dinner while I cleaned up. It brought a warm smile to my face to see her play and read to Lupe who loved her grandmother as much as I once loved mine. After that miracle, I never forgot the power of praying a novena.

One Sunday as we washed the dishes after our dinner, Gloria stared out the kitchen window. "Teresita, I always thought that you were the problem. But I'm beginning to understand that it was me. I have always been too proud. I thought that I was better than you, that I had more culture and more money. But you . . . you had more dignity . . . more *valor* and *aguante*— courage and endurance. I can see that now. I wanted a grandchild, a white grandchild. This was not a grandmother's love . . . this was false pride."

I stood there speechless.

"I thought that you were just low class. I didn't want you to embarrass me in front of my white Cuban friends. I didn't want a mulatto grandchild. But after Billy died, I began to see you and Lupe in a different light. I felt not only my own pain, but also my son's. I realized through my own grief as a mother and grandmother that you, too, had suffered for your child—my grandchild. You risked everything, without any family support to bear Lupe and make a real family. I just want to say it very simply: I'm proud of you and I'm proud of Lupe. I love you both, and I'm proud to have you for a daughter-in-law and Lupe for a grandchild. Saying I'm sorry will never make up for what I did. But I ask you to forgive me . . . so that we can be a real family. Will you please forgive me, Teresita?"

"Of course, I forgive you. To tell you the truth, Gloria, I could have used your support, but I'm glad to have it now. That's what's important." There was no more talk between us about what had happened in the past; we were too caught up in the present and far too excited about the future.

Fifty-two

*H*ello, Teresita? This is Dad!" It was a late Sunday morning, one year later, in the spring of 1992. We had just arrived home from Mass when I received a phone call from my father. The more time I spent with Gloria over the past year, the more I thought of my own mother. I hadn't seen or heard from Mom or Dad since I ran away almost eight years before. But I thought of my mother more and more, and I felt that I should really make the effort to contact her. Then Providence worked it out for me. Dad called.

"How did you find me?" I blurted out. I really wanted to say, "I'm so happy that you found me!" But as usual with my parents, it came out wrong, and we got off on the wrong foot.

"Never mind how I found you. That's not important right now. With a little money, you can find anybody. I'm just glad I found you."

"So am I. In fact, I'm really happy that you called. I've finally gotten my life together, Dad, and I want to share it with you and Mom."

"Well," he emotionally sobbed, "mine's falling apart!" Without warning he blurted out, "Your mother had a stroke—a thrombosis, the doctors say— just like your grandmother. She's in a coma, and the doctors want to pull the plug. She has to live! I can't deal with these doctors. I keep breaking down. I can't think straight. I need you, Teresita, right now! Please come!"

"Well . . . uh, sure Dad. . . . I'm so sorry for you and . . . and for Mom. But I don't know if I can come immediately."

"Teresita, we were at a cocktail party and she turned to me, pointed to her face and said, 'I feel nauseous. Do I look pale?' You know how she's always concerned about her looks. Then she just keeled over and dropped to the floor. When the rescue people placed her on the stretcher, she whispered to me and said, 'Jim, find Teresita. I want to see her. Get her, Jim!' They were her last words. You've *got* to come, Teresita!"

"Well, when should I come?"

"Tomorrow, there's not much time."

"*Tomorrow?* But Miguel, he's my husband, and Lupe, she's my daughter, I uh, I gotta' figure things out."

"There's no time to figure anything out. I bought you a ticket for tomorrow morning's 10 a.m. flight to Boston. For God's sake, Teresita, please be on it. I'll pick you up at the airport, and we'll go straight to the hospital in Hyannis. I've got to go now . . . your mother . . . thanks, Teresita. . . . See you tomorrow."

"Okay," I said, surrendering in confusion and sadness as I hung up the phone thinking, *He's the same old Dad. Can't communicate. Just orders and demands—even though he did say "please" this time.*

The next morning I left Lupe with Mary and, as a dutiful daughter, took the plane to Boston and met Dad at Logan Airport. He greeted me with an awkward hug, and we left directly for the hospital. On the way, he provided me with more details about Mom's sudden stroke and the ambulance ride to the emergency room. Evidently, by the time they got to the hospital, she was already in a coma. They admitted her and hooked her up to a life support system. She never regained consciousness. But the doctor told Dad that she might be able to hear and understand us. Dad sobbed so much through the story that I had to ask him to stop the car so I could drive. He kept repeating through his tears, "I can't lose her, Teresita . . . I need her . . . the doctors won't help. She's too young to die! She's only 45 years old!"

When we arrived at the hospital, we went directly to Mom's room. I barely recognized her. She was lying on the bed with tubes coming out of her from everywhere. Her eyes were closed. Her face was haggard and drawn. She didn't seem to hear anything. She was on a ventilator and was receiving liquid food and hydration through an IV in her arm.

I walked up and stood beside her. It felt like time had turned upside down. She was so helpless! Here lay the mother that I had feared so much while growing up. The mother who had tried to abort me and hit and abused me for no apparent reason during my childhood. All of my old resentment, bitterness, and anger against her rose up like a powerful wave, but it crashed just as quickly in my compassion for her.

The memory of all those painful years was not just my history but hers as well. It was the playing out of choices and their consequences. By our abortion choices, each of us had chosen our own destructive wave to surf. Each of us rode it out, and crashed hard on the shore. Only God, the Great Lifeguard, could save us. I was confident that He would do it for Mom as He had done it for me.

I stood there staring at her in awe and wonder as she lay on her deathbed. Her ventilator went *wissssh, whoosh* in and out sounding like an elderly asthmatic's wheezing. I heard the *beep, beep* of the blood pressure monitor, and I smelled that distinctive antiseptic hospital scent.

I gently lifted my hand to her forehead and felt her taut and cool skin. I stroked her hair as she might have stroked mine while I slept as an infant. Then I held her limp hand and said, "Hi, Mom, it's me, Teresita. I'm home!" I began talking to her as if she were perfectly well and understood everything I was saying.

"I love you, Mom. I'm a mother now, too! I have a five-year-old daughter. Her name is Lupe. It's short for 'Guadalupe' and, like you and Grandma taught me, I pronounce her name *loo-pay*. She's the joy of my life—she and my husband Miguel. He runs a Cuban restaurant in Miami. . . ."

I summoned all my courage and apologized for the past. "I'm sorry that I ran away, Mom. Please forgive me. I forgive you. I forgive you for trying to abort me. I can understand now. I know the pressures that you were under. I was scared and did the same thing myself. The apple doesn't fall very far from the tree, does it? In many ways I'm just like you, although I never wanted to admit it, and I tried my best to be different.

"Since I broke the relationship between myself and my son with my own abortion, I can understand your problem in never being able to establish one with me. But without that relationship, Mom—that special grace between a mother and her child instilled in us by God—there wouldn't be any continuation of the human race. Now I can see, through my relationship with my own daughter in comparison to ours, that you and I never really connected . . . we never bonded, and I feel sad about that.

"It seems unnatural that the child should re-establish the bond with the mother, but that's what you and I need to do. We need to make peace with each other. We need to love one another. So as your daughter who really loves you, I'd like to restore the bond that we should have had all along."

I suddenly realized that as my mother helped bring me into this world, I was helping her to leave it—like a midwife for her birth into eternal life.

"I'm sorry that we never bonded, Mom. But it's never too late." I held her hand in both of mine and said, "I love you Mom. Life is full of second chances.

"We can try to make up for our bad choices by making good ones. I tried to make up for my abortion of Luke by giving birth to Lupe. I tried to make up for my fornication by being chaste with Miguel and marrying him. I tried to make up for my drug and alcohol abuse by abstaining. Let's make up for our estrangement by bonding NOW."

As I said this, she squeezed my hands. She had heard me, and she was responding to my love . . . at last. We were no longer estranged. I felt great relief . . . and then my tears began to flow.

Fifty-three

*D*ad and I never left Mom's side. It was like a birth vigil. Her face was etched like a mother in labor. She seemed intent on whatever was happening inside of her. She seemed absorbed in an intense struggle, a fearful, physical battle to live, just like a mother caught up in the tidal wave of labor. I prayed that she would surrender peacefully to the struggle and not fight against it, just like in childbirth.

I was struck by how much the dying process was so much like a birth experience. Just as it is so good to have helpers for the birthing mother, I thought it would be good if all the dying had helpers, too. And how appropriate for their own children to be those helpers. It seemed natural that the children who were once helpless and received care from their parents should return the same act of love to their helpless, dying parents.

I thought, *Too many people die alone without family and friends, surrounded only by medical technology and personnel, just like too many mothers give birth in the same way. We need each other, and there is a great need to have family and friends present at both birth and death. Tending to Mom's death process is teaching me that, just like in childbirth, there is nothing to fear. What is needed is trust. It reminds me of the words of Our Lady of Guadalupe, "Have no fears or anxiety . . . am I not here who am your mother?" And here is my earthly mother teaching me to die without fear—naturally, with dignity and peace. Even though she's unconscious, she's teaching me that death is a natural event not much different from birth. It's just a transition from one form to another, from a living body with oxygen to a living soul without it, just like from a living fetus without oxygen to a living child with it. I know that Mom will live on after death.*

Eventually Dad fell asleep out of sheer emotional and physical exhaustion. So I left him asleep in the chair next to Mom and went to speak with her doctor. I asked him a lot of questions. He said that Mom's situation was hopeless. Only artificial life-support was keeping her alive, and they were just maintaining her in a coma. There was no hope that they could improve her condition over time and, if the life support were removed, she would die a natural death within a day.

As I processed what the doctor was saying, it didn't make much sense to me to keep her alive just for the sake of keeping her alive. Despite her brief response in squeezing my hands, Mom no longer demonstrated any brain activity, and her internal organs were quickly shutting down, one after the other. I am pro-life to the core, but that philosophy has also led me to believe that we should allow life to end naturally, the way God intended. I didn't want to hasten Mom's death, but I also didn't want to prevent it.

Dad was too emotionally involved to think clearly about what was best for Mom. He was in denial and didn't want to let go, even if, for all intents and purposes, she was no longer here. He kept chanting over and over again, "She's going to make it . . . everything will be all right . . . she's not going to die, Teresita . . . we've got to find doctors who can help her. . . . I need her, Teresita. . . . Oh my God, this is a nightmare. . . . I can't live without her!"

So I talked to the Catholic chaplain about the moral considerations. He said that heroic or extraordinary measures didn't have to be used if there was no hope for recovery or improvement of Mom's condition for an appreciable length of time. He said, "Just as we shouldn't interfere with life by preventing it through killing, as with abortion, we likewise shouldn't interfere with death by preventing it through extraordinary heroic means. Based upon what I know about your Mom's condition, she should be allowed to die a natural death as comfortably as possible with pain medication and her family's caring presence."

Knowing that it would be hard to convince my father of this, I trudged back to Mom's hospital bed and relayed what the chaplain had just explained to me. Initially, Dad responded with an expression of horror and panic, but said nothing. Finally, he looked at Mom and then at me with the look of one who has reluctantly surrendered, and nodded his head ever so slightly. We decided that we should allow Mom to die naturally and with dignity at this time, if that was God's will, and that we shouldn't prevent it. We also decided that she shouldn't die alone and that we'd care for her and keep her as comfortable as possible. I went back and asked the chaplain to come and administer to her the sacrament of the Anointing of the Sick.

He came right down to Mom's bedside and anointed her forehead and hands with holy oil. He prayed for God's support, comfort and help so that she would find hope in suffering. Then he led us in reciting Psalm 23:4 and John 17:24 three times each. I wrote them down.

Though I walk in the shadow of death,
I will fear no evil, for you are with me. . . .
"I desire that where I am, they also may be with me,"
Says the Lord Jesus.

Then the chaplain prayed,

Lord Jesus Christ, Savior of the world,
We pray for Your servant Maria,
And commend her to Your mercy.
For her sake You came down from heaven;
Receive her now into the joy of Your kingdom.
For though she has sinned,
She has not denied the Father, the Son, and the Holy Spirit,
But has believed in God and has worshiped her Creator. Amen.

The chaplain left, and Mom's life supports were removed that afternoon. For the next few hours, I held her hands, wiped her face with a warm washcloth, spread moisturizing cream on her face, and moistened her mouth with peppermint-flavored swabs to ease her thirst. I also talked to her and prayed for her, repeating the ejaculation to God the Father, "For the sake of Christ's sorrowful passion, have mercy on her and on the whole world." Dad was only able to sob and to sleep intermittently.

After a few hours, the nurse came in, checked Mom, took me aside and said, "Her circulation and breathing have slowed down. It won't be long now." Just before dawn, Mom began to breathe erratically with a gurgle. It sounded like she was snoring. Her chest heaved with each irregular breath as she gasped for oxygen, failed, lapsed into stillness, and then rose again. It reminded me of Lupe as a baby with the croup. I thought that she was choking, so I pushed the call button for the nurse. She came in, listened to Mom and softly said, "That's her death rattle."

After she left, I suddenly remembered that Our Lady of Guadalupe had appeared to Blessed Juan Diego's dying uncle, Juan Bernardino, and healed him. So I asked her not for a healing, but for a happy death for Mom, *Our Lady of Guadalupe, please come for Mom as you came for Juan Bernardino.*

As I continued praying, Mom's breathing slowed down until it nearly stopped. Then, to my shock, she opened her eyes. She looked right into mine, and I felt like she was drawing light from them. Our eyes locked and we stared at each other for the longest time. I, her daughter, was cementing the bond that should have been made by her. She looked at me as she probably never did while she bottle-fed me so many years ago.

Then to my utter astonishment, she stared at the foot of the bed, she lifted her head, opened her arms as if welcoming someone, and said in loud and clear Spanish, *La Morenita, tú estás aquí!*—"Little Brown Girl, you are here!"

She lay back on her pillow and seemed to be peacefully asleep with a little smile on her face. Suddenly, a great stillness pervaded the room. I felt a sense of awe and peace. I couldn't hear or move. I felt like time had stopped and my feet were glued to the floor. Then I saw a flash of blue light, heard a popping in my ears and the normal hospital sounds and movement returned. My mother was dead. I was dumbfounded. I gently closed her mouth and eyelids and sat there staring at her as I thanked God for giving her such a peaceful death. Then I gently woke my father, told him that Mom was gone, and led him to her bed so he could say his last goodbye.

Fifty-four

I stayed with Dad on the Cape to make all of the funeral and burial arrangements. The funeral Mass was at St. Joan of Arc's church. Mom hadn't been there in a long time, but God was her judge, not me, and His mercy endures forever. We prayed for her soul to rest in peace. The words of the funeral readings touched me deeply and echoed through my mind. . . . *The souls of the just are in the hands of God and no torment shall touch them, chastised a little, they shall be greatly blessed, because God tried them and found them worthy of himself. Jesus said, "I am the resurrection and the life: whoever believes in me, though he should die, will come to life. . . . "*

As we processed behind the casket to the rear of the church, the organist led us in singing, "I will raise you up on the last day. . . . " I went outside of the church and stood there with Dad. We greeted the mourners as they left. After everyone had dispersed, I walked in a dreamlike state toward the statue of St. Joan of Arc that overlooked the town. I thought of my romantic, feminist virgin heroine and my happy years in grade school across the street, and afterward with Julie on our surfing, fishing, hiking and skiing expeditions . . . until that last beach party.

As I relished my happy memories, I saw him out of the corner of my eye. He was walking briskly toward me wearing a blue blazer and a red power tie. I felt a chill go down my spine. It was Brian.

"Hey, Terry, how ya' been? Long time no see. Sorry I'm late and about your mom and all. I got to know her through my real estate business. I'm giving your dad as much competition as I can! Doing pretty good at it too. Livin' in a big new house overlooking Pleasant Bay. The environmentalists don't like our houses—they're awful sarcastic, you know. They call them 'trophy homes.' But that's okay. Hey! After all, it *is* my trophy! It's big and comfy for my girl and me. And I'm driving a BMW, fishing out of a Grady

White and partying at the Orleans Inn. No more beach parties for me. Hey, we had some good ones, didn't we Terry?" He winked his right eye and gave me a knowing smile.

"Well, I just wanted to say hello and express my condolences. Hope you have a nice visit with your dad. Tell him I said hello. See ya'."

He walked away as rapidly as he had approached. I stood there stupefied. He never asked anything about me or my life. It was all about him. I never got a word in.

My God! How could he be so insensitive? He just broke the reverie of my happy youth like he broke it in real life. It's still a big joke to him—"We had some good ones, didn't we Terry?" No apology, no regrets, no maturity. And unfortunately, no healing or forgiveness . . . and no true freedom. He's still just a self-absorbed boy.

There are worse sins than those of the flesh like mine were. There are sins of pounding an invisible nail into the heart of another, like he did to mine—"I'll pay for the abortion . . .That's my promise." Those words changed my whole life and broke my spirit.

*He reminds me of Chillingworth—*The Scarlet Letter *again. He was Hester's cruel husband. Like Hester, my sins of the flesh have been revealed, and I wear them on my heart. But, like Chillingworth, Brian's sins remain hidden because he carries them inside of his heart. I've been forgiven, but he can't even see the need for forgiveness. Or else, he's genuinely afraid to. He's blinded by his own bright light of self-absorption, and he can't see that from deep within his own heart, he violated in cold blood the sanctity of mine. Thank God our relationship ended!*

I walked slowly to the car where Dad was waiting for me and got into the driver's seat.

"I saw Brian and he said to say 'hello.'"

"Oh . . . he's doing very well . . . my biggest competitor. . . ."

"Yeah," I replied. "You both probably came from the same mold." I started the car and drove to the cemetery.

When we got to the open grave, the priest prayed, "Lord Jesus Christ, by Your own three days in the tomb, You hallowed the graves of all who believe in You and so made the grave a sign of hope that promises resurrection even as it claims our mortal bodies. Grant that our sister, Maria, may sleep here in peace until You awaken her to glory, for You are the resurrection and the life. Then she will see You face to face, and in Your light will see light and know the splendor of God, for You live and reign for ever and ever."

We all responded with a sad but hearty, *"Amen!"*

Then Dad threw a rose onto Mom's casket as it was lowered into the grave. After that, he threw in some dirt. He seemed more able to accept the finality of her death. I took him home for our post-funeral luncheon reception. Later I decided that I'd go for a walk on Nauset Beach.

Fifty-five

*A*s I drove towards Nauset Beach, I noticed the signs of spring on the Cape—yellow forsythia bushes and the brighter yellow daffodils and multicolored tulips. Bright red cardinals and red-breasted robins hopped on the ground. I arrived at the beach, got out of the car and started walking. Memories started flowing. The dark memory of my one night with Brian was quickly overshadowed by the sunny memories of swimming and surfing with my old high school friends. I remembered Julie. Somebody told me after the funeral that she had married a college classmate and moved west with him to L.A.

I looked out into the ocean that seemed as endless and infinite as God's mercy and love for us. The ocean never failed to quicken my heart in a mysterious reverence and peace. I took a deep breath of the fresh salt air, and started walking along the shoreline. The comforting and clean smell of salt air instantly reconnected me to nature. Somehow, I felt renewed and alive. Tension left my body, and my soul was refreshed.

I took off my shoes and walked along the edge of the surf, like Julie and I used to do. I felt the moist sand between my toes and let the cold surf wash over my feet. Soon I noticed an information sign higher up on the beach that I had never seen before. I walked up for a closer look. It read:

This place marks the spot of The Outermost House of Henry Beston where he spent the year of 1926 and wrote, "The world today is sick to its thin blood for lack of elemental things, for the fire before the hands, for water welling from the earth, for air, for the dear earth itself underfoot. In my world of beach and dune these elemental presences lived and had their being, and under their arch there moved an incomparable pageant of nature and the year."

Yes, I thought, *our technological culture takes nature for granted and not as a gift from God to provide for us and to refresh and heal us. We can explain the "how" of sunrise, sunset, and the ocean, but we can't explain the "why." It's simply beauty that should be appreciated and not analyzed and understood. It speaks to our hearts and not to our heads. It certainly speaks to me today of life and death, of choices and consequences, of change, renewal and eternal life.*

As I walked further down the beach, I came upon yet another informational sign. This one read:

Here stood Henry David Thoreau in 1850 and wrote, "A man may stand here and put all America behind him."

Right, I thought, *and a woman too. And I too have put everything behind me—my mother's attempt to abort me, my own abortion of Luke, and the attempted abortion of Lupe by Miguel and later by his thugs. I don't blame you, Mom. I forgive you and I forget. I don't blame anyone. I forgive you, Dad. I forgive you, Brian. I forgive you, P.A. I forgive you, Miguel. I forgive you, Gloria. I take full responsibility for myself. The past is all behind me now.*

And then I prayed, *Eternal rest grant unto, Mom, O Lord and may perpetual light shine upon her. May her soul and the souls of all the faithfully departed rest in peace. Amen.* I had reached closure on Mom's death. I felt no bitterness, no regrets, just sadness for a broken relationship that was finally re-established on her deathbed. It seemed that Jesus and Our Lady of Guadalupe had taken the broken pieces and shattered glass of our lives and made them into a beautiful stained glass window.

I felt safe leaving Dad the next morning to get back to my own family. I flew home from Boston with the hope that Mom had entered into eternal life in heaven.

As soon as I got home, there was a phone message to call Dad. I called him, and he said he was lonely already. It was harder to live without Mom than he had thought. Couldn't we move closer, he asked, so he could see more of us? I told him it wasn't possible with my own family, a lonely mother-in-law, and Miguel's restaurant. I said that it would be much easier for him to move to Florida than for us to move to Cape Cod. But he didn't want to retire from his real estate business. So I invited him down for a visit, so he could meet everyone. Much to my surprise, he accepted. We planned it for the Fourth of July weekend. But, first, I had a few things I needed to say to him. I chose to do it in a letter.

Dear Dad,

I'm writing you this letter because I think it's the best way for me to say what I need to say to you and for you to "listen" without interrupting me. I don't want to wait until you're dying, like with Mom. In the hope of starting a new relationship with you as your adult daughter, I need to tell you these things, so you can understand where I'm coming from.

I always longed for your love and approval. I'm not saying that you didn't love me, but you didn't really show it much. You never told me that you loved me, you never hugged me, and you never came to my piano recitals. You were always too busy with your work. I never got to know you. The only talk we ever had was that time on summer vacation in Isle La Motte. How I wish that it could have always been like that!

Because you were so cold and distant, I thought you had rejected me just like Mom had since the time she tried to abort me. Of course, you were part of that decision, too. You were never there for me, and I didn't think that I could confide in you or trust you. So I didn't.

Then when I really needed your support, advice, and encouragement when I got pregnant, I couldn't seek it because I thought you'd reject me again, and I couldn't have handled that. So I took what I thought was the easy way out. I got an abortion. But it was a disaster, so I ran away. Then, to make matters worse, you never even tried to find me or contact me. But when you needed me for Mom, you sure found me quickly enough!

I've had a hard life, but I've endured. I never quit. I always tried to do better, and that's what I hope to do with my relationship with you. My feelings of anger, hurt, sadness, resentment, bitterness, and regret have all slipped away. I'm just left with a great sadness that we never knew one another. But it's not too late to try!

And, Dad, there's your granddaughter Lupe! You can start with her the way you should have started with me. Life is full of second chances, Dad, and she's your second chance. You're welcome to my home, and I'm looking forward to your visit. No need to answer this. I just had to say it.

Love,
Your Daughter, Teresita

Dan Lynch

Soon Dad came for his visit. He never mentioned my letter. He seemed to take a liking to Miguel, as they talked much about running their respective businesses. It also seemed as if he did more with Lupe in one weekend than he did with me during my entire childhood. He took her to some of her favorite places, including the Seaquarium and the Miami Metrozoo, a mini animal kingdom on islands that you view from an elevated monorail. It had a special petting zoo for Lupe to touch and learn about small animals. The innocence of childhood seemed to help him to forget his attachment to Mom. Our relationship remained superficial, but at least he became a positive factor in my life, for which I was thankful. He still pestered me about moving north but he went home with a smile on his face. Then something happened to make me re-think a move to the north.

Fifty-six

Hurricane Andrew ripped across southern Florida in August of 1992 at 160 miles per hour and caused the worst natural disaster in the history of the United States. It flattened wooden buildings and crumpled mobile homes causing billions of dollars in damage, leaving 150,000 people homeless and 35 dead. Miraculously, the city of Miami was spared. But people were scared.

I saw the news on TV. A witness said, "The hurricane looked like the blade of a buzzsaw on the TV weather map, and when it hit my mobile home, the wind sounded like the high-pitched whine of a real buzzsaw. I was inside of what sounded like a loud, speeding and shaking freight train. All I could see was black dirt flying through the air with pieces of wood of every shape and size. After it ended, all I could smell was propane gas from the disconnected tanks. The horizon was pink all around from the many fires and our mobile homes were piled like crumpled paper in the corner of our park. I was lucky to get out alive!"

This hurricane was too close for comfort for me. I got nervous about living in southern Florida and, as my father had pestered me, I started to pester Miguel to take us north. My feet were itching to get the sand out of my shoes and move on. I didn't want to return to the Cape. It was too close to Dad and held too many memories. I thought that we needed a fresh start.

I began to think of the only other state that I had visited except for California—Vermont. My thoughts drifted to Burlington, but I immediately dismissed that idea because it was the scene of my abortion and imprisonment. But then I began to think that the only way to conquer these painful memories was to confront them. So I began to think positively of Burlington. I had read that it was one of the most desirable small cities in America, if you could take the harsh winters.

It was located right on Lake Champlain—good for swimming, boating, and fishing. Yet it was only a half-hour from the Green Mountains and hiking and skiing. It had a low crime rate and was considered as a safe city for children—that is, if you didn't count unborn children. It had good schools and open spaces with all of the advantages of a city with its libraries, museums, shops, and colleges. And it was only one and a half hours from Montreal, Quebec, a major international city.

I started to read more about it and sent for listings from real estate brokers. Then I started to work on Miguel. He was open to a move since the recession in Florida was affecting our business. I told him that it was important for Lupe to have a safe city, and Miami was not known as "Miami Virtue" but as "Miami Vice." I told him that the economy was good in Burlington, and it was known for the international cuisine of its restaurants—a Cuban restaurant would probably be a great success up there.

To please me, Miguel did a market survey of Burlington restaurants and found that they were very successful. He started to get interested, but then he faltered and began whining about his mother. "How can I leave my mother? I'm her only son. Miami means everything to her."

I simply said, "We can take her with us." Immediately I had second thoughts. I couldn't believe that I had said that. *Me. . . live with my mother-in-law?* But I held my tongue. Miguel approached his mother with the idea and, amazingly, she was open to it. She, too, had a good scare with Hurricane Andrew and was ready for a change. I couldn't retract my offer now. It was all systems go. We sold the restaurant and our house, bought a former Italian restaurant in the heart of downtown Burlington on Church Street, and a large house on the outskirts of the city in South Burlington.

Shortly before we moved, I went to say goodbye to Mary. I was going to miss her friendship, and I wanted her to know it. I consoled myself with the thought that she'd give me an excuse to bring my family down to Florida for Christmas vacations.

On the Sunday after that, I went down alone to Little Havana early in the morning after Mass. I wanted to say goodbye to my old neighborhood. As I walked along the *Calle Ocho*, I stopped at the memorial column for the Cuban 2506th Brigade in the memorial park. Then I noticed a four-foot white statue of Our Lady about fifty yards behind the column in the shade of a tree. She was holding the Baby Jesus in her arms. I had never noticed it before. So I went right up to it for a closer look. At its base was an engraving in granite. It said:

Ser Madre Es Una Bendición De Dios—"Motherhood Is God's Greatest Blessing"

I smiled and nodded my head in agreement as I reflected on that simple message. *Yes, motherhood is God's greatest blessing, and His greatest gift is the gift of life. He loves us into being through our mothers! Even if they don't love us, He does! His heart is like the heart of a mother from which we are conceived in love. His love feeds us through His Son, Jesus, just as a mother feeds her baby through her umbilical cord. We are cradled in His heart like a baby in the womb of its mother. So we can really be called "children of God." Just like St. John said in his first letter, "See what love the Father has bestowed on us in letting us be called children of God!" And we can call Him Abba—Daddy!*

As I turned and left my old neighborhood and all of its memories behind me, I resolved to draw a picture of my meditation.

We moved north on Columbus Day Weekend in 1992. It was the same weekend that I had first gone to Burlington for my abortion eight years before. As then, the foliage would be at its peak, but this time I would savor its beauty without any anxieties, pain, sadness, or regret. Now it would be with anticipation, joy, excitement, and happiness.

As we drove north in Florida, I asked Miguel to stop in St. Augustine since it was the oldest city in the United States and I had never been there. As we entered the city, my attention was drawn to the largest cross that I had ever seen. It stood 208 feet tall overlooking the Atlantic Ocean. I learned that this spot marked the place where my Spanish ancestors landed and celebrated the first Mass in North America on September 6, 1565. Here they founded the oldest continually occupied city in North America. I asked Miguel to stop at the 35-acre park named *Mission Nombre de Dios* – "Name of God" – in honor of the Holy Name of Jesus.

He stayed in the car with Lupe and Gloria while I got out. As I walked through the beautiful park towards the Great Cross, I passed a life-sized colored mosaic image of Our Lady of Guadalupe. There she was again! I passed under the Cross and walked towards what appeared to be a small Spanish Mission church complete with a bell at the top of its ivy covered front. I walked to the door that identified it as the oldest shrine to Mary in the United States. It was named The Hermitage of *Nuestra Senora de La Leche y Buen Parto* – "Our Nursing Mother of Happy Delivery." I walked into the simple Hermitage and saw a three-foot statue of Our Lady sitting atop a wooden column. She was sitting in a chair nursing the Baby Jesus! Her eyes were glued to His.

I reverently walked up to the statue and fell on my knees at her feet and prayed, *Dear Mother, you formed your mother's bond with your child by nursing your Son with your own breast unlike my own mother who broke her bond with me by her attempt to abort me and by nursing me with a bottle! May all mothers bond with their children – both unborn and born – and may you protect them in their pregnancies and childbirths. Amen.*

I got up off my knees and returned to the car and we drove off to Vermont.

Our new home was a restored 1830 brick farmhouse nestled into ten acres of land. It had original, wide-plank wood floors, three fireplaces, and a large kitchen. It was big enough to divide into three units—one for us, one for Gloria, and one to rent out to help pay the mortgage and to be available in the future for my father, if he ever wanted to come to live with us.

The yard had a vegetable garden, flower beds, and shade and ornamental trees. It also had a shed suitable for raising small animals for Lupe. It was a romantic, back-to-nature, dream-come-true home with all the benefits of my husband's restaurant and a city nearby. We all adjusted and made the transition with surprising ease. We had a very thankful Thanksgiving, and Dad even came up from the Cape to join us in our official housewarming.

Then our first long, hard and cold Vermont winter set in . . . and I began to feel a mysterious urge to nest.

Fifty-seven

*A*s December 12 approached, all kinds of thoughts and memories came to me. It was the Feast Day of Our Lady of Guadalupe, my birthday, and the anniversary of my completed abortion and the death of my first baby, Luke. I wanted a happy memory of this day for the rest of my life to overcome the memory of Luke's death. I wanted another baby.

I had been practicing Natural Family Planning, and I periodically self-examined myself to see whether I was fertile or not. With time, I really got the hang of it and realized how amazing and even exciting it was to be in touch with your own natural fertility signs. I didn't follow my mother's bad advice to use a condom "for safety," as she said. I didn't want my sex with my husband to be "safe" but to be "sacred." I didn't want any artificial pills, condoms, and IUDs going into my body . . . only my husband.

As the 12th drew nearer, my vaginal mucus was long and stretchy when pulled between my thumb and index finger. I could tell this just by checking for a second after I used the bathroom, just like the NFP books had illustrated. Also, my cervix was dilated which was also easy to tell by a self-exam, and my vaginal temperature had increased. All of these natural signs indicated that I was in my fertile period, and that I could get pregnant.

I started my birthday off by reading the story of Our Lady of Guadalupe to Lupe. I read it from Tomi de Paola's beautifully illustrated book. It was a tradition that I started with Lupe when she was 3. Now that she was almost 6, she knew the story by heart. I also told her about how her grandmother would go out as a little girl pretending to be the Virgin Mary and looking for lodging for the Baby Jesus—*Las Posadas.*

After that, we all went as a family to Mass in honor of Our Lady of Guadalupe. Then Miguel dropped Lupe and me off at home and went to work. We made *Ojos de Dios*—"The Eyes of God," to later hang on our Christmas tree. This was another tradition that I reestablished in our family.

That evening, Miguel took me out for dinner to celebrate my birthday. I used all of my feminine wiles to attract him—a new hairdo, makeup, perfume, my best jewelry and a new black dress. We went to the Radisson Hotel on the waterfront of Lake Champlain. It had a beautiful view of the starlit lake. We had dinner and then wine with big band dancing. I had the strongest desire to have Miguel take me home and make love to me. I didn't tell him that I was fertile. I wanted to surprise him. I knew that he loved Lupe so much that he wanted another child to be the fruit of our married love and to make up for our unmarried lust.

When we got home, we made love. It was shortly before midnight on December 12. My period never came the next month. I was pregnant. Life begins at the moment of conception, so I would have the memory of this new life on December 12 to overshadow the sadness of Luke's death on the same day. I shared the good news with Miguel. He was ecstatic.

Soon, my hormones started changing, and my body and emotions as well. The "early pregnancy factor" hormone kicked into my bloodstream. This altered the cells within me, and my body began to make different demands on me. I craved different foods and needed more rest. New cells began to grow in my breasts, cells that would mature and secrete milk specifically formulated for the needs of my newborn baby. What a miracle new life is. To think that my body could provide an environment for a baby's growth, and that I would be able to "feel" that growth.

I began to think "baby" and started noticing babies everywhere—babies on the streets and babies in the stores. I also dreamed and daydreamed about my baby. *What sex will my baby be? Will my baby be healthy? What will my baby look like?*

The month after I got pregnant, our new President, Bill Clinton, did a horrible thing. He repealed all of the prior Presidential Executive Orders that had prohibited abortions in the military and fetal experiments, and he granted millions of dollars to international agencies that promoted abortions. He did this in a grand ceremony on January 22, 1993. That was the anniversary of the United States Supreme Court decision that overturned state laws prohibiting abortion and legalized abortion in every state of the union.

Just like the Supreme Court, without any say from the people in our so-called "democracy," Bill Clinton reversed the decisions of Presidents Reagan and Bush, legalized military abortions and experiments on innocent unborn children and funded abortion promotion internationally. He hadn't learned from the history of Nazi Germany, whose horrors began by experimenting and killing innocent people. I resolved that I would bear the pain and suffering of my childbirth in reparation for his horrible act.

I chose to go to a midwife in order to have a more natural birth. I had experienced the cold technology of abortion clinics and the Green Mountain

Hospital, and even good Dr. Espinoza's hospital. I wanted a drug-free, monitor-free, and IV-free birth. I wanted to experience it all naturally in a warm and welcoming environment with my husband, the father. So I chose the midwife route for a more personal and caring birth in the comfort, security, and familiar surroundings of my own home.

My midwife explained that the job of a midwife is to be a guide toward an ideal birth—*I* would deliver the baby, and *she* would just catch it! That sounded much better to me than having a doctor "deliver" my baby. In her opinion, an ideal birth was a mother surrounded by people who love her— her spouse, her mother, her siblings, and her children—all without technological intervention. The mother should be able to deliver in any position that is comfortable for her, with her spouse helping and comforting her. She said that when birthing is filled with awe and appreciation, the family has a greater chance of remaining stable and intact. Healthy and happy families make for healthy and happy communities that make for a healthy and happy world. I looked forward to my child's birth with my midwife and my chance to do my part to make a healthy and happy world.

On September 8, 1993, Feast of the Birth of the Virgin Mary, my midwife rubbed my back and had me sit in a tub of hot water to relax me. I had a powerful backache. I got out of the tub and, on my hands and knees, count-breathed. Then I seemed to come to some primeval point of desperation. I looked the midwife right in the eye and screamed, "Help me through this pain!" Somehow, I was able to push that pain away and asked her to help me to the bed. Miguel stood behind me wiping my forehead with a warm washcloth. Gloria and Lupe stood at the foot of the bed.

Unlike with Dr Espinoza, I had full "permission" to do whatever I wanted to help the pain. So I got into comfortable positions of my own choosing. I was able to relax myself and really participate in the final labor. I didn't force the push, but I didn't fight it either. At one point, I actually just had this overwhelming *need* to push, like I couldn't "hold it" any longer, and I just let it happen. It was just like surfing and staying with the wave. I lay on my side and pushed after every other pain. No one could have told me "when" to push any better than myself, just as no one can tell you "when" it's your time to use the bathroom! Suddenly, the baby slid out—just like when your head slides out through a turtleneck shirt as you pull it on.

Raaaah, erraaaaaaaaah! "It's a boy!" yelled Gloria. "And he's got your blue eyes and your father's white skin." The midwife plopped him on my stomach and said, "There are many colors in God's rainbow of children. He looks like a Mickey to me."

"That's it, Miguel . . . we'll name him after you, but we'll call him . . . Mickey."

"Sounds good to me," he said, as he deftly cut the umbilical cord. I immediately pressed my son to my swollen breast. The sticky-sweet clear fluid ran out of it initially, and he followed the trail on my breast with his little pink tongue until his mouth seemed to swallow my nipple. We bonded as I looked into his unblinking, bright blue eyes. All of the fear and pain of the birth melted away into the miracle that I was blessed to hold, to bond with and to love.

My own midwife stood smiling down at me just as my midwife great-grandmother must have smiled upon so many mothers herself. Her *bendición* had indeed carried to the fourth generation, just as she had prayed. It passed from her to my grandmother on her pilgrimage from Mexico to America, to my mother on her pilgrimage to heaven, and to me on my pilgrimage through the culture of death to new life.

I lay there nursing my newborn son, and I vowed to become a midwife—a *comadrona,* just like my great-grandmother. Then I passed on her *bendición* to the *fifth* generation—to my children—and I prayed aloud, "May *La Virgen de Guadalupe* watch over and protect you and your children and theirs, to the fourth generation. May the circle be unbroken!"

As I prayed this, my midwife overheard me. She said, "That was a beautiful blessing! You know . . . God honors those who protect children."

"I certainly hope so!"

"He does. In the Old Testament, the Egyptian Pharaoh ordered the Hebrew midwives to kill all the male babies at their birth. Do you know that they refused to obey him?"

"Yes, and I told Judge Titus about Moses being rescued by the Pharaoh's daughter. But it didn't keep me out of jail for rescuing unborn babies."

"Well, read this," she said. "It may give you some consolation."

As she left, she handed me her card. I cuddled Mickey in my left arm, and I read the card from my right,

So God dealt well with midwives; and the people multiplied and grew very strong. And because the midwives feared God, He built up families for them. (Exodus 1:15-21).

Afterword

When I look back upon my abortion experiences, I'm continually amazed at my survival from pain, grief and guilt through God's grace. After the abortion, I felt like I was bleeding from a knife that was cutting me from the inside out. So I pushed down the lid and kept the wound hid. But the memories would slip into my mind, and my conscience would be ashamed.

Now I feel a deep peace, joy, and gratitude for my healing from post-abortion traumatic stress syndrome. Through my healing, I have learned not to judge but to have more compassion and mercy for other mothers like me who have aborted their children. I don't judge anyone because I know that I deserve judgment, but I received compassion and mercy. Somehow, God made all things work toward the good, and He brought goodness out of the evil in my life. I always try to remember that our God is a God of mercy and that He'll forgive us for anything, if we're truly sorry.

I hope that you never experience the painful, empty loss of your baby by abortion. But if you have, turn off the TV and music, find a quiet place, and tell God and your baby, "I'm sorry, please forgive me." Believe that you've been forgiven by them, forgive yourself and live on in freedom and peace.

Famous actresses have expressed their loss after their abortions in a few words better than I ever could:

> *The greatest regret of my life has always been that I didn't have my baby. . . . Nothing in the whole world is worth a baby. I realized it as soon as it was too late, and I never stopped blaming myself.*
> —Gloria Swanson.

> *If I had only one thing to do over in my life, I would have that baby.* —Patricia Neal.
> *I would give up everything—my money, my academy awards, my career— if only I could have those children now.*
> —Shelley Winters.

I took up my pen and wrote because I was inspired by the words of Harriet Beecher Stowe, author of *Uncle Tom's Cabin,* who wrote about the injustice of slavery:

I was oppressed and brokenhearted, with the sorrows and injustice I saw, because as a Christian I felt the dishonor to Christianity— because as a lover of my country I trembled at the coming day of wrath.

The injustice of slavery brought its own "day of wrath"—the Civil War. What day of wrath will come from abortion? Those who do not learn from history are doomed to repeat it. Although God's mercy endures forever, His goodness and mercy will not be forever mocked by the legal killing of innocent unborn children.

I have added two Appendices. The first one shows contrasting quotes that I found by Abraham Lincoln and Pope John Paul II that show the similarities between slavery and abortion. The second is a list of helpful contacts.

Don't be afraid to ask for help. You are not alone. What I have freely received, I now freely pass on to you.

Appendix One

"Those who choose not to learn from history, will have the consequence of repeating it."

—Teresita Gonzalez, summer 2000

"Can we, as a nation, continue together permanently—forever half slave and half free? The problem is too mighty for me. May God, in His mercy, superintend the solution."

—Abraham Lincoln, summer 1855

"President Lincoln's question is no less a question for the present generation of Americans. Democracy cannot be sustained without a shared commitment to certain moral truths about the human person and human community."

—Pope John Paul II, October 1995

"A house divided against itself cannot stand. I believe this government cannot endure, permanently half slave and half free."

—Abraham Lincoln, June 16, 1858

"The condition for the survival of America is to respect every human person, especially the weakest and most defenseless ones, those as yet unborn."

—Pope John Paul II, September 19, 1987

Under the United States Constitution, a Negro is not a citizen of the United States.

—United States Supreme Court, Dred Scott decision, March 6, 1857

"We think the Dred Scott decision is erroneous."

—Abraham Lincoln, June 1857

Under the United States Constitution, an unborn child is not a person.

—United States Supreme Court, Roe v. Wade decision, January 22, 1973

"When the sacredness of life before birth is attacked, we will stand up and proclaim that no one ever has the authority to destroy unborn life."

—Pope John Paul II, October 7, 1979

"Woe unto the world because of offenses! . . . this terrible war [is] the woe due. . . . Yet, if God wills that it continue, until all the wealth piled by the bondman's two hundred and fifty years of unrequited toil shall be sunk, and until every drop of blood drawn with the lash, shall be paid by another drawn with the sword, as was said three thousand years ago, so still it must be said, 'the judgments of the Lord, are true and righteous altogether.'"

—Abraham Lincoln, March 4, 1865

"Woe to you if you do not succeed in defending life."
—Pope John Paul II, August 15, 1993

"We are facing an enormous and dramatic clash between the culture of death and the culture of life. We find ourselves in the midst of this conflict. We are all involved and we all share in it, with the inescapable responsibility of choosing to be unconditionally pro-life. . . . 'For your own life-blood, too, I will demand an accounting . . . and from man in regard to his fellow man I will demand an accounting for human life' (Gn 9:5). . . . The deepest element of God's commandment to protect human life is the requirement to show reverence and love for every human person."

—Pope John Paul II, The Gospel of Life

"The greatest destroyer of peace in the world today is abortion. If a mother can kill her own child, what is there to stop you and me from killing each other? The only one who has the right to take life is the One who has created it. Nobody else has that right. . . . When we die, we will come face to face with God, the Author of life. Who will give an account to God for the millions and millions of babies, who were not allowed to have the chance to live, to love and be loved."
—Mother Teresa

"Today, I call heaven and earth to witness against you: I am offering you life or death, blessing or curse. Choose life, then, so that you and your descendants may live, in the love of Yahweh your God, obeying his voice, holding fast to him; for in this your life consists. . . . "

Deuteronomy 30:19-20

224

Appendix Two

Crisis Pregnancy Help

Birthright, Inc.
686 North Broad St.
Woodbury, N.J. 08096
National Hotline 1.800.848.5683

Care Net
109 Carpenter Drive, Suite 100
Sterling, VA 20164
1.800.395.4537
www.care-net.org

Post-Abortion Hope and Healing

The National Office of Post-Abortion Reconciliation and Healing, Inc.
PO Box 07477
Milwaukee, WI 53207
Hotline: 1.800.593.2273
www.marquette.edu/rachels

Elliott Institute
1.217.525.8202
www.afterabortion.org

Project Rachel Offices in US:
www.hopeafterabortion.com

Priests for Life
P.O. Box 141172
Staten Island, NY 10314
1.888.735.3448
www.priestsforlife.org

Gabriel Communications
Box 283
Cheltenham, PA 19012
215-379-5683
www.gabrielcommunications.org

Retreat Programs

Rachel's Vineyard
1.877.467.3463
www.rachelsvineyard.org

Blanket of Love

DeMarillac Center
PO Box 226
Emmitsburg, MD 21727
1.301.447.1811
www.blanketoflove.org

Hope for Former Abortion Employees

The Centurions
P.O. Box 75368
St. Paul, MN 55175
651.771.1500
www.plam.orglid6_m.htm

The Missionary Image of Our Lady of Guadalupe Inc.
144 Sheldon Road • St. Albans, VT 05478
1.802.524.5350
www.ourladyofguadalupe.org • missimag@together.net

Dan Lynch

The *Heart* of God Our Father

Teresita

This is my drawing of my meditation on the heart of the Father of All Mankind that is on page 214.

226

*****

This book is a dramatic testimony. Teresita's character is a composite of
several women who have confided their true stories to the author. All of
the abortion experiences and the healing experiences really happened
substantially as told. Otherwise, names, characters, places and incidents
are fiction or used fictitiously. Any resemblance to actual persons, living or
dead, events or places, is entirely coincidental.

*****

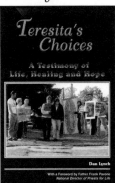

231

233

Production assistance by:
COME ALIVE COMMUNICATIONS, INC.
West Grove, Pennsylvania 19390
www.comealiveusa.com

Printed in the USA
REGAL ART PRESS
St. Albans, Vermont